INSIDE THE WHITE HOUSE

Books by Ronald Kessler

*Inside the White House**
*The FBI**
*Inside the CIA**
*Escape from the CIA**
*The Spy in the Russian Club**
*Moscow Station**
*Spy vs. Spy**
The Richest Man in the World
The Life Insurance Game

*Published by POCKET BOOKS

INSIDE THE WHITE HOUSE

The Hidden Lives of the Modern Presidents and the Secrets of the World's Most Powerful Institution

RONALD KESSLER

POCKET BOOKS
New York   London   Toronto   Sydney   Tokyo   Singapore

POCKET BOOKS, a division of Simon & Schuster Inc.
1230 Avenue of the Americas, New York, NY 10020

Library of Congress Cataloging-in-Publication Data

Kessler, Ronald, 1943–
  Inside the White House : the hidden lives of the modern presidents and the
secrets of the world's most powerful institution / Ronald Kessler.
    p. cm.
  ISBN: 0-671-87920-0
    1. Presidents—United States—History—20th century. 2. White House (Wash-
ington, D.C.) 3. Washington (D.C.)—Social life and customs—1951– I. Title.
E176.1.K45 1995
973.92'092'2—dc20   94-36327
                                                                          CIP

First Pocket Books hardcover printing February 1995

10 9 8 7 6 5 4

POCKET and colophon are registered trademarks of
Simon & Schuster Inc.

Printed in the U.S.A.

For Pam, Rachel, and Greg

Contents

Acknowledgments   ix

Prologue   xiii

1 The Most Mysterious Eighteen Acres in the World   1

2 "The White House Is Full of Arrogance"   38

3 Smuggling Coors   65

4 A Theft from the Presidential Suite   84

5 "Don't You Ever Point a Finger at My Dog"   104

6 A Rat in the Pool   130

CONTENTS

7 Bimbo Eruptions   158

8 "God! God! God!"   237

  Notes   261

  White House Dates   271

  Presidents and Their Wives   277

  Rumsfeld's Rules   281

  Index   289

Acknowledgments

HAVING PROBED TWO POWERFUL, SECRETIVE INSTITUTIONS—THE FBI and CIA—I was looking for another challenge. I found it in the White House.

Even though the White House and its occupants appear on television almost daily, what really goes on in the White House rarely comes out. Indeed, I found that, fearful of the consequences of talking, the people who surround the president and first family—the Secret Service agents, maids and butlers, *Air Force One* stewards, and the chefs and ushers—are actually more secretive than CIA and FBI officials who have access to classified information.

Luckily, I began the book with good sources. As a *Washington Post* reporter, I had probed the mysteries of the White House's finances and had developed some critical contacts. I had also reported on the General Services Administration, which maintains the east and west wings of the White House, and had longtime sources there. Most important, when I had finished my book on the FBI, FBI agents introduced me to Secret Service agents who knew practically everything about what goes on behind the scenes at the White House.

ACKNOWLEDGMENTS

While they cannot be named, I am grateful to those sources, without whom this book could not have been written.

My editor, Paul D. McCarthy, senior editor at Pocket Books, is as much responsible for this book as I am. He not only immediately recognized the idea as worthwhile but also came up with an organizational structure that made all the difference. He then applied his awesome talents to editing the manuscript, giving it greater clarity and depth.

My agent, Robert Gottlieb, executive vice president of the William Morris Agency, supported the project strongly and was a source of wisdom.

My wife, Pamela Kessler, a former *Washington Post* reporter who is the author of a book on Washington's spy sites, initially edited the manuscript and shared her exceptionally good judgment with me. I am fortunate to have her as my colleague, friend, and wife.

My children, Rachel Kessler Englehart, now a Washington reporter, and Greg Kessler, a New York artist, were sources of pride and support.

My friend Daniel Clements read the manuscript and offered helpful insights, as did several other friends who cannot be named.

Those who were interviewed or who helped in other ways include:

Ralph Albertazzie, Raleigh D. Amyx, Toinette (Toi) Bachelder, William M. Baker, William P. Barr, Robert E. Barrett, Paul W. Bateman, William J. Bell, Shirley Bender, John V. (Jack) Brennan, Jimmy R. Bull, Stephen B. Bull, James A. Buzzelli, William J. (Joe) Chappell, Daniel M. Clements, Clement E. Conger, Kenneth L. Cox, John Cronin, Jr., James U. Cross, William F. Cuff, Lloyd N. Cutler, John W. Dean III, Jan Du Plain, Mary Ann A. Esperancilla, Fred F. Fielding, Marlin Fitzwater, Gennifer Flowers, Gerald Ford, Ron Geisler, and Stanley J. Goodwin.

C. Boyden Gray, Shirley Green, Bill Gulley, Sean T. Haddon, W. Robert (Bob) Hall, Henry Haller, Robert T. Hartmann, George Hertzog, William J. Hopkins, Lew Hubbard, Frank A. Hughes, Joseph A. Jaworski, James R. Jones, Representative Paul E. Kan-

ACKNOWLEDGMENTS

jorski, David Hume Kennerly, Kenneth L. Khachigian, Laura Kopelson, James F. Kuhn, Joseph Laitin, Louis J. Lawrence, Robert A. Lazaro, Donald F. McKeown, Lester C. McLelland, Robert M. MacMillan, Ed Menken, Morton Mintz, J. Bonnie Newman, D. Patrick O'Donnell, Terrence O'Donnell, Charles Palmer, Lillian Parks, Bradley H. Patterson, Jr., Carl A. Peden, Anthony J. Pellicano, Don Penny, Nelson C. Pierce, Jr., John E. Pinkerton, Gerald F. Pisha, and Milton Pitts.

John Podesta, Lucille B. Price, Glenn A. Quigg, Michael Reagan, George E. Reedy, Russ Reid, Oliver B. (Buck) Revell, John F. W. Rogers, Donald H. Rumsfeld, James R. Saddler, George E. Saunders, Dr. Morris C. Shumiatcher, Lee F. Simmons, Jack W. Smith, Joseph J. Sofet, Larry Speakes, Elliot W. Spence, Arthur Spitzer, Rodney R. Sweetland III, David C. Tiffany, Lieutenant General Richard G. Trefry, Charles G. (Chase) Untermeyer, Buddie L. Vise, Gary Walters, Frederick H. Walzel, W. David Watkins, Mary E. Weaver, Mark D. Weinberg, Brad Wells, and Raymond Young.

Prologue

A MONTH AFTER BILL CLINTON WAS ELECTED, THE SECRET SERVICE sent a teletype to all of its 2,051 agents, warning them not to talk to the press without first clearing it with headquarters. After Clinton had been sworn in on January 15, 1993, another teletype went out. The Secret Service had a "one-voice policy," the message said. In other words, only those Secret Service officials anointed to talk to the press could do so. In April, after *Newsweek* quoted Secret Service agents as saying Hillary Rodham Clinton had thrown a lamp at her husband, the Secret Service sent out a third teletype repeating the previous warnings. The message was clear: anyone caught talking to the press would be fired.

The level of concern was unprecedented but understandable. The Clintons had a chilly marriage. At night, ushers on the first floor of the White House were shocked to hear yelling from the second floor, which, together with the third floor, is the residence portion of the White House. The screaming reverberated through the 201-year-old structure. Moreover, while Hillary Clinton had not thrown a lamp at her husband, she had thrown a briefing book at him. If such details ever leaked through the Secret Service, the agency could find itself in jeopardy.

Yet there was nothing unusual about a president and first lady leading a life that departed radically from the image they sought to project. In private, no modern president or his family has matched its public persona. Indeed, each of the presidents has engaged in elaborate charades to conceal his true character, actions, and words. From marital infidelity to corruption, from official deception to stealing, from arrogance to incompetence, modern presidents have managed to mask their real faces, manipulating the press to conceal the truth.

In *The Twilight of the Presidency,* George E. Reedy, press secretary to President Johnson, said the "splendid isolation" of the president within the White House had turned the presidency into a monarchy.

"The atmosphere of the White House is a heady one," he wrote. "By the twentieth century, the presidency had taken on all the regalia of monarchy except robes, a scepter, and a crown."

The people who know what really goes on in the White House are the Secret Service agents; the White House maids, butlers, and ushers; the military aides who carry the so-called football containing codes for unleashing a nuclear war; and the *Air Force One* stewards who attend to the first family's needs. Like video surveillance cameras, these nonpolitical aides are there but forgotten, observing what goes on when the press conferences and public speeches are over. For the White House is a stage, where the stars adroitly play their roles. Only the producers, directors, and stagehands know what the actors and actresses are really like. For the most part, this infrastructure continues from administration to administration. Dedicated to maintaining their own power, the permanent staff presides over an institution that remains largely unchanged, regardless of who is president.

Known by the Secret Service code name Crown, that institution is the White House, the physical manifestation of the American presidency. Protected by some of the most sophisticated intrusion devices ever invented, it is the most powerful spot on the globe and the most visible symbol of America. Yet what goes on inside the White House and its outposts—*Air Force One,* the presidential motorcades, Camp David, and the presidential vacation homes—rarely comes out.

"If the general public knew what was going on inside the White House, they would scream," a Secret Service agent said. "Americans have such an idealized notion of the presidency and the virtues that go with it, honesty and so forth. That's the furthest thing from the truth."

"I'll guarantee you," the agent continued, "the public doesn't know what is going on most of the time. When you are into power and that close, nobody is going to give you the answers. Nobody will talk."

But they did. What they revealed raises profound questions about the modern presidency.

Inside the White House

1

The Most Mysterious Eighteen Acres in the World

LYNDON JOHNSON WAS FURIOUS. JOHNSON'S WIFE, LADY BIRD, HAD caught him having sex on a sofa in the Oval Office with one of the handful of gorgeous young secretaries he had hired. Johnson blamed it all on the Secret Service, which guarded the Oval Office and the rest of the White House.

"He said you should have done something," recalled a Secret Service agent. "We said, 'We don't do that. That's your problem.' "[1]

After the incident, which occurred just months after he took office, Johnson ordered the Secret Service to install a buzzer system so that agents stationed in the residence portion of the White House could warn him that his wife was approaching.

"The alarm system was put in because Lady Bird had caught him screwing a secretary in the Oval Office," the Secret Service agent said. "He got so goddamned mad. A buzzer was put in from the quarters upstairs at the elevator to the Oval Office. If

1

we saw Lady Bird heading for the elevator or stairs, we were to ring the bell."

Lyndon Johnson was not the first American president to engage in dalliances in the White House. Franklin Roosevelt regularly visited with Lucy Mercer Rutherford when his wife, Eleanor, was out of town.

"Lucy Rutherford came only when Eleanor was away," recalled Alonzo Fields, who was a White House butler at the time. "I would always know when she was coming. It was usually around three or four in the afternoon. I would be told the president would like you to serve his party tonight, which would mean it would be the two of them in his study, and he would not have an assistant. Usually I would direct the service, but in this case I would have to serve the meal. That way, they would know who talked [if the encounter appeared in the press]."[2]

Meanwhile, Eleanor Roosevelt had a long-standing lesbian relationship with Lorena Hickok, who lived in the White House across from Eleanor's room on the second floor.

John F. Kennedy, while married to Jacqueline Kennedy, had sex with dozens of women, including two secretaries known as Fiddle and Faddle; Judith Campbell Exner, who was then seeing Mafia kingpin Sam Giancana; and Marilyn Monroe. According to Secret Service agents, Monroe never entered the White House. Instead, she had sex with Kennedy in New York hotels and in a loft above the office of then Attorney General Robert F. Kennedy, the president's brother, at the Justice Department. Between the fifth and sixth floors, the loft contains a double bed that is used when the attorney general needs to stay overnight to handle crises. Because it is near a private elevator, it was easy for Kennedy and Monroe to enter from the Justice Department basement without being noticed.

"He [Kennedy] had liaisons with Marilyn Monroe there," a Secret Service agent said. "The Secret Service knew about it."

Robert Kennedy became attracted to Monroe and began having sex with her as well.

JFK's scheming was not limited to sex. Though he'd placed an embargo on goods from Cuba, Kennedy made sure he continued to be supplied with Upmann petite cigars, the Havana cigars that he favored, even though he knew that the *Air Force One* stewards who supplied them were violating the law by obtaining them.

"He never asked us to get them," said Robert M. MacMillan, then a steward on *Air Force One.* "But he [Kennedy] would say, 'Jesus, I'm sure going to miss my cigars. Too bad I didn't exempt them.' Kidding, you know."

MacMillan said he bought Upmann petites from a tobacconist in Bermuda when *Air Force One* went there. Because the trips were training missions, Customs inspectors paid no heed.

"We kept the humidor [on *Air Force One*] full," MacMillan said. "He would say, 'Jesus, are we ever going to run out of these?' We would say, 'Don't ask.' He would say, 'I get the message. I won't ask that question again.' We had them until the day he died. He knew damn well we were pulling shenanigans. But he could remain out of it if a newsy got ahold of it, and we would take the heat," MacMillan said. "It was illegal to bring it into the country," he said. "If you didn't violate a law, you were going to be canned and your career would be over under virtually all of them."[3]

But if presidents before Johnson had engaged in deceit on occasion, it was Johnson who turned fooling the public into a wholesale operation. Johnson viewed the White House as a private fiefdom and his Texas ranch as an extension of that fiefdom. The fact that he broke the law by using taxpayer money to fund that fiefdom never bothered him. It was during the Johnson administration that presidential security became omnipresent, further isolating the president from the public. Johnson transformed the White House and its operations into a house of mirrors—a spectacle that continues to this day.

The stage set for this pageant is at 1600 Pennsylvania Avenue. Workers laid the cornerstone for the White House on October 13, 1792. It is perhaps symbolic that today the cornerstone cannot be found.

The original building, based on a Georgian design by James Hoban, consisted of a sandstone box that measured 165 feet from east to west and 85 feet from north to south. The elegance

3

of Georgian buildings comes from the simplicity of their shallow-pitched roofs and symmetrically arranged windows and doorways. Gray in color, the home was referred to as the President's House. That was the name preferred by George Washington, who never got to live there but who guided the project through Congress. When the building received a coat of whitewash in 1797, people began referring to it as the White House.

Home to forty-one presidents and their families, the White House over the years has been sacked and burned, gutted, extended, modified, improved, renovated, and redecorated. In 1902, Theodore Roosevelt officially changed the name of the president's home to the White House. That same year, the west wing was added to house presidential offices. In 1909, the Oval Office—the president's office—was added at the southwest corner of the west wing.

As if purposely to confuse, no one ever refers to the front or back entrance of the White House. Instead, they refer to the porticoes—colonnades that protect from the rain—added to the structure. In 1824, the south portico was added to the rear of the house, and in 1829, the north portico was added to the front. Finally, in 1942, the east wing was built to house the offices of the first lady as well as the White House military office.

When Margaret Truman's piano began to break through the second floor, the District of Columbia's commissioner of public buildings said the floor was "staying up there purely from habit." A renovation, finished in 1952, included gutting the inside of the house and installing a steel frame to support the floors. A balcony on the second-floor level of the south portico was also built.

Other changes have reflected technological progress. When John Adams, the second president, and Abigail Adams first moved into the White House on November 1, 1800, with their eight servants, they had an outdoor privy. In 1803 Thomas Jefferson replaced the privy with two custom-made water closets. In 1834, indoor plumbing was installed. Gaslights were installed in 1848, and in 1845, the White House got its first refrigerator.

In 1879, a telephone was installed—number 1—but it got little use because the country had so few telephones. In 1880, the White House got its first typewriter. To cool the fever of James Garfield as he lay dying from an assassin's bullet, a primitive air-conditioning system was invented for the White House in 1881. Ten years later, the White House got electric lights.

Today the 132-room White House is a four-star hotel complete with priceless paintings. The White House Situation Room can instantly retrieve reports electronically from the CIA, State Department, or Defense Intelligence Agency. In real time, monitors track troop movements by satellite. Any movement on the White House grounds is detected by infrared, electric eye, audio, and pressure sensors. Video cameras on the roof and on the grounds record every movement. A SWAT team on the roof is ready with machine guns any time the president leaves or enters the White House. A digitalized locator box tracks each member of the first family from room to room within the White House and around the world. The White House operators, who handle an average of 48,000 calls a day, even accommodated Caroline Kennedy when, at age five, she asked to speak with Santa Claus. They connected her with a gruff-voiced man in the White House Transportation Department, who is said to have taken her order for a helicopter for John-John.

Nancy Reagan has described the White House with awe. "There's a feeling of wonderment," she said. "Are you really in this beautiful house where so many have lived before you, so much history has been made? The first few weeks you're really in a daze."

In Reagan's memoirs, *My Turn,* she detailed the perquisites that made the White House feel like a palace. "If we needed a plumber, we'd call the usher's office, and he'd be there in five minutes. There were people to wrap packages and wind clocks. And just as soon as the president took a suit off, it would be whisked away for pressing, cleaning or brushing. The sheets are changed after every use, even a catnap."

But just as the cornerstone cannot be found, what the White House consists of is open to question. It sits on 18.1 acres that the District of Columbia government has assessed at $314,975,600. Together with the $25,024,400 assessment given to the building, this gives the property at 1600 Pennsylvania Avenue NW a total value of $340,000,000. The second and third floors, which are the living quarters, are referred to as the executive mansion, while the first floor, used for entertaining, is called the state floor. But that is only part of the constellation known as the White House. When referring to the White House, people may mean the residence, but they may also be referring to the current administration, the west or east wing, the new or old Executive Office Buildings, or other annexes such as the Winder Building on Seventeenth Street, all of which house employees of the Executive Office of the President.

Even to insiders, the White House remains a cipher. Over the years, presidents have sought to expand their domains while making it appear that they are shrinking. By setting up different accounts and borrowing funds and employees from other agencies, they have successfully hidden the true cost of the presidency.

The president himself receives a salary of $200,000 a year plus $50,000 for expenses, a reasonable sum considering his responsibilities. But he also receives $9.7 million a year to run what is known in the U.S. budget as the Executive Residence at the White House, and another $38.9 million for the White House Office. That does not include another $24.8 million for the Office of Administration, which supports the White House Office and other entities within the Executive Office of the President. Nor does it include another $93.8 million for the remaining entities—from the Office of Management and Budget to the National Security Council—that advise the president.

Even these figures are but a token of what the White House really costs. The real costs are unknown even to Congress and the General Accounting Office, the audit arm of Congress, because dozens of other government agencies help support the White House.

"The total cost of the White House isn't in any records," said

John Cronin, Jr., who directed the GAO's audits of the White House for twelve years. "The navy runs the mess and Camp David, the army provides the cars and drivers, the Defense Department provides communications, the air force provides airplanes, the Marine Corps provides the helicopters. The State Department pays for state functions, the National Park Service maintains the grounds, the Secret Service provides protection, and the General Services Administration (GSA) maintains the east and west wings and the old Executive Office Building and provides heat."[4]

Hundreds of people from other agencies are detailed to work for the White House on specific projects, either full-time or part-time. "It's pretty hard in some cases to determine what is a White House expenditure and what is an expenditure of an agency working closely with the White House," Cronin said.

Moreover, the costs of functions within the White House are often allocated to different accounts. The $260,000 in salaries for the White House's five calligraphers, for example, comes from the budget of the Executive Residence; the calligraphers' supplies come from the White House Office.

Mary E. Weaver studied the White House's finances for a year for Congressman Paul E. Kanjorski, a Pennsylvania Democrat who headed a subcommittee of the House Post Office and Civil Service Committee. She was horror-struck.

"The starkest realization we had was that basically the budget numbers you see are not representative of what is really spent," she said. The subcommittee held four hearings and questioned White House officials at length about the size of the White House budget. "Even today we are not able to tell you what those numbers in the budget do represent," Weaver said.

In 1992, the Office of Personnel Management tried to total all these additional costs. The personnel agency came up with a figure of $978.5 million. But even that was a gross underestimate. OPM said it could not calculate the costs of support some agencies provide. Further, the cost of Secret Service protection was not included because the figure is classified. OPM listed only the $15 million spent by the Secret Service to protect former presidents. But Secret Service sources estimate that, because most of the Secret Service's expensive technical service division supports the White House and the president, the cost of protecting the president, the vice president, and their families alone is probably 75 percent of the agency's $475 million annual appropriation—another $356 million.

It was not until 1857 that Congress approved the first salary for an employee to handle secretarial duties in the White House. The amount was $2,500 a year. Prior to that, presidents paid secretaries from their own pockets. When Herbert Hoover was president, the White House had fifty employees, according to William Hopkins, who was executive clerk until 1971. Even then, presidents covered up how much they were spending by using employees temporarily detailed from other agencies. Half of the employees tended to be detailees. Under Harry Truman, the total staff had increased to two hundred.

Almost every president has claimed he would cut the size of the White House staff, and most have ended office with a higher number than their predecessors. As will be discussed later, President Clinton raised the stakes in this shell game. Claiming he reduced the White House staff by 25 percent, he actually *increased* the total cost of running the White House.

Today the Executive Office of the President employs about 1,600 people, but again, this is only the tip of the iceberg. The White House Communications Agency, a Defense Department entity that provides the president with instant worldwide communications, has another 1,003 employees.

While administrations come and go, three-fourths of the White House staff remains, forming an infrastructure with its own culture, rules, rituals, and secrets. Together with appointed White House aides, this hidden government helps set the agenda for the nation, framing the issues that the president will address and propounding solutions. Like the court of Louis XIV, the staff forms its own alliances, trading favors for information, power, and proximity to the president.

The dizzying combination of power and perquisites is corrupting. The percentage of White House aides who have had to consult psychiatrists is far out of proportion to the general population. Simply being able to tell family and friends that

8

one has been invited to attend a White House dinner is intoxicating. Being able to say that one works in the White House is a power trip that many find difficult to deal with. The White House is an environment that magnifies character flaws, a catalyst that has led to such scandals as Watergate and the Iran-contra affair.

"The White House is the ultimate example of where you have derived power, which can be confused with real power or earned power," said Dr. Bertram S. Brown, a Washington psychiatrist who has a unique perspective on the phenomenon. As a special assistant to President Kennedy, he worked in the White House and saw close-up the effect it has on people. A former director of the National Institute of Mental Health, Brown has been a consultant to the Secret Service on threats to the president. Most significantly, through informal referrals by the Secret Service and others, he has been consulted over the years by dozens of White House aides.

"Most of the staff is around thirty and in the age group I worry about," Brown said. "The White House is a crucible that will mold you or break you in terms of identity, growing up, recognizing the difference between self and derived power, or the ability of power to corrupt. The question is, Does it corrupt you the rest of your life? Do you want to be that important again? Are you smart enough to have some mentors who tell you it is evanescent, enjoy it while you can?"[5]

If anyone was corrupted by power, it was Lyndon Johnson. Having been sworn in as president after the death of John F. Kennedy, Johnson was elected president in his own right in 1964, winning 61 percent of the popular vote. During the campaign, he portrayed himself as a peace candidate in contrast to his opponent, Barry Goldwater.

"Some others are eager to enlarge the conflict [in Vietnam]," Johnson said during the campaign. "They call upon us to supply American boys to do the job that Asian boys should do."[6]

A master manipulator, Johnson promptly enlarged the conflict and turned the White House into a chamber of deception, using Pentagon money to fund improvements to his ranch, lying about the costs of running the White House, and stealing government furniture and other items from the White House. In doing so, Johnson—whose Secret Service code name was Volunteer—enlisted the aid of Bill Gulley, one of those anonymous White House aides who continue from administration to administration.

Born on a dirt farm in southern Illinois, Gulley was a country boy with a laugh that sounded as if it were being filtered through marbles. He joined the marines and served as executive assistant to Brent Scowcroft when he headed the White House military office. Scowcroft recommended him to Johnson as someone who could impose order on chaos, and Johnson named Gulley to succeed Scowcroft as head of the military office. Gulley became a civilian and—in a classic example of how presidents try to minimize the White House staff—was placed on the payroll of the U.S. post office. Gulley wound up doing the job for four presidents.

As the keeper of the nuclear football and the person in charge of communications and transportation, Gulley presided over a fiefdom that ate up the largest share of the government's expenditures for the White House. His domain included *Air Force One,* the marine helicopters, the White House drivers and garage, Camp David, communications and computers, the White House mess, the nuclear football, the White House medical unit, the White House TelePrompTers, and the White House television unit, which films the presidents for historical purposes. In effect, Gulley was the mayor of the White House. While he admits to engaging in extensive illegal acts to fulfill presidential whims, Gulley himself was regarded by those who worked with him as honest and credible. From Larry Speakes, President Reagan's press secretary, to Scowcroft, who became President Bush's national security adviser, presidential aides have vouched for his veracity.

Gulley quickly realized that the fragmented nature of the White House gave him an opening to enhance his own power and that of the presidents he served. For the White House is a cauldron of competing interests, each vying for influence with the president.

"Those are the most mysterious eighteen acres in the world," Gulley said. "It's mysterious to secretaries of state, generals, admirals. They all wonder. Nobody really knows what goes on there. A lot of people who come to work for two or three or four years don't have a clue what is there. The White House is compartmentalized. The chief of staff sees most sides of things on the west side of the White House, but he doesn't have a clue as to what happens with the first lady's staff, the Defense Department, or the Secret Service."

When Gulley came to the White House in 1966, he decided he would try to penetrate its secrets, parlaying his knowledge into more personal power.

"I tried as much as I could to involve myself in the whole White House," he said. "It was not too hard because the military provides so much support that they have to go to you to get things done. You stay as the staff turns over. When they leave, they say, 'Call Gulley in the military office.' "

The maids, cooks, and butlers do the same thing.

"They ingratiate themselves with the new president and his family," Gulley said. "They start by telling them how important they are. 'If you want to know anything, just call me.' Some are very successful at this, especially with the first lady. There is a total difference between a Pat Nixon, who had seen the hangers-on and the phonies, and Rosalynn Carter, who did not have a clue what was going on. She thought the best thing was to bring in people who had worked around the mansion in Georgia. Then you have a battle between the old and new people. They all work for their own benefit. No one really cares about the first lady."

As another way of extending his influence, Gulley had one of his aides dispense trinkets to key players in the White House. Manufacturers contributed many of the items he distributed, such as cigarettes imprinted with the presidential seal.

"The aide knew what they smoked, what kind of gum they chewed," Gulley said. "He had cough drops, sunglasses. He had cuff links with *Air Force One* on them."

Secretaries to the president or the chief of staff were favorite recipients.

11

"It's important to know what the president will do," Gulley said. "A secretary may know. A presidential assistant may not know for two weeks. She won't tell you unless she trusts you. But he [Gulley's assistant] kept the communication going. By giving tie clips for her husband and cigarettes for her mama or papa, I knew things before anyone else did."

To bolster his power further, Gulley would arrange for the secretary to the president and her family to stay at Camp David. Code named Cactus by the Secret Service, Camp David is in Catoctin Mountain Park seventy miles north of the White House. Franklin Roosevelt had first used the retreat, calling it Shangri-la. Dwight Eisenhower named it Camp David for his grandson. Gulley's gesture ensured a steady stream of inside tips.

"It's damn important that you know who is going to be fired or is close to the president," he said. "Sometimes it's important to know if an aide is really quoting the president or has made up a story about what the president said. It's great to know if the president said something," Gulley said. "You can get the president to say yes to anything in the personnel area. By phrasing it right, you can get them to say yes or no."

Gulley said some aides would claim the president had authorized a request when he really had not.

"You can't call the president and say, 'Did you tell [Bob] Haldeman this?' But you can call a Rose Woods or Juanita Roberts. They'll say, 'That's bullshit.' "

Ralph Albertazzie, an *Air Force One* pilot under Nixon, said Gulley was a master at using the president's name to get what he wanted.

"He had been there long enough so he knew where the keys were to unlock the secret doors and where the bodies were buried," Albertazzie said. "If he said the president wants this, you didn't dare challenge it."

Gulley used the press as another lever. Apparently to impress friends, one aide asked Gulley's office to arrange a trip on an SR-71, a spy plane used by the CIA.

"The Pentagon made the arrangements and then got shaky about it," Gulley said. "They said, 'We thought you ought to know about this.' I checked to see if he had asked the president. He had not. So I just called Helen Thomas of UPI. I said, 'I need a favor.' She knew in return I would leak something of more importance. You tell her something at 1 P.M., at 1:10 it's gone all over the world. I said, 'This guy has arranged for a flight on the SR-71.' She flashed it. It scared the shit out of him. You're never going to have trouble with him as long as he lives."

Among the many secrets Gulley learned were the day-to-day sexual activities of the presidents. In the case of Lyndon Johnson, they were extensive.

"Johnson would pick women out of a crowd," he said. "He would spot them and send [an aide] to be the pimp."

Gulley said Johnson would spot pretty secretaries in the White House, make a play for them, and if they went to bed with him, place them on his personal staff. Of the eight secretaries around him, only three were not having sex with the president, Gulley said.

A press officer recalled that Johnson became enamored with the press officer's secretary.

"All I know is the next day, she was his secretary," the former press officer said. "One day she said, 'Mr. President, I won't be here after next week,' " the press officer said. "He said, 'Why not?' She said, 'I'm getting married.' Winking, he said, 'Well, if it doesn't work out, come back.' "

Johnson did not limit himself to women he transferred to his personal staff.

"We had gals on my staff he screwed," Gulley said. "One . . . showed up when she wanted to show up. I couldn't tell her to do anything."

Johnson took the woman on a long weekend trip, and she put in for fifty-six hours of overtime, which Gulley felt obliged to approve.

"One weekend, Johnson brought three women back from Texas with him who couldn't even type," Gulley said. "They had to be sent to a commercial school by the State Department to learn to type. They were all knockouts. They could have been *Playboy* centerfolds."

A month after they had been hired, Johnson took one of the women with him on a trip to the Philippines.

"He sent for her from his bedroom," Gulley said. "She went with her pad and pencil. He was ready in his bedroom. She ran out of the room. They sent her by commercial airline to San Francisco, and I sent a military plane to San Francisco to pick her up," Gulley said. "After that, all she did was run the automatic signing machine. Johnson wouldn't have anything more to do with her. He kept her in the old Executive Office Building."[7]

The other two women apparently met with Johnson's approval. According to Gulley, they remained on the west wing staff until Johnson left office.

With the exception of one female reporter for the defunct *Washington Star,* Johnson kept the press at bay in the west lobby. Several times a month, he had the reporter come into the Oval Office. He would close and lock the door, and the secretaries in the next office would stop their work and listen. After less than an hour, the toilet in a bathroom off the Oval Office would flush, and the woman would leave.

"He [Johnson] would screw anything that would crawl, basically," said William F. Cuff, Gulley's executive assistant in the military office. "He was a horny old man. But he had a totally loyal White House staff. There was one common enemy everyone in the White House had, and that was he. Therefore, everyone got along fine because they were afraid of him."[8]

In his role as a power broker, while Presidents Johnson and Carter were out of town, Gulley said he arranged for select White House aides to sleep with girlfriends in the Lincoln Bedroom. Decorated primarily with American Victorian furnishings, the room was never used by Lincoln as a bedroom. Instead, he used it as his office, where many of the major decisions during the Civil War were made. Mary Todd Lincoln, the president's wife, purchased the imposing rosewood bed, which is eight feet long and six feet wide. When Lincoln learned the price, he was aghast and banished it to a guest room. However, several other presidents—including Woodrow Wilson and Theodore Roosevelt—used the room, which is said to be haunted by Lincoln's ghost.[9]

Gulley made the arrangements through a White House butler who controlled the living quarters. In return, Gulley gave the butler and his family trips on *Air Force One* during training missions. Each time, the butler got a certificate saying he had been the guest of the president on *Air Force One.*

"Maybe you want to impress a woman by screwing her in the president's Lincoln Bedroom in the family quarters," he said. "So he has the certificate, and in exchange for the ride, he'll let you spend the night in the Lincoln Bedroom with your girlfriend."[10]

Gulley said White House aides and their girlfriends would enter the White House through a subterranean tunnel. The tunnel—which is ten feet wide and seven feet high—extends from the basement of the Treasury Department into a subbasement of the White House under the east wing.

Originally, the tunnel was planned as a bomb shelter. It is also used to sneak people into the White House so they are not seen by the press. After Tricia Nixon married Edward F. Cox in a Rose Garden ceremony in 1971, they used the tunnel to escape photographers and reporters.

Today, in the event of a nuclear threat, presidents are supposed to be whisked from the White House by helicopter, then taken to either a "doomsday" plane or one of a handful of bomb shelters or "relocation centers." Officially known as National Airborne Command Posts, "doomsday" planes are Boeing 747 jets specially configured so a president may direct a nuclear war from them.

Chief among the relocation centers is the one inside Mount Weather within the Blue Ridge Mountains of Virginia, fifty miles southwest of Washington. The not-so-secret installation is supposed to shelter the president, Supreme Court justices, Cabinet secretaries, and other high-ranking government officials. A self-contained community, Mount Weather has its own clinic, reservoirs of fresh water, computers, communications, dormitory, and cafeteria. A television studio is provided so the president can send messages of hope to any survivors.[11]

While the Secret Service scans the tunnel to the Treasury Building with cameras and protects it with alarms and cipher locks, it is under the jurisdiction of the military office. Small rooms off the tunnel are equipped with cots, and once a month, Gulley invited White House aides and what were then known as airline stewardesses to spend evenings there.

"They partied in the bomb shelter," Gulley said. "There might be six or eight couples. There were bedrooms under the east wing off the tunnel leading to Treasury."

The couples would end their revelry with the ultimate power breakfast—champagne and caviar in the White House mess. With space limited to ninety seats, the mess in the west wing is one of the White House's greatest perquisites.

A Secret Service agent confirmed that at least into the Carter years, the White House was a microcosm of Peyton Place.

"Butlers arranged for staff to sleep with girlfriends upstairs while the president was out of town," the agent said. "It was in the Lincoln and guest bedrooms, especially if they wanted to score big time. The president's bedroom was off limits. . . . That has been going on for a long time—sexual favors. You didn't have to do much for the butlers. You could give them a ride on *Air Force One.* To me the certificate is not a big deal. Those don't cost anything. To some people that is very important."

To retain his power, Gulley made sure he knew the peccadilloes of each member of the first family. For example, Johnson's brother, Sam Houston Johnson, was an alcoholic who would sequester himself on the third floor of the White House while drying out. He was constantly getting into trouble.

At four one morning, local Maryland police called Gulley at home. The president's brother had been in an auto accident with someone else's wife. The police wanted to verify that he was the president's brother. The story never made the papers, but Gulley let everyone know that he was aware of such secrets.[12]

Gulley made sure the press learned very little about the way the White House operates. Each administration regards the White House's finances and perquisites as state secrets, to be guarded even more jealously than classified information. Requests for seemingly trivial information like the number of cars in the White House motor pool are invariably turned aside. When a *Washington Post* reporter tried to find out the true number of White House cars—about thirty-five—by staking out the Secret Service garage, Gulley was ready for him. Having gotten reports that the reporter was watching from across the street from the garage, then at 1222 Twenty-second Street NW in Washington, "I stationed the cars at the White House, at Fort Myers, and in Anacostia so he wouldn't see them," Gulley said.

While the president's military aides carried the so-called nuclear football, Gulley, as chief of the military office, was the person at the White House who was in overall charge of its operation. The football consists of a locked briefcase, which contains a code book. The code book lists a number of nuclear strike options. When the president calls the Pentagon to launch a nuclear strike, he is supposed to begin by reading codes from a plastic authentication card, which he is supposed to carry. This verifies that he is the president. Then he is supposed to read off the code beside the option he wants to use. For example, during the cold war, he might have wanted to bomb only Moscow. Or he might have opted for a strike at five major Soviet cities.

Gulley found the system laughable. For one thing, few presidents had the skill to use the cumbersome codes. More worrisome, the Soviets presumably would have launched a surprise attack at night, when the president was asleep. Yet during the night, the football was kept by a communications watch officer in the subbasement of the White House near the military switchboard. If alerted by phone of an impending attack, the aide was to meet the president with the football in the Oval Office. Even if the president awoke immediately, it would take ten to fifteen minutes for the president to rush to the Oval Office. In that time, the Soviets could have already hit the United States.

"The flaw was trying to find the guy who had the authority, the president," Gulley said. "The Russians weren't going to attack on a sunny day when the president was in the situation

17

room. Submarines could hit Washington in five minutes, but everything was predicated on a thirty-minute launch from Russia itself.''

"It could be a good ten minutes [to get to the Oval Office]," a Secret Service agent agreed. "A submarine could be offshore. We would be tracking it. If we had a sub off the coast, the president won't be sleeping."

The emergency plan consisted of a three-inch-thick looseleaf notebook that was so secret few people in government were cleared to see it. But because they thought it could enhance their careers, military people who had anything to do with it would all try to change it.

"Military assistants became enamored of the emergency plan," said William Cuff, Gulley's executive assistant. "Their eyes got shiny. They thought, 'This is the important stuff.' They all wanted to play with it. That meant rewriting it and moving material from this chapter to another. They envisioned they had helped the national security. Occasionally, a substantive change would creep in."

Gulley was equally skeptical of the military's plan to evacuate the president in the event of an attack.

"I had helicopters three minutes from the White House when he was in town," Gulley said. "All this supposedly was going to take place simultaneously. You would bust in on the president at 3 A.M. and say the Russians have launched. He's going to worry about his wife and kids. It was never practical."

By his own account, Gulley helped Johnson swindle the government. Using a classified fund that was supposed to maintain classified bomb shelters. Gulley said he illegally spent the money on improvements to Johnson's ranch, including an extension to the landing strip, a theater, a roadway, and a water pump. Gulley's records show at least $3.7 million spent this way. When Johnson left office, Gulley arranged for secret flights to ship government property to the LBJ Ranch in Johnson City, Texas.

Referring to the improvements to the ranch, Gulley said, "Johnson got personally involved. Very few knew. He put it in a way that you knew you better get it done. He would deny any knowledge. We put in a sprinkler system at the ranch and showerheads [for his] head, legs, and belly. It cost $125,000 to put the water pump in. We resurfaced a road."

Gulley recalled that Johnson called a military duty aide at four one morning.

"This is the president, and I'm going blind," Johnson said.

"Yes, sir," the aide said.

"Well, goddamn it. Didn't you hear me? I said I'm going blind."

"I'll get the doctor," the aide said.

"I don't want the goddamn doctor," Johnson said. "Don't you want to know what is making me go blind? The military is tearing up the roads, and the dust is getting in my eyes. Anyone with an ounce of brains would know it has to be fixed."

Gulley said he ordered the air force to fly in water trucks that constantly sprayed water on the roads.

"They [the trucks] never left that ranch," he said.[13]

Gulley said Johnson asked the Secret Service to wash his car. When the agents refused, saying that was not their job, Johnson had Secret Service headquarters pay for a car wash machine.

"A theater was installed," said Cuff, Gulley's former assistant. "The justification was he had a lot of military people assigned to him who needed to watch training films. It was paid for by the government. Of course, the purpose was to show him movies. I don't think anyone would have dared to show a training film in it."

Johnson also ordered marine helicopters to herd his peacocks.

"There were things that you probably wouldn't do today," said James R. Jones, who acted as Johnson's chief of staff. "For example, he wanted peacocks. They brought helicopters in to control them or capture them."

"Johnson was the grand thief," Gulley said. "He knew where the money was. He had us set up a fund code named Green Ball. It was a Defense Department fund supposedly to assist the Secret Service to purchase weapons. They used it for whatever Johnson wanted to use it for. Fancy hunting guns were bought. Johnson and his friends kept them."

Joseph Laitin, Johnson's deputy press secretary, said an admirer had sent to Johnson at his ranch an expensive grandfather clock.

"Johnson said it would look good in the library," Laitin said. "Jack Valenti [one of Johnson's top aides] said, 'Sir, there's a rule we can't accept anything over fifty dollars.' " Saying he would keep it, "Johnson turned around and said, 'I wouldn't pay fifty dollars for that thing.' "[14]

Johnson did more than any other president to cover up the true costs of the White House by loading up the staff with detailees from other agencies, according to Gulley.

All the while, Johnson fostered the image of a penny-pincher who was saving taxpayer money. The January 21, 1964, *New York Times* announced, "President Johnson, as part of economy drive, orders cutback in use of electricity." As part of the economy drive, the April 23, 1965, *Times* carried a story saying Johnson had ordered the lights turned off inside the press office ladies' room.

"He [Johnson] had a fetish about lights," said Nelson C. Pierce, Jr., who was an assistant usher in the White House. "If there was a light on in a room and no one was in that room, he went into orbit."[15]

"If he saw a light on in the old Executive Office Building, he would say, 'Who is that person?' " said Frederick H. Walzel, a member of the White House Police who later became its chief. "You find out some poor soul forgot to turn the light out."

One evening, Johnson came back to the White House drunk, screaming about the lights.

"He is the only person [president] I have seen who was drunk," said Walzel. "He [Johnson] was asking about the lights and was cussing and cursing. He was drunk."[16]

One of the more bizarre events during Johnson's presidency took place when a Central American dictator sent Johnson a Chinese cook as a present. Known only as Mr. Wong, the cook did not speak English and seemed only dimly aware of his intended purpose.

Gulley said he first learned of the cook when the military aide on *Air Force One* told him to meet the cook at the White

House on a Saturday afternoon. Gulley was to arrange to fly Wong to the LBJ Ranch.

"I went in, and here is a four-foot-eight-inch-tall Chinaman," Gulley recalled. "He had a straw hat and a suitcase. He was in the lobby at the north door. He couldn't speak English. He didn't know what the White House was."

Gulley arranged for Wong to sleep in a third-floor room of the White House, then flew with him to the ranch the next morning.

"He arrived at 7:30 A.M.," Gulley said. "LBJ and Lady Bird came to the trailer that was used for support. He said, 'Did my Chinaman arrive?' He [Mr. Wong] didn't stand up. He didn't know who the president was. LBJ said, 'Bird, see if you can talk to him. He is here to work. Clean up this trailer.' "

Johnson asked the other cooks to teach Wong to cook his favorite dishes—tapioca and chili. Then he flew Wong back to the White House to help out as a chef.

"So he stayed at the White House," Gulley recalled. "One time he was supposed to go to the ranch for the weekend, and he hid behind the drapes in the East Room," Gulley said. "He would play hide-and-seek. He didn't see the seriousness of keeping LBJ waiting. He was like a child, although he was in his late twenties." After several months had passed, "He began to realize that this is the president, and he worked for him," Gulley said.

Catalino Minor, a houseman at the White House, recalled that Wong actually did very little when he was at the White House.

"He did nothing in the White House," he said. "He would walk around."

When Johnson left office, Gulley said, he arranged for at least ten flights to fly government property to Johnson's ranch.

"A lot was sent by State," he said. "We sent LBJ tie pins and busts and lots of furniture. There were wristwatches, rings, cuff links, ladies' bracelets, lipstick dispensers. It was not cheap stuff. They all had presidential seals," Gulley said, estimating that the gold cigarette lighters cost $1,000 each. "There was *Air Force One* toilet paper, soap, and furniture," he said.

While Gulley said he was not sure in every case that the

property belonged to the government, he knew that Johnson's personal furniture and belongings had been sent separately by van to Texas. He said many of the items sent by plane were, in fact, government property.

"In the White House," Gulley said, "you never worry about the law. . . . My thinking was, if the president wants it done, it's right."[17]

"There is an unreality to the White House, more so now, that does make you think you are above the law," said Jim Jones. "You have so much power at your command. You have all the perks of office—the cars, the White House mess. Any time you go to a party and a White House operator calls, the host is thrilled. 'I must be something important.' There is an unreality to it."[18]

"Lyndon just took things [from the White House]," said Clement E. Conger, who became the White House curator under President Richard Nixon.

D. Patrick O'Donnell, an *Air Force One* flight engineer, said he flew what he had been told were White House items back to the ranch.

"We flew White House furniture back," he said. "I was on some of the missions. The flights back were at 7:50 or 8:50 P.M. and early in the morning. I had three of the missions. . . . I think he even took the electric bed out of Walter Reed Army Hospital. That was a disgrace."[19]

Cuff, one of Gulley's aides, said he arranged for two of the flights. He said he was told by those who loaded the goods that they came from the State Department and the White House.

If Johnson's behavior in the White House was shocking, his conduct on *Air Force One* was scandalous. Known by the Secret Service code name Angel, *Air Force One* had gotten its name when Dwight D. Eisenhower was president. Prior to that, the aircraft used by Franklin D. Roosevelt and Harry S Truman had been known by air force designations. Because a flight controller had mistaken the president's plane for a commercial one, the pilot suggested calling the plane the president was using *Air Force One*. Boeing 707's were used from Kennedy until President Bush, who used a Boeing 747.

The crew that flies *Air Force One* is part of the air force's Eighty-ninth Airlift Wing under the Air Mobility Command. The unit provides transportation for government officials, including members of Congress. Based at Andrews Air Force Base east of Washington, *Air Force One* costs $41,875 per hour to fly for fuel and supplies alone. The total annual cost of *Air Force One* and its crew is estimated by the Office of Management and Budget at $185 million.

Crew members are handpicked for *Air Force One*.

"They have a history on you [within the Eighty-ninth] before you are selected to go on the crew," said Jimmy R. Bull, who was chief communicator on *Air Force One*. "Everybody watches everybody."[20]

Despite the pressure, there has never been a serious problem with a crew member.

"The worst thing you ever saw was a guy getting a ticket for drinking and driving. A lot of people were history. They don't kick them out of the air force, but you're not a part of this organization anymore. If you want to have a drink, you better be in for the night. You can have a cocktail or two the night before a flight, but keep in mind you are flying the president. I never saw any abuse of that. It is one of the things you learn."

The plane is specially maintained as well.

"The maintenance goes beyond specifications," Bull said. "The treatment it gets from the beginning is white glove. It is looked at more. If there is a hint of metal when they check the oil, the engine is changed. They might change the oil filters at halftime. On the president's plane, you don't use recapped tires. All the commercial airlines and most trucks use recaps."

Under Federal Aviation Administration regulations, *Air Force One* takes precedence over other aircraft. When approaching an airport, it is placed ahead of other planes that got there first. Before landing, the Secret Service agents on the ground check the runway for explosives or objects like tires. Generally, other aircraft may not land on the same runway for fifteen or twenty minutes before *Air Force One* lands.

"The airport authority at JFK in New York got so fed up with us that they didn't want the president coming in there anymore, so we started going to Newark," Bull said. "With the planes arriving and departing, it messes up schedules, which costs the airlines money."

Air Force One is accorded special treatment by other countries as well.

"The last thing a legitimate government would want to do is shoot down *Air Force One*," Jimmy Bull said. "Obviously, there are enough kooks out there with shoulder-fired missiles that that was a big concern. Air traffic all over the world would provide any head of state sufficient air space. They would keep other aircraft away from you. They were protecting themselves. To have a midair collision on their watch would not look good."

When flying over the Soviet Union and Syria one day, *Air Force One* suddenly found itself surrounded by fighter planes.

"That made our cockpit a little nervous," Bull said. "They didn't let us know in advance. It made you nervous to look up and see half a dozen MiGs."

Because of the president's unpredictable schedule, working on *Air Force One* can be enervating.

"It burns you out," said Stanley J. Goodwin, a communicator on *Air Force One.* "It causes a lot of personal hardships. When the president of the United States wants something, you are there to serve him, and you do your best. Getting up at 3 A.M., we get old fast. But I don't regret one day of it. It's probably one of the best experiences that anyone could have."

It was in *Air Force One* that President Clinton committed one of the worst gaffes of his presidency, resulting in diversion of air traffic at Los Angeles International Airport while Cristophe, a Beverly Hills barber, cut his hair for $200. Even more than in the White House, presidents think they have privacy in *Air Force One* and can do as they like.

MacMillan, the steward on *Air Force One,* recalled that once he was on the plane, Johnson would make outlandish demands.

"One warm afternoon in Texas, Johnson asked for a diet root beer," he said. "We had ten or fifteen cans on board. The staff around him was monkey see, monkey do. When they saw him drinking that, they all decided they wanted that. A little while later, he decided he wanted a second one, and there wasn't one on board. He acted like a child. He ranted and raved. He told [the chief steward] to get 8,700 cases of root beer and keep it on the airplane. He [the chief steward] ended up buying eight cases, and Johnson never ordered another root beer."

"Only one person could make his chili," said Russ Reid, another steward. "He had to have a certain kind of root beer. One time they landed somewhere just to buy root beer."

MacMillan said Johnson's favorite way of referring to a staff member was "you damn fool."

"Regardless of how old you were, he liked to call you 'boy' just because he knew it upset you," MacMillan said.

Johnson was obsessed with finding leaks. He would purposely float stories to individual staff members to see if they showed up in the papers, then rip into the offenders and fire them.

"We were coming back from the ranch," said Laitin, Johnson's deputy press secretary. "It was 2 A.M. He called me into his office on the plane. He said, 'What do we have to make a headline tomorrow?' I said, 'How about the fact you'll make Gronouski ambassador to Poland and Larry O'Brien the new postmaster general?' He said, 'Where did you hear that?' I said, 'Bill Moyers [then Johnson's press secretary] told me.' He said, 'I told Moyers not to tell anybody.' I said, 'He told me not to tell anyone.' Johnson said, 'But you're telling me now.' "

Laitin wondered if Johnson was serious when he made such absurd criticisms. According to George E. Reedy, Johnson's press secretary, he was.

Of all the presidential watchers, none is more astute and experienced than Reedy. Having worked for Johnson when Johnson was in the Senate and when he was vice president, Reedy knew many of Johnson's predecessors. Having served for most of his term as Johnson's press secretary and then as counselor to the president, Reedy knew firsthand how the White House works. Having studied former presidents, he knew their history. As a former newspaperman, Reedy understood the press as well.

In 1970, Reedy wrote *The Twilight of the Presidency*, a brilliant analysis of how presidents become consumed by the office. Just as Niccolò Machiavelli's *The Prince* is the classic tome on the use of power, Reedy's book is the definitive critique of the presidency.

Almost as soon as he began working there, Reedy became uneasy about the White House atmosphere. But it was not until he had temporarily left the Johnson White House and had run into Senator Richard Russell at a party that it all came together in his mind. By then, it was clear to Reedy that Johnson had lost the political skill he had had when he was in the Senate. Because of opposition to Johnson's policies in pursuing the Vietnam War, Johnson would later decline to run for reelection.

When Reedy encountered Senator Russell at the party, Johnson had just made a major miscalculation in trying to end a strike by machinists.

"He had the best brain I have ever encountered in my whole life," Reedy said of Russell. "He was really brilliant." Referring to Johnson's latest misjudgment, Reedy said, " 'Senator, do things look as bad as they seem to be?' He said, 'Yes, they are probably even worse.' I said, 'Why don't you go down to the White House the way you did in the Senate and tell him what you think?' He said to me, 'George, I cannot talk to a president the way I talk to a senator.' "

That night, Reedy had difficulty sleeping, leading to his decision to write his book on the presidency.

"I thought, 'Why was it that Russell, who had more brains than Johnson and had fought the Ku Klux Klan when it was strong, could not talk to Johnson in the White House the way he could in the Senate?' If you understand that story fully, you understand the White House. . . . Johnson was a moody, impulsive man. If he started getting impulses in the Senate, there was Senator Hubert Humphrey on one side of him and Senator Richard Russell on the other side coming at him from different angles. Eventually, he would come up with sensible solutions."[21]

For example, Reedy said Johnson would make an undiplomatic speech or try to push a bill that had no chance of passage.

"In the Senate, there were people who would take him into

26

the cloakroom and talk to him in the mother tongue," Reedy said. "In the White House, that didn't happen because in the White House, nobody talks to the president in the mother tongue. In the Senate, fifteen or thirty of his colleagues would back him into a corner and let him know what was happening. In the White House, everyone would say, 'Yeah, verily.' "

Reedy said that at first Johnson continued to prosecute the Vietnam War because he thought Kennedy would have, and he wanted to demonstrate that no crackpot assassin could alter American policy.

"When he first came in, he had a big meeting with all of the top Kennedy people and all his top people," Reedy said. "I had the feeling I was sitting in a big poker game. Everyone was trying to hide his cards from the other guy and get a peek at the other guys' hands. He had decided he wanted to continue Kennedy's policies. He was looking to them to find out what Kennedy would have done. They, on the other hand, were looking to him to see what he wanted done. I think a signal got mixed up somewhere. He got the idea that Kennedy was going to prosecute the war in Vietnam to a greater extent than he would have, which was against Johnson's own feeling. He had visited there, and I was with him. He thought it was pretty silly."

It was not long before Johnson's ego became involved.

"Once a president makes a decision, the decision is going to grow and grow even if it's foolish," Reedy said. "When a president does something, he commits the United States. Suppose the president issues an order to make an attack on something in Vietnam. Fifty men get killed. The order may have been stupid. The president is not going to say to himself, 'They died in vain because I was stupid.' They died heroically, and he is going to send 100 to make up for this so they won't have died in vain. So the 100 get killed. Before you know it, you send 100,000 men in to demonstrate the original men did not die in vain."

Often, the information coming to a president is distorted because aides tell him what he wants to hear.

"The information is accurate, but it doesn't come to him with the overtones it should," Reedy said. For example, the figures given to Johnson on the number of Vietnamese villages that had been "pacified" and could be counted on to support the South Vietnamese were skewed. To begin with, the villagers told the Americans who came to analyze them what they wanted to hear in order to get rid of them.

"They told them what they knew would please Saigon," Reedy said. "What would please Saigon would please the Pentagon. What would please the Pentagon is what would please the president."

As it happened, the Central Intelligence Agency repeatedly gave Johnson gloomy assessments of American prospects in Vietnam, but the president found it easy to ignore the CIA's warnings because so many other people around him were telling him what he wanted to hear. The same applied to the press.

"As a rule, the only place a president gets real reactions from is the press," Reedy said. But, surrounded by obsequious courtiers, presidents develop rationalizations for ignoring the press.

"A president can always blame the press," Reedy said. "It's either the damn liberal press or the damn conservative press or the damn northern press.

"You had these college students in the park jumping up and down yelling, 'Hey, hey, LBJ. How many kids have you killed today?' " Reedy said. "The White House was full of young college students who were there on various fellowships. They would say, 'Those people don't represent America's youth,' because they were the ambitious types or they wouldn't be there. I think he sometimes thought the anti-Vietnamese protesters came from Mars.

"You'll get plenty of speeches in Congress by his political opponents attacking him," Reedy said, "but when they come in the White House, they immediately become obsequious. During the 1964 campaign, both Barry Goldwater and George Wallace had to come into the White House for different reasons. They had been campaigning against Johnson. If you followed their campaigns, you thought they just wanted to get their hands on his throat. I was at both meetings. All they said was, 'Yes, sir, Mr. President.' 'Yes, sir, Mr. President.' "

Simply being in the Oval Office intimidates most people.

"You walk in and see the president standing behind that desk," Reedy said. "There are flags of the marines and navy and air force behind him. All of a sudden your knees start knocking. This is your country. To be nasty or critical of him is almost like blowing your nose on the American flag. He is your country. Then when people get out of the White House, they get their nerve back."

The contrast makes presidents feel that everyone around them is duplicitous.

"Someone will come in and could not be nicer, and then go out and denounce the president," Reedy said. "That makes the president cynical and mistrusting."

Indeed, there is some reason for a president to become wary. Besides the fact that almost everyone is constantly asking him for things, the White House staff usually engages in its own power plays.

"If you have any sensitivity at all, you can't help but see that almost everyone in the White House is engaged in a plot of some kind," Reedy said. "It's palace politics."

In the White House, all the leavening influences that keep people balanced are missing. Even spouses who normally can be counted on to keep politicians balanced experience the same sense of exhilaration and lose touch with ordinary people.

"The White House confines people to the White House," Reedy said. "The president's wife can't go down to the local department store and buy a dress. She doesn't go to the local grocery store and talk to other people.

"In your ordinary everyday life, what keeps you from being a damn fool are all the people you run into that give you a hard time or question you," Reedy said. "American politics is very plebeian. We scuffle. All of a sudden, presidents get into one area where they do not get direct heat. That's the White House. Everything there is set up to make his life easy on the grounds he has so many burdens."

In part, presidents' obsession with secrecy is rooted in the fact that so much of what they deal with is, in fact, secret.

"You have an entire area of government that is secretive—

the CIA, FBI, Defense Department," Reedy said. But, impressed by their own power, presidents tend to become irrationally secretive as a way of asserting control.

"Secrecy can get ridiculous," Reedy said. "I remember all the secrecy we had about the bases we had in Thailand. The South Vietnamese knew about them, the North Vietnamese knew about them, the Chinese and the Thais knew about them. Just about everyone knew except the American taxpayer, who was paying for it."

When Johnson criticized his deputy press secretary, Laitin, for repeating to Johnson his plans to nominate O'Brien and Gronouski, he meant it.

"He could be very serious about a thing like that," Reedy said. "He could really get very silly about things like that."

Johnson was never satisfied with the way the press portrayed him.

"Johnson had had a heart attack, and the doctors told him to walk a mile every day," Reedy said. "Being Johnson, he got in his car and measured a half mile. That put him within a hundred feet of his cousin Auriole. She was an elderly lady who lived all alone. Every evening, he took that half-mile walk. He would pound on her door and whoop and holler. She loved it."

On one such visit, Johnson took Helen Thomas of United Press International. "She was captured by the whole spirit of the thing," Reedy said. "There was this pioneer setting. His cousin came to the door without slippers on. I thought, 'Any public relations man should get $100,000 for arranging the story.' But Johnson got mad as all get-out. He interpreted it as meaning these Johnsons were a bunch of hillbillies."

In general, Reedy said, "to a president, a good story is one that says he is noble, forward-looking, and honest and took another step today to rescue the country."

"We were serving roast beef one time," MacMillan, the *Air Force One* steward, said. "He [Johnson] came back in the cabin. Jack Valenti [Johnson's aide] was sitting there. He had just gotten his dinner tray. On it was a beautiful slice of rare roast beef. Johnson grabbed that tray and said, 'You dumb son of a bitch. You are eating raw meat.' He brought it back to the galley and said, 'You two sons of bitches, look at this. This is raw. You gotta cook the meat on my airplane. Don't you serve my people raw meat. Goddamn, if you two boys serve raw meat on my airplane again, you'll both end up in Vietnam.' He threw it upside down on the floor. He stormed off.''

A few minutes later, Valenti went back to the galley.

"I said, 'Sorry about your dinner, Mr. Valenti.' He said, 'Do we have any more rare?' 'We have plenty of rare.' Valenti said, 'Well, he won't be back. He's done his thing. Don't serve me any fully cooked meat.' We cleaned up the mess and ignored him [Johnson]. He never came back.''

Gerald F. Pisha, another *Air Force One* steward, said that on one occasion when Johnson didn't like the way a steward had mixed a drink for him, he threw it on the floor.

"He said, 'Get somebody who knows how to make a drink for me,' '' Pisha said. "He [the other steward] said, 'Sir, if you show me how to make that drink, I'll make it that way from here on out.' It was Cutty Sark and soda. It was just too weak. Johnson filled his glass three quarters with Scotch and filled it with soda water.''

Johnson then ordered the steward to throw away the remaining soda water. He said, " 'I want fresh soda water each time,' '' Pisha said.

"He had episodes of getting drunk," Reedy said. "There were times when he would drink day after day. You would think this guy is an alcoholic. Then all of a sudden, it would stop. We could always see the signs when he called for a Scotch and soda, and he would belt it down and call for another one, instead of sipping it.''

Because he spent more time with him when Johnson was in the Senate, Reedy said he observed him getting drunk more often there. Others said that when he became president, Johnson generally confined his drinking sprees to his visits to his ranch.

"He needed attention," MacMillan said. "He needed to assert his authority.''

Dr. Brown, the psychiatrist who has seen many White House aides, said Johnson's humiliation of his employees was a way of exercising his power. He would, for example, issue instructions to his aides while sitting on the toilet.

"Johnson was a megalomaniac," Brown said. "He was a man of such narcissism that he thought he could do anything."

As another way of asserting control, Johnson was always late.

"He would be an hour late and would expect the crew to make it up so he would be on time," MacMillan said. "We hedged our bets and would add forty-five minutes to an hour for every stop. He finally figured that out. He said, 'How come it takes the [commercial] airplanes an hour, and we take two hours?' We said, 'Mr. President, that's because you are often an hour late.' He would say, 'That's my business.' "

At the same time, Johnson demanded that the second he walked on board *Air Force One* or one of the marine helicopters, the aircraft was to take off.

"He had all the pilots intimidated," Laitin, the deputy press secretary, said.

Having been forewarned about Johnson's demands, a new helicopter pilot lifted off from Johnson City, Texas, near Johnson's ranch, the moment the helicopter door had closed on Johnson. In their haste to let the helicopter take off immediately, the ground crew had forgotten to remove the telephone cord that now dangled from the helicopter.

"They slammed the door shut and had forgotten to disconnect the phone," Laitin said. "The helicopter went up, and there was this thirty-foot cord dangling. It was frightening because there were high-tension wires. They called the pilot, and he had to come back."

Reedy said Johnson was a great mimic.

"He would mimic Bobby Kennedy," he said. "When he would start mimicking Bobby, you would think he was right in front of you. It was his voice and his mannerisms. God, he was good at it."

Johnson thought that if he mimicked what successful people did, he would be as successful as they were.

"Jack Kennedy always wanted soup," Reedy said. "Johnson really did not like soup, but he finally found a chili soup. It was a diluted chili con carne. And by God, every place we went, we had to load cases of it on the airplane. It was a lousy soup.

"He was always trying to get me to write speeches like Winston Churchill's," Reedy said. "That was absolutely silly."

Johnson, like other presidents, would often reveal his true motivations in asides that the press never picked up. During one trip, Johnson was discussing his proposed civil rights bill with two governors. Explaining why it was so important to him, he said it was simple: "I'll have them niggers voting Democratic for two hundred years."[22]

"That was the reason he was pushing the bill," said MacMillan, who was present during the conversation. "Not because he wanted equality for everyone. It was strictly a political ploy for the Democratic party. He was phony from the word go."

MacMillan said Johnson's younger daughter, Luci, then seventeen, was a "wretched witch." On one stopover in Florida, she was having a tantrum because she did not know where a servant was. She blamed MacMillan for it.

"She said, 'Damn you. You go find my nigger right now,'" MacMillan said. Playing dumb, MacMillan asked for a description of the man.

"She screamed again. 'Find my nigger.' People around were smiling. She drew her hand back as if she was going to slap me. I said, 'Miss Johnson, I don't think that would be a good idea.' She said, 'Damnit, I'll find him myself.' This was the attitude of these people who were championing civil rights."

Asked for her comment, Luci Johnson denied that such an incident ever took place.

"I do not now, nor have I ever, subscribed to such feelings or such language and therefore could not use it," she said in a letter to the author.

"Luci was his favorite to the detriment of Lynda," a Johnson aide said. "Lynda was the ugly duckling. It was heartbreaking to watch it. But George Hamilton [the actor] did a lot for her. . . . Once, they went away to Acapulco and *Life* had a six-page spread on them taken secretly. She called me and said, 'How did *Life* know where we were? George said he never told *Life*.' I said, 'Of course he didn't. His press agent did.' She said,

'Some people say he is using me.' I said, 'Sure he is. But you are using him, too. If you are getting enough out of it, fine.' "

MacMillan said that when military leaders raised questions about the wisdom of Johnson's policies in Vietnam, the president brushed them off.

"He had an attitude of, 'Don't confuse me with facts, my mind is made up,' " he said. "When they tried to steer him away from something, he would unload on them and let them know who was chief.

"Johnson called the South Vietnamese those 'poor little boogers,' " MacMillan said. "He said, 'We're going to liberate those poor little boogers, and I'll be known as the great emancipator.' "

According to MacMillan, the *Air Force One* steward, in contrast to Johnson and other recent presidents, Truman and Eisenhower listened to people and went out of their way to obtain the views of ordinary citizens.

"We had been asked to take Mrs. Kennedy and former president Truman to Greece for the inauguration of their president," MacMillan said. "We left shortly before Kennedy was killed. In the middle of the night, I was sitting on the ice chest, and this figure appeared in his pajamas. It was Truman. He said, 'Where is the crapper?' I said, 'I'm sorry, sir?' 'Where is the crapper? Where do you go?' "

MacMillan told Truman that there was a lavatory near the presidential stateroom. But Truman said he was afraid to wake Jackie.

"I'm an old artillery captain, and I want to go where the crew goes," Truman said.

When he came out, Truman asked if MacMillan had any Jack Daniel's. Holding up two fingers and looking around, Truman said he could have a drink since "the boss"—his wife— wasn't around.

As MacMillan poured him a drink, Truman said, " 'There is only one.' I said, 'That's what you asked for.' Truman said, 'No, you don't understand. I'm not supposed to drink alone.' "

MacMillan told the former president that he was not supposed to drink on duty.

"Well, tell them the old captain told you to," Truman said.

The two talked for the next hour and a half as MacMillan pretended to sip his drink.

"It was probably the most enjoyable conversation I had with anybody in my life," MacMillan said. Referring to Truman's forceful leadership and honest approach, MacMillan said, "I just admired the man because of the way he conducted his life and what he did."

"With Truman, there was not the slightest breath of scandal," Reedy said. "He was exactly what he looked like—a proper midwestern husband and father. But even he changed in the White House. I think he lost some of his political feel," as demonstrated by the indecisive way he handled charges that he had Communist ties. "The White House robs people of their political instincts," Reedy said. "It's like a flower being raised in a hothouse. You have people who won't give it to you with the bark off."

John F. Kennedy's bedroom activities were well known to the White House and *Air Force One* staff, as well as to the press, but it was not until after his death that the details began to emerge.

"JFK had Fiddle and Faddle," said Reedy, referring to the two White House secretaries—a blonde and a brunette—who had threesomes with Kennedy and swam nude with him in the White House pool. "Everyone in Washington knew about them. In those days, the press did not write about those kinds of personal relationships. I think stories about personal relationships are justified because they reveal something about a man," Reedy said. "The way a man reacts toward women is governed by gut instincts. He can present all sorts of fronts to the press and public at large, but when he is with a woman, he can't. The way he relates to women is something the public should know. I think a president who goes from woman to woman is not a serious man. All he is interested in is going to bed."

While Kennedy treated the staff with respect, the *Air Force One* crew had trouble with Bobby Kennedy's black Labrador, which constantly had to be played with to keep it from running up and down the aisles and bothering passengers.

"After the second trip, we were serving cocktails and had mixed a batch of martinis," MacMillan said. "Someone had changed his mind and didn't want his. So we gave it to the dog in a plate. He lapped it up and went to sleep. So after that, we always gave him two martinis. We had work to do, and he wanted to play."

"The only thing that astounded me was JFK's lack of consideration about Jackie and the kids," said Ralph Albertazzie, an *Air Force One* pilot. "He would come aboard the plane and grab some papers and start reading. She [Jackie] would be struggling to get in the plane with the kids, and he could care less."[23]

But that was nothing compared with Johnson's antics.

"Johnson would come on the plane, and the minute he got out of sight of the crowds, he would stand in the doorway and grin from ear to ear, and say, 'You dumb sons of bitches. I piss on all of you,' " MacMillan said. "Then he stepped out of sight and began taking off his clothes. By the time he was in the stateroom, he was down to his shorts and socks. It was not uncommon for him to peel off his shorts, regardless of who was in the stateroom."

MacMillan said Johnson did not care if women were in the area.

"He was totally naked with his daughters, Lady Bird, and female secretaries," he said. "He was quite well endowed in his testicles," MacMillan said. "So everyone started calling him Bull Nuts. He found out about it. He was really upset."

While in Texas, Johnson had ordered a new pair of pants. As he put them on in *Air Force One,* O'Donnell, the flight engineer, said Johnson bellowed, " 'I need some more goddamn ball room in these pants.' He was a real uncouth individual, absolutely a disgrace," O'Donnell said. "All these gals and his wife and one of the children were on board. You could hear him all over the airplane."

Late one afternoon, Johnson called an impromptu press conference at his ranch.

"He whips his thing out and takes a leak, facing them sideways," O'Donnell said. "You could see the stream. It was embarrassing. I couldn't believe it. Here was a man who is the president of the United States, and he is taking a whiz out on the front lawn in front of a bunch of people."[24]

MacMillan and other *Air Force One* crew members said Johnson commonly closed the door to his stateroom and spent hours alone locked up with pretty secretaries, even when his wife was on board.

"Sometimes a message came in, and the radio operator could not deliver it to the old man in his room because he was fooling around," O'Donnell, the flight engineer, said. "He could lock it. He would be in the partitioned area with some broad. Lady Bird would get up and try and get in."

A member of Johnson's press office recalled seeing Johnson engaged in intense conversation on *Air Force One* with one of the curvaceous secretaries he was known to be having sex with.

"Across the aisle was Lady Bird reading a book," the former press officer said. "She was a very tolerant woman."

The press officer said a White House photographer always knew when another Johnson secretary had had sex with the president in the Oval Office.

"[The secretary] would go in to take dictation, and when she came out, the seams in her stockings were not straight the way they were when she went in," the former press officer said. "The door was always closed."

When he was vice president, Albertazzie said, Johnson tried from *Air Force Two,* the vice president's Boeing 707, to get a female NBC correspondent to meet him in Europe.

"He located her in Vienna and wanted her to come to Paris," Albertazzie said. "He almost begged on the radio. The radio operator got so embarrassed he lost the communication, deliberately. I knew about that firsthand."

"I doubt that there was a day in Johnson's life in the White House that he didn't do something that was dishonest," MacMillan said.

2

"The White House Is Full of Arrogance"

ASSIGNED TO PROTECT PRESIDENTS TWENTY-FOUR HOURS A DAY, SE-cret Service agents see presidents—and former presidents—in their most private moments. With only a hundred agents assigned to the presidential detail, guard duty is an exclusive club, with its own rules and culture. While club members freely share stories among themselves, they fiercely resist talking to the press or other outsiders about what they know.

Of all the presidents, the Secret Service found Richard Nixon and his family to be the strangest. Like Johnson, Nixon did not sleep in the same bedroom with his wife. But unlike Johnson, who consulted Lady Bird on issues he faced, Nixon seemed to have no relationship with his wife, Pat, who had taught typing and shorthand at Whittier High School in California, and he barely spoke with his two daughters, Tricia and Julie.

"He [Nixon] never held hands with his wife," a Secret Service agent said. After he left the presidency, the agent said, "in

San Clemente, he walked a nine-hole golf course with his wife and daughters, and not a word was spoken among the four of them. It was an hour and a half, and he never said a word." He added, "Nixon could not make conversation unless it was to discuss an issue. . . . Nixon was always calculating, seeing what effect it would have."

"I never witnessed affection with the Nixons," said Charles Palmer, the chief steward on *Air Force One*.

"Nixon kept to himself," said Russ Reid, another steward. "He stayed in his compartment, and the first lady stayed in her compartment by herself. Occasionally, they would hold hands when they were getting off the plane just for show. There was little conversation."

During his election campaign, Nixon successfully portrayed his opponent, George McGovern, as a radical leftist who would "cut and run" from the Vietnam War. Nixon also campaigned for sharp cuts in defense spending and tax reform.[25]

As president, Nixon expanded the fighting in Vietnam beyond the borders of Vietnam into Cambodia and Laos before finally ending U.S. involvement there. He neither cut defense spending nor reformed the tax structure.

Nixon's greatest accomplishment was his decision to alter U.S. policy toward Communist China. He agreed to support the Communist regime's admission to the United Nations, and in February 1972, he undertook what he called a "journey for peace," a widely publicized visit to China. But Nixon lost the presidency when he became embroiled in the Watergate scandal, which included a wide range of illegal acts from breaking into Democratic National Committee headquarters at the Watergate Office building in Washington to using government agencies to retaliate against Nixon's perceived "enemies." Only after the House Judiciary Committee had approved three articles of impeachment against him—including charges of obstructing justice and abusing his power—did Nixon agree to resign on August 9, 1974.

During Watergate, said a Secret Service agent, "Nixon was very depressed. He wasn't functioning as president any longer.

[Bob] Haldeman [Nixon's chief of staff] ran the country. Nixon was only interested in international issues."

Even before Watergate, Haldeman said in his memoirs, Nixon—code named Searchlight—would have trouble sleeping and would wander outside the White House in the middle of the night, a sign of depression.

In 1970, he wandered out at 4 A.M. to talk to some antiwar demonstrators. Haldeman said he was sure Nixon did not go out for the purpose of talking with the demonstrators. Rather, "He was restless after a particularly difficult TV press conference and couldn't sleep." Haldeman called these disappearances "Nixon's unique way of letting off steam when things were very tense or he was very tired."[26]

But Nixon was on the edge, said psychiatrist Bertram Brown, who was consulted during Watergate by a group of senators led by the late Jacob Javits.

"Towards the last hundred days, it wasn't clear what Nixon's mental status was," Brown said. "Whether he was going crazy, becoming psychotic, whether he would start a war. One level of concern was in the Senate. I had breakfast with a half dozen senators. It was to talk about these issues—whether he would lose his cool. I gave them some clues on what to watch out for. The clues were irrational statements, disappearing—not knowing where he was—and not eating."

"Towards the end, Nixon got very paranoid," a Secret Service agent said. "He didn't know what to believe or whom to trust. He did think people were lying to him. He thought at the end everyone was lying."

While Nixon rarely drank before the Watergate scandal, he began drinking more heavily as the pressure took its toll. He drank a martini or a Manhattan.

"All he could handle was one or two," a Secret Service agent said. "He wouldn't be flying high, but you could tell he wasn't in total control of himself. He would loosen up, start talking more, and smile. It was completely out of character. But he had two and that was that. He had them every other night. But always at the end of business and in the residence. You never saw him drunk in public.

"Pat Nixon had a problem," the agent said. "I think at one point she was almost an alcoholic. She had to have counseling, arranged through her friends. It was during the first term. After she left the White House, she had a big problem in San Clemente [where they temporarily settled]. . . . She was in a pretty good stupor much of the time. She had three to four martinis a day, for lunch and through the day."

At times, the agent said, Pat Nixon did not recognize people she knew because she was so inebriated.

"It began in the White House, especially as Watergate got worse," the agent said. "I think it became a problem then. She was depressed."

Throughout Nixon's career, Pat Nixon managed to hide from the public the fact that she was a smoker. She died of lung cancer in June 1993. She was eighty-one.

Like most presidents, Nixon made a show of going to church or having services held in the White House. As soon as he left office, he stopped going.

"Going to church was more show than anything else," an agent said. "That was not unusual with most of them. It was more to give the appearance you are a good Christian. Nixon went the least of all. They [the Nixons] wouldn't go after they got out of the White House."

Before Ronald Reagan made his bid for the presidency, he called Nixon practically every day for advice and support.

"We would pick up the calls," a Secret Service agent said. "That was when Reagan was out of office and doing radio shows. I remember Nixon saying, 'I'll give you all the support I can. I can raise the money, but we can't be seen together.' It was at San Clemente. Nixon still had the control and contacts with the people in the Republican party."

Of all the people guarded by the Secret Service, Nixon's son-in-law David Eisenhower, the grandson of Dwight Eisenhower, was considered the densest.

"David Eisenhower was as dumb as the day is long," an agent said. He related an incident that occurred at David Eisenhower's home in California. He said the light in his remote-control electric garage door opener was not going on.

41

"Do you know anything about garage door openers?" he asked a Secret Service agent. "I need a little help. I've had it two years, and I don't get a light. Shouldn't the light come on?"

"Maybe the light bulb is burnt out," the agent said.

"Really?" David said.

The agent looked up, and there was no bulb in the socket. The agent said, "Do you have a light bulb?"

"He would play Axis and Allies all night with the midnight shift," an agent said. "He had nothing else to do."

"We did a loose surveillance or tail on David Eisenhower when there were a lot of threats on the president, and he was going to George Washington University School of Law in Washington," an agent said. "He was in a red Pinto. He comes out of classes and goes to a Safeway in Georgetown. He parks and buys some groceries. A woman parks in a red Pinto nearby. He comes out in forty-five minutes and puts the groceries in the other Pinto. He spent a minute and a half to two minutes trying to start it. Meanwhile, she comes out, screams, and says, 'What are you doing in my car?' We were smiling. We were doing nothing. Our attitude was, this guy doesn't even know his own goddamn car.

"She said, 'This is my car.' 'What are you talking about?' He said, 'This is my car. I just can't get it started right now.' She said, 'I'm going to call the police.' She finally got in, started it, and drove off. He was still dumbfounded. He looked at us. We pointed at his car. He got in and drove off like nothing happened."

Gulley, then over the White House military office, said that over the objections of the White House maître d', David Eisenhower one day borrowed a camel-hair coat of Nixon's, one of Nixon's favorites.

"John Ficklin [the maître d'] tried to stop him, but David overrode him," Gulley said. "Julie was in Indianapolis. He [David] was going to Andrews Air Force Base to get a JetStar we set up for him. He burned a hole in this coat [with a cigarette]. John Ficklin was hiding for months."

In contrast, the Secret Service and White House staff respected David's grandmother Mamie Eisenhower, whom the Secret Service guarded for many years after Ike died.

"We would say, 'We are going to the Mamie Eisenhower Finishing School,'" an agent said. "Everything had to be correct and proper. The car had to be driven correctly. Manners at the table had to be correct. She would correct us. 'We don't raise our voices. The fork goes on the left.' But she was nice."

Because she was afraid of flying, Mamie traveled overseas by ship. On the trips, she invited the wives of her Secret Service detail.

"She said, 'I'm paying for it. I want them [the agents] to enjoy the trip.'"

To the Secret Service, Nixon's daughter Tricia was the prototypical White House child, spoiled and aloof. Noting that Nixon walked on the beach in San Clemente in his dress shoes, a Secret Service agent said Tricia Nixon wore a cape and broadbrimmed hat when she went on the beach. To go swimming, he said, "She actually got in the water [in San Clemente] and wouldn't untie the cape until she was immersed. She was afraid of the sun. It was a joke.

"Most kids become spoiled," the agent said. "They know they are somebody and have special privileges. It's the White House aura. It takes a real good kid to be able to handle himself. Most of them can't."

Kenneth L. Cox, one of the *Air Force One* pilots under Nixon, said a special leather chair had been designed for Nixon on *Air Force One.* When Tricia saw a prototype, she said the leather had a "'funny smell. I don't like that. I'm going to see what Dad thinks.' She found Nixon, got him out of a meeting, and came back and said, 'I won.'"

Cox said that one evening, Tricia was supposed to meet a smaller plane in New Haven to bring her back to Washington.

"She was late two and a half hours in New Haven. She got to the airport at 11 P.M.," Cox said. "She didn't apologize. She wore her daddy's rank."[27]

Gerald Pisha, an *Air Force One* steward, said Tricia reported another steward to White House aides for staring at her legs.

"Tricia always thought she was better than anyone else," said

Russ Reid, an *Air Force One* steward. "She had a regal attitude."

Tricia Nixon seemed to lack common sense.

"Somewhere in Kentucky, we were waiting for Eddie [Tricia's husband] to show up at the plane," said Reid, the *Air Force One* steward. "Tricia Nixon started walking across the parking ramp and wound up heading for the active runway. The Secret Service ran her down. She didn't say, 'Can I walk this way?' "[28]

In contrast to Tricia, Nixon's other daughter, Julie, was a "lovely lady, very gracious," Kenneth Cox said.

Buddie L. Vise, an *Air Force One* steward, said that after he was hospitalized with a collapsed lung, Julie Nixon called him at home to see how he was doing.

"Julie was my favorite in the family," he said.

Carl A. Peden, an *Air Force One* pilot, said he often flew Julie to Providence, where David Eisenhower was attending school.

"We parked near the airport fire station," he said. "They [the firefighters] asked why she didn't wave to them. I said, 'Probably because she doesn't know you are there.' So I talked to the Secret Service, and the firemen got out in their best, and she shook their hands and had her picture taken with them. She had them wrapped around her little finger."

"Julie was down-to-earth, but she was very defensive about David and her dad," a Secret Service agent said. "The only thing we could never figure out was why she married him. Maybe it was the place in history."

When Nixon became president, the crew of *Air Force One* immediately noted a difference.

"Nixon was easy to approach when he was vice president, but the morning after the election, when we were sent to New York to pick him up, we found out there was a new gang around him of real hardball players," said MacMillan, the *Air Force One* steward. "They built a wall around him. Those of us who had come to know him over the years [when he was vice president] couldn't approach him. We had the suspicion things were not going to be well at the White House. . . . They were arrogant."

"He was isolated," said Jimmy R. Bull, the chief communicator on *Air Force One.* As a communicator, Bull placed calls for presidents from *Air Force One.*

"He [Nixon] would not on most occasions be openly friendly," Bull said. "He went right into his office on the plane and closed the door."

Nixon would tell Bull to place a call to an individual. When the person was on the line, Bull was not supposed to ring Nixon directly. Instead, because Nixon's staff wanted to filter all contacts with the president, Bull had to tell a staff member or the chief steward that the caller was on the line. The staff member would then tell Nixon to pick up the phone.

"Other presidents had no problem," Bull said. When calls came in for Nixon, "In many cases, the [Nixon] staff said, I'll talk to him first. They did a lot of filtering. I probably saw that more with the Nixon administration than with any other president," said Bull, who served from the Nixon to the Reagan administrations.[29]

In his book *Blind Ambition,* John W. Dean III, the White House counsel under Nixon, described the heady experience of being connected with the White House. Summoned to San Clemente for his job interview with Nixon, he landed in Los Angeles. While passengers were still fumbling for their luggage, an officious airline executive stepped on board.

"Excuse me," he said to the startled passengers, "would you wait just a moment please?" He whispered to the stewardess and followed her to Dean's seat.

"Mr. Dean?" he asked. "Are you going to San Clemente?"

He then took Dean's bag and whisked him off the plane. As the flight crew stared, he was then escorted onto a marine helicopter as a corporal in full-dress uniform stood at attention at the foot of its boarding ramp.

"I figured if nothing else came of this trip, I could at least call the stewardess whose name and phone number I had managed to acquire," Dean, who was then single, wrote. "I wouldn't have any trouble getting a date—she must be wondering just who I was. I was wondering the same thing."[30]

"The White House is full of arrogance," said Steve Bull, one of Nixon's aides. "The nicest people can come to the White

House, and after a few weeks, they start [becoming arrogant]. I think it is an infirmity endemic to any administration, that they start confusing their personal importance with institutional importance. But it doesn't happen to everybody. To some people."

Under Nixon, the White House police were given silly uniforms to make them look more important and regal. The uniforms included double-breasted tunics trimmed with gold braid and gold buttons. They were to be worn with helmets that made the officers look Prussian.

The first formal attempt to provide security for the White House began during the Civil War, using four officers of the Metropolitan police and members of the 150th regiment of the Pennsylvania Volunteers. In 1930, Congress placed the White House Police under the supervision of the Secret Service, which had been guarding presidents since William McKinley was assassinated in 1901. Besides protecting presidents, the Secret Service investigates counterfeiting of currency, forgery of government checks, and credit card and computer fraud.

Under Nixon, the White House Police was renamed the Executive Protective Service and was given responsibility for protecting foreign missions. In 1977, the Executive Protective Service was renamed the Secret Service uniformed division, largely because the officers wanted the status of Secret Service agents.

Still, guards try to give the impression of being in the Secret Service. For example, Gary Walters, the chief White House usher, said in an interview that he began his career as a Secret Service agent. In fact, he later admitted that he was in the uniformed division.[31]

At any given time, a hundred uniformed officers and thirty-five Secret Service agents guard the White House and old Executive Office Building. The uniformed officers are responsible for the security of the buildings, while Secret Service agents are responsible for the security of the first family and vice president and his family. If a criminal investigation is required, the Secret Service usually takes over from the uniformed division. Both uniformed division and Secret Service can obtain backup from their Washington field offices. Secret Service headquarters is on the top four floors of 1800 G Street NW.

Besides guarding the White House, armed uniformed officers give the White House tours, screening more than a million visitors a year for weapons and radioactive material.

"They find weapons," a Secret Service agent said. "All the doors have magnetometers. They send a silent alarm to the guards. People with weapons are charged under the D.C. Code. We turn them over to the Metropolitan police. There are about twelve cases a year of people trying to bring in weapons. Most of the people are just tourists. They say, 'I carried that gun all my life.' We used to be tolerant. Then we saw it was a problem. They are charged for carrying a concealed weapon, even if it is licensed. We have signs saying weapons are prohibited."

Besides magnetometers and Geiger counters, the White House has a system that screens water for chemical and other impurities. The air is constantly checked for radioactivity or poisonous substances.

"There is a backup generator and a backup water supply," an agent said. "We can shut off the water and use the backup. We monitor the water constantly. We have a purifier also that filters the water and tests it for chemicals. If harmful impurities are detected, an alarm goes off. Then we shut it down."

The uniformed division maintains a canine unit in Beltsville, Maryland, which provides German shepherds that sniff cars that enter the White House grounds for explosive devices. Occasionally, the dogs mistake fertilizer that people lug in their trunks for bombs, causing embarrassment to visiting guests. In December 1990, the Secret Service sealed the entrances to the White House for an hour because an explosives-sniffing dog detected something amiss in the car of Representative Herbert H. Bateman, a Virginia Republican. It turned out to be fertilizer for azaleas.

The uniformed division controls the White House garage at 1310 L Street—code named Headlight—and another garage at the old Anacostia Naval Air Station. There, the division screens mail for explosives before it goes to the old Executive Office Building, where it receives another screening.

Contrary to published reports, no missiles protect the White House. Aircraft are not supposed to fly over the White House, but if one did, there would not be time to launch missiles before a plane dropped its bombs.

"There are no missiles to shoot down airplanes," an agent said. "There are electronic eyes and ground sensors six feet back that are monitored twenty-four hours a day. They sense movement and weight. Infrared detectors are installed closer to the house. You have audio detectors. Every angle is covered by cameras and recorded."

Uniformed officers, who are required only to have high school diplomas, do not have the background and training of Secret Service agents, who must be college graduates. The uniformed officers constantly get into trouble. The number of disciplinary actions for each of the uniformed division's 1,106 officers is roughly twice the rate for the Secret Service.[32]

Within the White House, uniformed officers are periodically caught napping on the job. One officer shot himself in the hand while cleaning his gun. Several uniformed officers have literally gone crazy. One threatened to jump off the ledge of an apartment house because he was having trouble with his girlfriend. Another handed over his badge and gun to a Secret Service agent and checked himself into Sibley Memorial Hospital.

The uniformed division runs a shop in room 68 of the basement of the old Executive Office Building that sells T-shirts and other White House mementos. Two officers have been caught stealing money from the till.

It was a uniformed officer who allowed Craig J. Spence, a Washington lobbyist, to bring homosexual friends and male prostitutes into the White House for tours at 1 and 2 A.M. The tours violated regulations, and because of the public exposure Spence committed suicide in Boston in 1989.[33] Another uniformed officer sold presidential trinkets and chinaware through a store in northern Virginia.

It is rarely clear whether White House property held by private parties was stolen or was a gift. Raleigh D. Amyx, a former trade association executive, runs a museum of White House and presidential memorabilia in Gainesville, Virginia. Many of the items—like JFK's cigar box or Franklin Roosevelt's cane—were donated or sold by maids and butlers who said presidents gave them the objects as presents.

When Nixon was president, the Secret Service investigated complaints that chinaware had been taken from the White House residence. The agents found that J. B. West, the longtime chief usher, had been letting friends in for tours, and they apparently had taken some of the items.

"He allowed some of his friends to come into the house after-hours upstairs," an agent said. "It was to show he was important, and then some things disappeared, some mementos. It was brought to our attention. Our investigation found there was unwarranted use of privileges."

The investigation also found that West was a homosexual. At the time, because of the belief that they could be blackmailed, homosexuals were considered security risks and could not work at the White House. West, who has since died, was dismissed.

Kenneth L. Khachigian, Reagan's chief speechwriter, recalled finding that the small cans of tomato juice he kept in a small refrigerator in his office in the old Executive Office Building kept disappearing.

"One night I had gone out late for a social event and came back at 11 P.M. to work," he said. "The office was dark, and the TV was on, and there was a uniformed officer with his feet on my coffee table watching TV and drinking from a small can of tomato juice."

The officer raced out of the office, and the next day, Khachigian's secretary insisted on reporting the incident.

"I was inclined to let it go," Khachigian said. "My secretary was very angry and reported it. It was outrageous behavior."[34]

Secret Service agents, as opposed to uniformed division officers, are not exempt from improper behavior. Some agents have made it a practice to submit phony claims for expenses incurred when moving to another city. One of those agents, William J. Bell, pleaded guilty in 1992 to a misdemeanor for submitting $7,000 in fictitious claims, which included about

$4,000 Bell had paid for closing and other costs that the government does not cover when employees move. Because the Secret Service found out about the phony claims, Bell never actually received the funds. As part of the same internal investigation, another nineteen agents who were polygraphers were also found to have submitted phony claims by either doctoring receipts or having friends sign receipts. In contrast to Bell's case, which was handled by the U.S. attorney's office in Newark, the U.S. attorney's office in Washington declined to prosecute the polygraphers. Bell was forced to resign from the Secret Service, while the others remained in the agency, and some have since been promoted.

"What I did was wrong," said Bell, who began as an agent in 1982. "But that is what I was told to do. That's what my supervisors did. That was the unwritten practice in the Secret Service."[35]

Indeed, in ruling on Bell's case, U.S. District Court Judge John W. Bissell agreed that submitting fictitious claims for moving costs was an "ingrained" and "systemic" practice among Secret Service polygraphers. While Bell was not a polygrapher, he said he and the polygraph examiners learned of the practice during Secret Service training.[36]

"Everyone knew that that was an accepted practice—to recoup legitimate expenses that were not covered by the government," Bell said. "Secret Service supervisors do it themselves. No one wants to lose money on a move."

Nothing about the improper claims has appeared in the press. Bell's allegations that some of his supervisors engaged in the same practices are still being investigated.

What makes the job of the Secret Service so difficult is that to many mentally unstable individuals, the White House is a mecca. Each year, twenty-five to thirty people try to ram the White House gates in cars, scale the eight-foot-high steel fence, break in with weapons, or cause other disruptions.

"The crazy people feel they have to be there," a Secret Service agent said. "When all else has failed, they take the last bus ride to Washington. We interview them in a special room at the northwest gate. We find out why they are here and what their intentions are. Can they care for themselves? They say they want to see the president."

During the Reagan administration, the gates were reinforced with steel beams that rise from the ground after the gates are closed. In addition, concrete posts reinforced with steel have been installed every few feet in front of the gates and around the perimeter of the White House.

"One reason we reinforced the gates is people have tried to drive their cars through the gates to see the president," an agent said. "An iron beam comes out of the ground behind those gates when the gates close. A two-ton truck could slam them at forty miles per hour, and they will withstand it."

During the Ford administration, a seventy-seven-year-old woman drove a car into the northwest gate at 6 P.M. She was put in St. Elizabeth's Hospital, which released her. By 11 P.M., she had rammed the gates again. She was then incarcerated.

The Secret Service intelligence division keeps extensive files on people who are potential threats to the president. As a rule, anyone who threatens any public official is considered a potential threat to the president.

"These individuals, if they are looking at one individual, are always looking at the president," a Secret Service agent said. "That is the top. He is the ultimate public official. We want to know about those individuals. Sooner or later, he will direct his attention to the president if he can't get satisfaction with the senator or governor."

The Secret Service is informed of any threat to a government official. In addition, threatening letters or phone calls to the White House are referred to the Secret Service. Upon hearing such calls, White House operators are instructed to put the caller on hold and have a Secret Service agent pick up the line. In most cases, the caller's telephone number can be traced.

"The next person you hear is an agent," a Secret Service agent said. "He is waiting for the magic word [that signifies a threat to the president]. He is tracing it. We can take it right back. We lock the line open. We have had that for the last two years. That is done immediately. You may make a threat and hang up. It's a good starting point. Most call from the house."

The Secret Service sorts potential threats into three categories. Category 3, with about a hundred people on the list, is the most serious. In all, the Secret Service lists about 50,000 potential threats. When a president is controversial, the number tends to go up.

"When Nixon ordered bombing raids in Vietnam, more threats came in by phone," an agent said. "It depends on conditions and what is going on and who is president."

In most years, the Secret Service receives 3,000 to 4,000 new threats against the president. So far, only four threats specifically mentioning Clinton have been considered serious enough to be placed in category 3. These four people are presently incarcerated for other crimes.

Under federal law, threatening the president is a crime. The Secret Service tries to differentiate between threats and the legitimate exercise of First Amendment rights.

"If you don't like the policies of the president, you can say it. That's your right," a Secret Service agent said. "We're looking for those that cross the line and are threatening: 'I'm going to get you. I'm going to kill you. You deserve to die. I know who can help kill you.' Then his name is entered into the computer system."

Before rating threats, the Secret Service interviews the people who made them. In many cases, that is enough to quiet them.

"Some say they really weren't thinking. 'It was a mistake. I was upset.' It [the file] will stay active for a year. If nothing else happens and he doesn't cause any commotion, the file is purged."

If that doesn't work, courts have given the Secret Service wide latitude in dealing with immediate threats to the president. Those who are in the most sensitive category are constantly checked on.

"We will interview serious threats every three months and interview neighbors," an agent said. "If we feel he is really dangerous, we monitor his movements almost on a daily basis. We monitor the mail. If he is in an institution, we put in stops so we will be notified if he is released. If he has a home visit, we are notified. I guarantee there will be a car in his neighborhood to make sure he shows up at his house."

At any given time, the Secret Service might give such close surveillance to thirty-five individuals.

"We know where they are all the time," the agent said. "If we know the president will be in the area, we put a monitoring team on them."

On the other hand, if people approach the White House gates and say they have a message for the president, "We read it, and if there are no threats, we give it to the staff," an agent said. "Three-quarters of the mail never sees the president's desk. If you have any credibility, don't do it that way. You address it properly."

Besides the threat list, the uniformed division maintains a "Do Not Admit List" of about a hundred people to be kept out of the White House because they have caused embarrassment. For example, the White House press office may place a journalist on the list because he or she made it a practice to disobey rules about where journalists must sit.

Before being allowed into the White House, visitors with appointments have their names checked against the computer lists. If they appear on Secret Service lists, they may not be allowed in. If they are going to see the president, the Secret Service first asks the FBI to check its criminal files to see if they are listed in them. This requires visitors to provide their Social Security numbers as well as their birth dates.

Occasionally, wanted fugitives make the mistake of entering the White House for appointments. Under the Bush administration, a man who was wanted for grand larceny accompanied a friend of Bush. The Secret Service promptly arrested him.

"If there is a warrant, the [computer] screen says, 'There is a warrant for this man's arrest. Call an agent,' " a Secret Service agent said.

The greatest embarrassment to the uniformed division came in February 1974, when U.S. Army Private First Class Robert K. Preston stole an army helicopter from Fort Meade, Maryland, and landed on the south lawn at 9:30 P.M.[37]

Instead of firing at the helicopter, uniformed officers called a Secret Service official at home, asking him what they should do. He told them to shoot at the helicopter. By then, the helicopter had flown away, but it returned fifty minutes later. This time, uniformed division and Secret Service officers shot it up.

"They riddled it with bullets," a Secret Service agent said. "They used rifles and handguns. When he landed [the second time], he opened the door and rolled under the helicopter. It probably saved his life. They put seventy rounds through that. There were twenty rounds in the seat. He would have been shot to death [if he had not rolled under the chopper]. It was not going to take off this time."

Preston was treated for a superficial gunshot wound. He was sentenced to a year at hard labor and fined $2,400.

Just after Reagan's second inauguration, a man sneaked into the White House by following a marine band entering the east gate. While he was caught, it was another embarrassment to the uniformed division.

The Secret Service cannot be blamed for every problem. When Frank Eugene Corder, flying a single-engine Cessna, crashed onto the White House grounds at 2 A.M. on September 12, 1994, questions were raised about the adequacy of White House security. But unless the White House is relocated to a military base, there is no adequate way to protect against such intrusions. Aircraft frequently stray into the forbidden airspace over the White House by mistake. Shooting down such craft would be foolhardy and would lead to the loss of innocent lives, both in the air and on the ground.

After Nixon became president, he made the usual noises about cutting staff and costs. On February 5, 1969, the *New York Times* ran a story saying the Nixons planned no remodeling of the White House and few changes. But what followed was a massive remodeling. Jacqueline Kennedy had started the job by hiring the first curator in the White House. To raise money for the project, she had solicited donations. Altogether, the Kennedy added 1,100 pieces of furniture and artwork to the White House collection.

Nixon asked Clem Conger, who had done an impressive job of turning the top floor of the State Department building into lavishly decorated diplomatic reception rooms, to become curator of the White House as well. During his tenure, Conger added 1,875 pieces of furniture and artwork.

"Mrs. Nixon called me on the phone and asked me to come on a Sunday afternoon," Conger said. "So I went in at 2 P.M. No one was around. She explained that they wanted the White House to be the most beautiful house in America. They didn't have the knowledge or time to do it. They thought Clem Conger could."[38]

Soon, Conger was raising millions of dollars a year to restore the White House and acquire paintings and furniture. As one vehicle, the White House Historical Association had been created during the Kennedy administration to receive donations. But the government paid for some of the work, including the cost of flying special military planes to Italy to acquire green watered silk Conger wanted used on the walls of the Green Room in the White House. A small parlor furnished in the Federal style, the Green Room was used by Thomas Jefferson as a dining room, where he introduced such delicacies as imported Italian macaroni and French ice cream served in warm pastry shells.

"I got a call from [Larry] Higby saying, 'Send an air force plane [to pick up the fabric],' " Gulley said.

The government also paid $5,000 for a bed for Nixon.

Unlike her husband, Pat Nixon was a genuinely warm person who was not self-serving.

"Every time we finished a room, I would say to Mrs. Nixon, 'We should have a press opening,' " Conger said. "Mrs. Nixon would say, 'I don't want to be compared with other first ladies.' So she didn't want publicity and didn't get it. She did more for the White House in the long run, building the collection, than any other first lady in history. This is amazing to the public because she was so modest."

"Pat Nixon was my favorite first lady," said Shirley Bender, who was executive housekeeper at the White House. "She was a lady through and through. She was interested in the operations of the house. She was generous to the staff. She brought jade back for us after her trip to China."[39]

But, said a Secret Service agent, "Pat Nixon couldn't cook to save her life. She used to put stuff in the oven for agents on the chef's days off. Then she burned it. It was in the upstairs kitchen [used only by the first family]. The fire alarms went off. They are all like that."

During the oil embargo, Nixon told the press he was flying to his San Clemente home on a United Airlines flight to save fuel. He then had the military fly him back on a JetStar, requiring the plane to fly empty to California before picking him up.

"I was on the JetStar," Lee F. Simmons, a former *Air Force One* steward, said. "There was publicity about the commercial flight but not about the flight back."

"It was to show we were saving fuel," Charlie Palmer said. "We sent the plane in [to California] empty."

"I spent a lot of time with Nixon after he resigned," Bill Gulley, the chief of the military office, said. "This guy is a consummate liar. I don't think he knows he is lying."

That conclusion echoed an earlier one by Harry Truman, who said, "Richard Nixon is a no-good lying bastard. He can lie out of both sides of his mouth at the same time, and if he ever caught himself telling the truth, he'd lie just to keep his hand in."

While Nixon was president, the government tried to conceal the cost of improvements to his two vacation homes, in San Clemente and Key Biscayne. After Nixon's resignation, the GAO totaled up the amount the government had spent under the guise of security to improve his homes. It came to $1.4 million. When other support such as communications was included, the total was $10 million. Among other items, the government put in hedges and fences, a flagpole, and an electric heating system. It also landscaped the lawns, paved walks and driveways, extended a sewer system, and bought furnishings for Nixon's offices in his homes, including lamps, chairs, tables, and a desk.[40]

Besides Bill Gulley's secret account, the money came from the General Services Administration and the Secret Service.

"The buzzword around the Nixon White House for projecting the proper image was 'presidential,' " according to Gulley. "If a thing or a place weren't dignified enough, or enough in keeping with somebody's—usually Haldeman's—idea of what was proper, then it wasn't 'presidential.' And that meant money had to be spent on it."

In contrast to Johnson, who Gulley said was an "out-and-out thief for his own personal gain," Nixon usually did not personally order improper or illegal expenditures. Instead, his staff did it.

"When we got these directives from Haldeman, I thought they were so ridiculous that I believed Nixon didn't know about them," Gulley said. "I was not in a position to ask the president directly. So I would ask Rose Woods. I would say, 'Haldeman has told me to set up *Air Force One* to take Haldeman, Ehrlichman, and [Ron] Ziegler with their families to California for a vacation and to pick them up after the vacation.' I would find Nixon didn't know about it, but then Nixon would approve the requests anyway."[41]

When the Nixon White House bought a new Boeing 707 as the presidential plane, Haldeman ordered special carpeting, seats, and wall panels that added to the cost. He designed the cabin layout so that he and his immediate staff sat near Nixon, while the first lady's cabin was farther back in the plane.

"Mrs. Nixon got on the airplane for the first time coming back from California," Gulley said. "She said, 'That might be a very nice airplane, but I'll never ride in it again.' Haldeman had set himself up between her and the president. He had people walking through her cabin. She had to go through the staff area to say hello to her husband. So we had to redo the airplane for $2 million." In the process, Pat Nixon's compartment was moved to the front of the plane.

The money came from the Defense Department, which is always available as a White House slush fund. But every White House uses sleight of hand to conceal even legitimate expenses.

"The reason the White House gets into this position of hiding the source of its funds is that there's no money to pay honestly for the things they want to do," Gulley said. "And there was no one who was able to check on what was going on. I could hardly believe it when I found out how dumb the General Accounting Office was and how easy to manipulate."[42]

John Cronin, who was in charge of GAO audits of the White House, said the Nixon White House concealed financial information, even altering vouchers.

"At one point, President Ford asked us to do an audit after Nixon resigned," Cronin said. "Knowing how bad the record keeping was, I basically refused. The comptroller general reversed me, and I did it. It showed a lot of the Nixon people walked out of the White House with everything except the furniture. There were typewriters missing, telephones, dictation equipment."[43]

When it came to his own money, Nixon was frugal. In the White House, presidents pay for nonofficial expenses such as their own food and grooming services. In contrast to the $200 Clinton paid Cristophe for a haircut on *Air Force One,* Nixon paid a mere $7.50 to Milton Pitts. Pitts had several shops in Washington when Alexander Butterfield, who would later reveal the existence of the Nixon tapes, recommended him to Nixon in 1970.

The White House has a ten-by-ten-foot barbershop in the basement of the west wing next to the Situation Room, and Pitts went there twice a week to cut the hair of the president and his staff. When Clinton fired him, Pitts was charging $25 for a cut, including shampoo.

"When I first met Nixon, he was wearing Brylcreem and Wildroot cream oil," Pitts said. "He would use one or the other. It makes wavy hair curl more."[44]

To Pitts, the perfect men's haircut contributes to making the head look oval.

"With Nixon, I shampooed the oil out and layer cut his hair and made it two and a half inches long and left it lower in the back and let the sideburns be fuller. He had a skeet nose. It was long. To de-emphasize it, I shortened the hair in the back and made it fuller on the sides," Pitts said.

"Nixon talked very little," Pitts said. "He wanted to know what the public was saying. We had a TV there. But he never watched TV. All the other presidents did.

"Nixon would be looking in the mirror, and he would say, 'Well, what are they saying about us today?' I would say, 'Mr. President, I haven't heard much news today.' This was during Watergate. I didn't want to get into what people were saying. I'm not going to give him anything unpleasant. He was my boss."

One afternoon, Butterfield came in for a haircut just before Nixon did. Motioning to the television set, Butterfield said to Pitts, " 'Leave that on. I want him [Nixon] to see what they are doing to us.' "

Pitts recalled that as soon as Nixon walked into the barbershop, "He pushed the button, and the TV went off. He said, 'Well, what are they saying about us today?' I said, 'Mr. President, I haven't heard much news today, sir.'

"Butterfield wanted Nixon to see that his people were being interrogated," Pitts said. "He thought it would be good for him to see it. It might change his thoughts. But he said he hated TV. I knew he would turn it off. He said, 'I get turned off by those people hounding me day and night.' "

If Nixon's conversation was dull, his taste in food was insipid.

Day in and day out, "[Nixon] had a pineapple ring and a scoop of cottage cheese on it for lunch. Period. No garnish, no parsley, no lettuce, no ketchup, plain," said Charles Palmer, the chief steward on *Air Force One.* For dinner, "Nixon liked Salisbury steak with gravy. Always plain. You don't decorate anything with him," Palmer said.

In the White House, Nixon liked lighter dinners than Johnson had had.

"When President Nixon came, I felt they liked fancy food," said Henry Haller, the White House chef. "That was my impression. The first couple of weeks, I served a first and second course, salad, and dessert. After a week, President Nixon said, 'Cut the first course.' In another week, he said, 'Chef, cut the dessert, too.' "[45]

Trained in his native Switzerland, Haller had been hired by the Johnsons, who continued to employ Zephyr Wright to make chili, barbecued ribs, and other Texas favorites. Johnson and

Lady Bird had divergent tastes, so Haller often had to serve them different foods, which they usually ate separately as well. For breakfast, Johnson liked chipped beef and freshly baked bread, while Lady Bird liked omelettes, pancakes, and waffles. For dinner, Johnson liked saucy beef dishes like beef Stroganoff and casseroles like seafood creole. Lady Bird, on the other hand, liked steak.[46]

The Nixons liked dishes made with fresh produce from Florida and California, including ripe avocados. Especially in the summer, they liked cold soups like gazpacho, cold poached salmon, and cold seafood plates for lunch. For dinner, they liked such simple American dishes as New England boiled dinner, braised Swiss steak, meatloaf, and Irish stew.

For dessert, Johnson liked tapioca, lemon or banana pudding, peach ice cream, and macaroons. The Nixons liked baked Alaska flambé, sponge cake, apple Charlotte, and macadamia nut ice cream.

Since he served in the Nixon and Ford administrations, Henry Kissinger was a perennial passenger on *Air Force One.* While the *Air Force One* crew enjoyed his dry humor, they did not enjoy cleaning up after him.

"Henry Kissinger . . . didn't like peas," said Charles Palmer. "If there were peas on his plate, he would take a knife and brush them on the floor. He was a real messy eater. There were a lot of things on the floor before he was finished."

MacMillan, the *Air Force One* steward, said he never saw Kissinger purposely drop his peas on the floor. Rather, he said, "Kissinger would push peas onto a napkin lying on the table. We would pick them up. I'm sure some went on the floor."

"He was on a diet, a quite frequent diet," said Louis J. Lawrence, another steward. "It would change based on what he wanted. We had some problems with candy. We would move them away from place to place depending on where he was. He would find them."

"When they went to the Sadat funeral, we had three former presidents on the plane—Nixon, Ford, Carter," said John E. Palmer, Jr., an *Air Force One* steward, referring to the funeral of Egyptian president Anwar Sadat. "I sat on the jumpseat and talked to President Nixon for a good hour while he was waiting for the lavatory. Kissinger was in there for almost an hour. He was shaving and cleaning up just like he had all the time in the world."[47]

Kissinger and other Nixon staff members became livid if they thought another staff member had gotten a bigger steak.

"The steaks all weighed the same, but some were thicker than others," MacMillan said. "He [Kissinger] was a man of great intellect but lacked common sense. He would take one sock from one pair and one from another. He would say, 'I don't have time [to worry about] that.'"

The Nixon people complained if they thought another staff member had received a steak that was cooked to the doneness they had wanted.

"I got notes from [Nixon aide Larry] Higby and other Nixon people saying, 'The guy next to me got a steak that was cooked better than mine,'" Charles Palmer, the *Air Force One* chief steward, said.

One Thanksgiving, Nixon was leaving Washington on *Air Force One,* so the crew served a Thanksgiving dinner. In the *Air Force One* galley, the stewards roasted the turkey from scratch.

"The wife of a Secret Service agent gave him three pies to share with other agents and with us," said William J. (Joe) Chappell, who began as a flight engineer on *Air Force One* with President Kennedy. "She had baked them for Thanksgiving. So he shared them with us and the press. It was pumpkin, apple, and mincemeat."

After the trip, Chappell said Higby wrote a memo to the crew criticizing the fact that they had had a choice of three kinds of pie, while Nixon was served only pumpkin pie. In response, the stewards explained that they ate the pies only because they didn't want to hurt the feelings of the agent whose wife had supplied them.[48]

Spiro Agnew, Nixon's first vice president, was known mainly for his large appetite.

"We were coming out of Palm Springs to Washington and we were taxiing out, and Spiro Agnew said, 'Can I have a sandwich?'" Russ Reid, a steward, said. "I said, 'Sir, we're going to serve dinner as soon as we get to cruising altitude.' He said, 'I want a sandwich now. I'm hungry.' I had people in the galley make him a sandwich, and as soon as we got to cruising altitude, he ate a hot meal, too.''[49]

In most administrations, candy and tobacco companies contribute their products. The preferred snacks varied by administration. Reagan liked jelly beans, while Carter wanted peanuts, a primary crop of his home state. Under Nixon, *Air Force One* served miniature Hershey bars and Baby Ruths in silver dishes.

"We got a memo from Larry Higby that Dr. Kissinger's table had miniature Baby Ruths, and Mr. Haldeman's had none," Chappell said.

Democratic administrations tended to prefer Coca-Cola, while Republicans liked Pepsi-Cola. Traditionally, Coke has allied itself with the Democrats, while Pepsi has allied itself with Republicans.

Several Nixon aides, including Steve Bull, would sip alcoholic drinks out of mugs to conceal what they were drinking.

"He [Bull] would sit with a white coffee mug in the afternoon with a drink in it," Charles Palmer said. "This was after Watergate. It was bourbon and water.''[50]

Lee F. Simmons, another steward, said, "He had it as soon as he got on. It could be in the morning. . . . He would have two or three."

"It became a joke with Jim Brown, a steward," Bull said. "I would say, 'I'll have black with soda.' "

Bill Gulley, the chief of the White House military office, believed Bull erased the crucial eighteen-and-a-half-minute tape of Nixon trying to cover up Watergate. While Presidents Roosevelt, Kennedy, and Johnson occasionally turned on tape recorders, Nixon is the only president to have recorded all conversations in the Oval Office.

According to Gulley, a military aide who was at Camp David the weekend the erasure occurred told him that Bull and Rose Mary Woods, Nixon's secretary, were working on the tape recorder, acting suspiciously.[51]

But Bull denied erasing the tape, saying he believes Woods accidentally erased it.

"There is a perfectly logical explanation," Bull said. According to him, it was easy to push the pedal of the transcribing machine Woods was using and simultaneously push the Record button by accident.

"She said, 'I was trying to make a transcription, and something happened,'" Bull said. "She said she never knew what happened. She was trying to do a transcription, and before she knew it, she was getting silent stretches of it."

"Nixon wanted to destroy the tapes," a Secret Service agent said. "Haldeman talked him out of it. He said, 'No, they will prove your side of the story.' Nixon said, 'I hope you're right.' He was wrong. This was early on. We did the recording."

In his book *RN: The Memoirs of Richard Nixon,* Nixon said the chief reason he did not destroy the tapes was that they would undercut false claims that others might make.[52]

Nixon was the only former president to have rejected Secret Service protection. He preferred in his last years to hire his own guards.

"Nixon got rid of the Secret Service because he was very private," an agent said. "He hated the press. He hate[d] to divulge anything."

According to the agent, Freedom of Information Act requests had been filed to find out how much Nixon's protection cost and where Nixon traveled.

"He wanted to get away from press inquiries and Freedom of Information requests," the agent said. "He said, 'It's nobody's goddamn business how much I spend and what I do.' [Gerald] Ford would call and ask how he gets around press inquiries. They would talk about how much they would spend and how they would do it. There were Freedom of Information requests all the time. He [Nixon] would get furious every time he saw that. Just wild."

"Nixon was an extraordinarily able man, one of the ablest of our presidents," George Reedy, Johnson's press secretary, said. "His problem was a feeling something was always going to go wrong. God, the way that man could worry."

Despite his suspicious nature, Nixon managed to give many the impression that he cared about them. Nixon made much of returning Vietnam War prisoners of war, inviting them to a dinner at the White House. When they were not listening, he would make disparaging remarks about them, throwing away gifts they had given him.

Nixon managed to fool even some members of the White House staff.

"A retired White House operator said, 'I still like Nixon the best,' " an agent said. "I didn't shatter her illusions. You don't know. You only know what they want to know. If Nixon lives long enough, we'll start building statues of him. Everyone will forget that he tried to obstruct justice, that he lied."

In fact, in the first flurry of stories on Nixon's death, that is exactly what happened.

It comes with the territory.

"Politicians are politicians," the agent said. "Do they really have your best concerns at heart? I don't think so. . . . I would see CEO's make asses of themselves trying to ingratiate themselves with the president," the agent said. "They would cut your throat back in the office. But before the president, they revert back to fourth graders. They grovel, they stumble over their words. They flush with embarrassment. It never fails. The staff recognizes this and rides roughshod. They demand free meals, free rides, free hotels. They lose their ability to say no [to presidential demands] for fear they will offend the president and not be considered teammates. Anything goes."

3

Smuggling Coors

THE SECRET SERVICE THOUGHT IT HAD HEARD EVERYTHING UNTIL
agents got a call at 3 A.M. from the Metropolitan police in Washington asking if one Robert T. Hartmann worked in the White
House and, if so, what he looked like.

The police had apprehended Hartmann, one of President Gerald R. Ford's top aides, slightly tipsy, and trying desperately to
get into what was then the Circle Restaurant at One Washington
Circle. First, Hartmann had tried to identify himself as a Secret
Service agent. But Hartmann—an older man with a bulbous
nose—did not look like one. When the police would not buy
that story, they threatened to put him in jail if he did not disclose his identity. Hartmann then said he worked in the
White House.

The Secret Service quickly confirmed that the man was indeed
Hartmann, counselor to the president and chief speechwriter. But
the story the police told the Secret Service got stranger. They said
that Hartmann had said he needed to get into the restaurant—
now the West End Cafe—because of a matter involving national
security. He would not give any further details.

Police had tried to get the restaurant owner, who lived in Maryland, to return to the restaurant and open it, but he refused. Much to Hartmann's dismay, the police took him to his home in Maryland. Meanwhile, the Secret Service sent agents to investigate. In talking with a clerk in the lobby, they learned that Hartmann had been dining in the restaurant that night with a well-built White House secretary who had an apartment in the vicinity.

When the agents first interviewed her, she denied knowing Hartmann.

"An agent said, 'Do you know this gentleman?' " according to an agent. "She said, 'No.' An agent said, 'We can place him in your apartment last night. You were having dinner with him.' "

Admitting that she had been with Hartmann that night, the secretary said she was married and her life could be "destroyed" if her husband found out.

The secretary told the Secret Service that Hartmann had left a briefcase containing top secret material in the restaurant. When he realized it was missing, he had tried to get into the back of the restaurant to retrieve it, and apparently tripped the alarms.

By 8 A.M., the restaurant owner had arrived. Agents found the briefcase under a table. Hartmann had left classified information in the restaurant that related to nuclear war.

Later that day, the Secret Service tried to return the briefcase to Hartmann and obtain a receipt for its contents. He put off the agents, trying to get them to give the material to his secretary. When the agents made it clear they would have to meet with him personally, he agreed to see them.

The Secret Service considered the incident highly sensitive, and no formal reports of it were written. Nor was Ford notified. However, Hartmann's influence within the White House had already begun to decline. While a brilliant speechwriter, Hartmann, who was Ford's chief of staff when he was vice president, was not considered a good administrator. He was also judged by White House aides and the Secret Service as a heavy drinker.[53]

Asked about the incident, Hartmann recently said he had no recollection of it. When prompted with details, he said he had a "vague recollection" of leaving sensitive material in a restaurant and having it returned by the Secret Service.

"I do have a vague recollection of leaving my notebook at a table at a restaurant and trying to recover it but finding the place closed," he said. "I think I called the police or the Secret Service."

Subsequently describing the material as being in a briefcase, Hartmann said he thought it merely "sensitive" information that the White House did not want released to the press.[54] But a Secret Service agent said the agency never would have become involved to the extent that it did unless the briefcase had contained classified documents.

Hartmann was not the only drinker in the Ford White House. As she later admitted, Betty Ford was an alcoholic, a fact that was kept under wraps while she was in the White House.

"She was in a stupor all the time," a Secret Service agent said. "We took her off *Air Force One* rigid as a board, carrying her down the steps. I blame Ford. He always seemed to be in another world. He never saw what was right behind him. She got counseling after he got out. Her kids intervened in Palm Springs. He says he did too. But he never took the time."

Betty Ford was taken to Long Beach Naval Hospital and began attending Alcoholics Anonymous meetings. While sons of Dolley and James Madison, Abigail and John Adams, and Eliza and Andrew Johnson, and brothers of Bess Truman, Eleanor Roosevelt, and Ida McKinley, William McKinley's wife, had suffered from it, Betty Ford was the first wife of a president known to have been an alcoholic. In a public statement, she said, "I have found I am not only addicted to the medication I have been taking for my arthritis, but also to alcohol . . ."

Since receiving treatment, said the agent, "She has been a changed woman."

"Most people didn't know she had a drinking and drug problem," said Larry Speakes, who was in the Ford press office. "The only evidence was long pauses in the conversation when she groped for a word. You learned quickly not to supply the word."[55]

"Mrs. Ford was a jovial and pleasant person," said Shirley Bender, the executive housekeeper. "I could not tell she had a drinking problem except sometimes her speech was a little slow."

Because of her penchant for bar hopping, Susan Ford caused problems for the Secret Service.

"Susan Ford was young and didn't know how to handle being daughter of the president," an agent said. "She was gregarious. She wanted to get out. She frequented taverns in Georgetown underage. A couple of places knew her and let her in when she was underage. On one occasion we said, 'You should realize the liability you have if you allow her on the premises.' Then she turned twenty-one."

Ford—whose Secret Service code name was Passkey—had a habit of flatulating that drove Secret Service agents crazy.

"He [Ford] used to let out gas a lot, fart, openly," an agent said. "Then he tried to blame it on one of the agents. He would say, 'Jesus, did you do that? God, show a little class.' Always joking. He just let it rip."

But unlike the impression Ford conveyed of being a dullard, "Ford was not dumb. He is klutzy," a Secret Service agent said.

Standing six feet tall and weighing 195 pounds, Gerald Rudolph Ford, Jr., as president had blond hair, which he combed straight back, and small blue eyes. Following Nixon's resignation, Ford was sworn in as president at 12:03 P.M. on August 9, 1974.

While Ford was not responsible for any great achievements, his honesty helped restore confidence in government after the Watergate affair.

"Of all the presidents, Ford was the most wholesome and down-to-earth," Dr. Brown, the psychiatrist who has seen many White House aides, said. "He would have gotten along well with Harry Truman."

Ford undermined that image when he granted Nixon a "full, free, and absolute pardon" for "all offenses against the United States" that Nixon committed or may have committed during his term of office. He said he issued the pardon because, should Nixon be indicted and tried, "ugly passions would again be aroused. And our people would again be polarized in their opinions." The action created a firestorm of criticism, leading to suspicions that Nixon had agreed to resign as part of a deal with Ford to pardon him. The pardon likely cost Ford election in his own right.[56]

Ever since the assassination of John F. Kennedy, the Secret Service had been tightening the security net around the president. After two women tried to shoot Ford in September 1975, security became even more stringent. Lynette "Squeaky" Fromme, twenty-six, a disciple of mass murderer Charles Manson, drew a Colt .45 from her holster and squeezed the trigger as Ford reached to shake her hand outside a hotel in Sacramento. The gun failed to fire, and Secret Service agents wrestled her to the ground. Then in San Francisco, Sara Jane Moore, forty-five, a political activist, fired a .38 revolver at Ford from forty feet away. A bystander pushed her, causing her to miss Ford by a few feet, and the Secret Service quickly arrested her.

After the two incidents, the Secret Service insisted Ford wear a bullet-proof vest when meeting the public, a practice that presidents since Ford have followed. When in public, Secret Service agents must wear the vests as well.

Until the Roosevelt administration, the White House grounds were open. Anyone could walk through the front door and be greeted by the chief usher.

"That was changed when the king and queen of England came over to visit the Roosevelts in 1939," said William Hopkins, who was executive clerk. "That was when they first issued White House passes. They also closed the gates. They increased the height of the fence."[57]

When President Johnson's aide Walter Jenkins was caught making a pass at another man in the men's room of the Washington YMCA, Johnson ordered the FBI to perform the first background checks on White House aides. Since then, George E. Saunders, a crusty former FBI agent, has acted as liaison between the White House and the FBI, prescreening White House aides by asking if they have anything embarrassing in their backgrounds. When White House aides get in trouble, it usually means a visit to Saunders' office in room 1 of the old Executive Office Building.

"You don't want to see George Saunders," said a White House aide.

Everyone except the president, the vice president, and their families must undergo a security check and obtain a pass to enter the White House. But the most visible sign of security is the presidential motorcade, which consists of a dozen to two dozen vehicles, many of them security-related.

The number of cars in the motorcade depends on the purpose of the trip. For an unannounced visit to a restaurant, five Secret Service cars, known as the informal package, make the trip. For an announced visit, the formal package of twelve to twenty-four cars is used. Including the president's limousine, at least five of the vehicles are Secret Service cars.

"We never want the motorcade over twenty-two cars and buses," an agent said. "It could get longer, but there are constraints moving through stoplights. I've seen it at forty vehicles. There has to be a good reason if it was that big. At twenty or twenty-two cars, we say it's enough. 'Why can't they go ahead of us or take a bus?' "

Each motorcade includes a car for the Secret Service counterassault team armed with machine guns. Another Secret Service car, known as the intelligence car, keeps track through computers of people who have been assessed as threats.

Generally, the second car is the president's limousine, while the first is a decoy. The president's limousine is armor plated, with bullet-proof glass and its own supply of oxygen. Every six months, the windshield is replaced because over time the sun clouds the bullet-proof glass. The limousine—code named Stagecoach—comes equipped with a secure phone, but no bar.

Before inaugurations, the Secret Service seals manhole covers along the motorcade route, soldering them shut. Every street leading to the parade route is blocked with concrete barriers.

"We go to every window and say, 'Every window must be closed when the motorcade passes,' " an agent said. "We have spotters looking at them with binoculars. For the most part they comply. If they don't, we have master keys to all those doors. We ask them why they are there and opening the windows. We have sweep teams, Park Police helicopters for crowd surveillance, agents all along the route."

Secret Service agents wear color-coded pins on their left lapels. The pins, which bear the five-pointed star of the Secret Service, come in four colors. Each week, agents change to one of the four prescribed colors so they can recognize one another in crowds. On the back of the pin is a four-digit number. If the pin is stolen, the number can be entered in the FBI's National Crime Information Center (NCIC), the computerized data base that police use when they stop cars to see if the cars are stolen or the occupants are fugitives. Besides listing fugitives, the NCIC lists stolen property.

When on protection duty, Secret Service agents wear the trademark radio earpieces tuned to one of the channels the Secret Service uses.

"There are five channels," an agent said. "Secret Service, White House staff frequency, military, intelligence. You always have a primary channel that everyone is on. The primary channel is called Baker. The Secret Service channel is Charlie. Oscar is staff."

Agents refer to members of the first family, the vice president and his family, and other top government officials by code names. It's tempting to draw a connection between the code names and the personalities of the people who have them. Occasionally, the press claims there is a connection. In fact, the code names are produced randomly by a Defense Department computer from a list of suitable everyday words. Words that are difficult to understand or are derogatory are not included in the list.

"There is no connection with the person," an agent said. "Sometimes it sounds like there is an association, but it is not there."

The code names for each family all begin with the same letter. For example, Clinton is Eagle, while Hillary Clinton is Evergreen. Chelsea Clinton is Energy.

The press also repeatedly claims that Roger Clinton, Clinton's brother, is code named Headache, presumably because he has replaced Billy Carter as the first family's black sheep. But because he is not protected by the Secret Service, Roger Clinton has no code name.

The military aide who carries the nuclear football sits in the limousine behind the president's. Occasionally, the aide and the president have become separated.

"One time I forgot it [the football] on *Air Force One* in France," said Robert E. Barrett, who carried the football for Ford. "I didn't have the football, and I was in a foreign country."

By the time Barrett realized it was missing, he and Ford had left the airport. Barrett said he was about to radio *Air Force One* when Herb Oldenburg, an *Air Force One* baggage handler, radioed to him.

"He said cryptically, 'Do you have everything you need?' I said, 'Negative on that.' The motorcade was rolling. He said, 'I'll get it to you.' He came up along the motorcade, and he handed it out the window," Barrett said.[58]

During the Reagan administration, the motorcade acquired another car. Under the cover of the White House Communications Agency, the super-secret National Security Agency (NSA) operates it. In addition, a plane operated by NSA accompanies *Air Force One.* The purpose of both highly classified missions is to monitor the airwaves for possible threats.

Whenever the president leaves the White House, the Secret Service designates a safe house to be used in case of a threat.

"If anything happens, that is where we go," an agent said. "It could be a fire station. It has emergency standby equipment. It's to evaluate the situation."

At least two weeks before a president travels, the Secret Service makes elaborate advance preparations, including taking over the hotels where he will stay.

"In the hotel, if the president will stay overnight, we secure the suite and floor he will stay on and make it as safe as the White House," an agent said. "We seal it off. No other guests can be on the floor. If the floor is huge, we will separate it. But no outside people will be on the floor, guaranteed. There won't be anyone underneath."

The Secret Service runs into trouble with people who live in hotel rooms on a long-term basis.

"We tell them to go to another room," the agent said. Hotels usually offer the permanent residents better accommodations free of charge. But some refuse to take them.

"If they say, 'We are absolutely not going,' then we will not bring the president," the agent said.

Before the president is allowed in a hotel room, a Secret Service countermeasures team sweeps it for radioactivity and electronic bugging devices.

"Bugs have been found in rooms. A lot are occupied by CEO's. They might have been bugged by the competition," an agent said.

Presidents hate to get stuck in elevators, so the Secret Service pays elevator repair companies $500 a day to station a repair person in hotels where elevators might get stuck.

When Chelsea Clinton graduated from the eighth grade at Sidwell Friends School in Washington in June 1993, the Secret Service uniformed division used hand-held metal detectors to check each guest.

Overseas trips require even more security. Because everyone in government wants to show his importance by traveling overseas with the president, as many as six hundred people have gone on the trips.

Presidential security has "gotten to the point where it is ridiculous," said Oliver B. (Buck) Revell, who was one of the FBI's top terrorism experts. "The amount of security that is imposed makes it impossible for a president to maintain contact with his constituents. The security has not prevented the assassination attempts in the past. If people are willing to forfeit their lives, they can still get to anyone. The best means to prevent that type of thing is through intelligence and appropriate planning. But this armed entourage taking over cities has become ludicrous. Around the world it has made us a laughingstock. They feel it is the imperial Americans coming in."[59]

"One thing that is harmful and destructive to the way our

system works is the system of security," said Donald Rumsfeld, chief of staff under Ford. "It has grown enormously since I went to Washington in the fifties. It happens incrementally. It may happen for good reason. I was with President Ford when he was shot at twice. It's no fun. President Reagan was hit. But the Secret Service and attendants have become so numerous and controlling that it is a put-off for the American people. A lot of people have stopped going to functions where the president and vice president are because there is so much security. There is something about the total number of people in your entourage that defines your importance. That is wrong. It is unhelpful to everyone. It inhibits communication."

In fact, only one presidential assailant—Sarah Jane Moore—had been listed as a threat in the Secret Service data bank prior to their attack.

"She had written [in a threatening way] about the president," an agent said. "We had interviewed her two days before the incident. The question is, did that trigger it? Was she aware he was coming before we interviewed her? We ask what are your feelings, what are your problems? His trip was publicized. But we ask ourselves if we started something. By giving them a feeling of importance, we may prompt them to think, 'I better follow through.' The rational person would say, 'Holy shit. I almost got arrested.'"

Secret Service agents believe that simply being there, scanning the crowds with a fierce look, deters would-be assassins.

"You have to be hyper-vigilant," said Jerry S. Parr, a former high-ranking Secret Service official. "Between 1963 and 1981, you had one president murdered, one shot and wounded, a governor shot and wounded and paralyzed, two attempts on Ford, and you had Martin Luther King killed. You know it's out there. You just don't know where."[60]

"You're protecting the office. That is our job. To keep this country running," another agent said. "The only excessive security is with the former presidents," he said. "They want protection for the convenience. We do their travel arrangements, we make it possible for them to catch trains, we are their fleet. We allow them to do things the ordinary citizen could never do. Ford and Carter could not do 75 percent of their travel if they didn't have the Secret Service. We are the facilitators. We make it work. They come to us because they have cut back on their staffs."

Instead of protecting former presidents for life, this agent and others said they thought the Secret Service should protect former presidents for just five years. Within months of leaving the White House, Barbara Bush told the agents who protect her husband that she no longer wanted constant protection.

Yet while no former president has been killed, antinuclear activist Rick Springer did lunge at Reagan after Reagan had left office. Reagan was speaking on April 13, 1992, at a convention in Las Vegas of the National Association of Broadcasters. Springer smashed a thirty-pound crystal statue of an eagle that had been given to Reagan. He was sentenced to 120 days in jail.[61]

Often, former presidents and other politicians think of Secret Service agents as personal servants there to act as gofers. When he was running for president, for example, Edmund Muskie demanded that the Secret Service carry his golf bags.

"He took vacations in Kennebunkport," an agent said. "He would play eighteen holes of golf every day. He would cheat and kick the ball in the hole with his foot and pick it up and put it in. An agent would not carry his golf bags [after Muskie asked him to]. It reduces our effectiveness."

William Bell, a former Secret Service agent, said agents protecting Lady Bird Johnson dial telephone calls for her because she is too frail to do it herself.

"It [Secret Service protection] becomes a glorified valet service," Bell said. "There were times when I felt it was a waste of taxpayer money. I absolutely refused to carry any shopping bags into the house. Other agents did that to ingratiate themselves. They [former presidents and their wives] were quick to identify that and see who they could manipulate. If Mrs. Ford had a heavy bag, I would do it out of respect for her. But I wouldn't volunteer to do that. They are quick to test you with that."

By asking the FBI to check its files, the Secret Service reviews the backgrounds of employees of suppliers that provide food to the White House. However, the White House chef and his helpers are not watched while they prepare food for the president. If the chef decides to buy a nice-looking eggplant for a presidential meal at the local grocery store, he may do so.

"We never had an official taster," Henry Haller, the White House chef, said. "The FBI and Secret Service are never in the kitchen. The chef is the official taster. If you can't trust the chef, whom can you trust?"

"You can't watch everything," a Secret Service agent agreed. "But the majority of stuff is checked. We have lists of the suppliers. We check the employees once and go back randomly and check them again to see if anyone has been added."

If a background check reveals that the employee has been arrested for child molestation, for example, the Secret Service tells the establishment either to fire the employee or the White House will change suppliers.

"It is to avoid embarrassment to the president and ourselves," an agent said.

President Reagan preferred that the navy stewards who operated the White House mess prepare most meals when he was outside the White House. With other presidents, including Clinton, Secret Service agents watch the people who prepare the food when the presidents leave the White House.

"We pick a plate at random and sample it," a Secret Service agent said. "We make sure it is the same as what the president is having. But Reagan never ate the food at a public function. The chefs who traveled with him supplied it. They cooked it in the kitchen. They used their ingredients, but we had checked the ingredients."

When the president goes to a restaurant, elaborate precautions are taken to check on the employees and watch patrons as they enter. The Secret Service visits the restaurant before the visit and searches the premises for anything suspicious. During the presidential meal, arriving guests are checked with metal detectors, explosives-sniffing dogs are stationed outside, and agents watch from rooftop perches.

President Bush favored two Washington restaurants, Peking

Gourmet Inn in Falls Church, Virginia, and Rio Grande in Bethesda, Maryland. Nixon liked Trader Vic's in Washington. Clinton ranges more widely, from Red Sage, a trendy southwestern restaurant, to Galileo, a pricey northern Italian restaurant, both in Washington.

Over the years, published reports have fingered Nixon for having ketchup with his cottage cheese at lunch. In fact, it was Ford, not Nixon, who used ketchup with cottage cheese.

"President Ford had A-1 sauce and ketchup, mostly A-1 sauce, with the cottage cheese," said Charles Palmer, an *Air Force One* steward. "We always had a vegetable garnish with spring onions, celery sticks, radishes. We always served ketchup and A-1 sauce with it. In most cases, he used A-1 sauce mixed in. . . . When we were going to land, he used mouthwash because of the onions."[62]

"President Ford had a hearty appetite," Haller, the White House chef, said. "He liked simple foods like pork chops and red cabbage, stuffed cabbage, wholesome dishes. He liked American-style cooking."

On Sundays, the Fords liked to have waffles with strawberries and sour cream for breakfast and later a rib roast with oven-roasted vegetables. For dinner, Ford liked navy bean soup, sweet-and-sour stuffed cabbage, and sautéed veal chops with mushrooms.

The Fords liked lemon sponge pudding, fruitcake, chocolate angel food cake, and orange chocolate cake for dessert.

On *Air Force One,* "Ford had a Gilbey's martini, extra dry. Maybe he had one or two. It was always the last stop of the day," Palmer said.

"I noticed that Mrs. Ford would get on board the plane at 10:30 A.M., and she might have a drink," said Simmons, an *Air Force One* steward. "They [the Fords] always had a drink before and after a meal. She had vodka tonic on ice."[63]

In Palmer's recollection, Ford got high only once.

"He had had some drinks prior to the flight," Palmer said. "He was in the Soviet Union. He was meeting with the Russian premier. We got away at seven or eight at night. We gave him two or three martinis flying home. We put him to bed. In the middle of the flight, he came out in his underwear and said, 'Where is the head?' Normally, he knew where the head is. He could walk. He was slurring words. It was the one time he overindulged and was tipsy."

As chief of staff, Donald Rumsfeld ordered the *Air Force One* crew to serve drinks only on trips returning to Washington. The crew believed the reason was a Ford staff member drank too much. But Rumsfeld said the order simply made good sense.

"I have had a policy wherever I have been that I wasn't comfortable with people drinking until the workday is over," he said.[64]

Like most rules in the White House, this one was soon ignored.

"Those things have a way of working themselves out," Palmer said, noting that the rule was forgotten after only a few trips.

Another rule that quickly vanished was Ford's wish that, in contrast to the way Nixon flew, all compartments on *Air Force One* should be open.

"He had heard compartments were closed on the plane," Palmer said. "He wanted them open. We started that way. Six weeks down the road, the doors to the [president's] stateroom were closed."

The Secret Service had long made it a practice to load up the aircraft with then-scarce Coors beer when the president was in Colorado. When Ford was president, a newspaper ran a photo of a Coors truck unloading cases of beer into a cargo plane that transports the presidential limousine and other Secret Service cars. That ended the practice.

"We smuggled Coors when Ford was President," a Secret Service agent said. "It was for personal consumption. It was a prestige item. People said, 'Where did you get this?' "

The *Air Force One* crew prided itself on being able to supply almost any food. Ford liked strawberries, so the crew had them flown in specially. But when Tricia Nixon asked for a Monte Cristo sandwich, the stewards were stumped.

"It was the first time any of us had ever heard of a Monte

Cristo sandwich, but we weren't going to let her know that we didn't know what it was," John Palmer, an *Air Force One* steward, said. "I told the chief steward, and he said, 'What in the hell are you talking about?' He said, 'Tell her we don't have anything to make it with.' We had every kind of bread and fresh sandwich meats you could think of. I said, 'What else can we make for you?' I named eight sandwiches. She looked at me and said, 'I'll have a hot dog.' "

When *Air Force One* was in California, the stewards investigated and found that a Monte Cristo—then popular on the West Coast—was made with sourdough bread and Monterey jack cheese, bacon, ham, and turkey or chicken. Like French toast, the sandwich is dipped in an egg-based batter and grilled. It is cut four ways like a club sandwich and sprinkled with powdered sugar and served with jam, the stewards learned.

"In California, we went to a restaurant that made them," John Palmer said. "We got the works, and she never asked for one again."[65]

While guests never got sick on *Air Force One* food, a Secret Service agent on one trip thought he had bitten into a piece of glass embedded in wild rice stuffing in a Cornish hen.

"We never bought from the supplier again," Charles Palmer said.

While presidents had always looked for jokes wherever they could, Ford was the first to hire a staff member primarily to write humor for him. Don Penny not only gave him lines but taught Ford how to speak publicly.

"I never met a politician who didn't know what he wanted to do. It's a question of how to teach them to deliver the spoken word," Penny said. "The attention span of the American public, because of TV, is that of a flea," he said.[66]

"I used to pace him," Penny said. "He had no ear. When you pause, you cause the listener to listen. Dead air is much more important than verbiage. The less you say before you have something important to say, the better. Take control of the audience. Let them know you are not going to move until they are paying attention."

Penny taught Ford to use his klutzy image to his advantage.

At one dinner, he had him drop his silverware on the way to the podium, then spill his papers all over the floor. The audience howled.

"Whatever he lacked in great intellect, he made up for with great humanity. He did not know how to lie," Penny said of Ford.

Penny went on to write humor as a consultant to other presidents, including Reagan. When presidents brought down the house at a Gridiron Club dinner, it was usually on jokes Penny or other professionals had supplied. Thus humor in the White House, like everything else about the place, has become contrived. The funny lines presidents deliver are almost entirely the work of professional humorists.

Each president has a personal assistant who schedules his time and works with him all day to make sure he keeps his appointments. Under Ford, that aide was Terrence O'Donnell, who caused a minor stir in the Oval Office one winter morning. Normally, a White House steward lights the fireplace in the Oval Office, but that morning O'Donnell did it because the steward had not yet come.

"I lit the fire in Ford's office without opening the flue, and the office filled with smoke," he said. "The Secret Service came in."[67]

Under their desks, presidents have a "panic button" that they are supposed to press if they need emergency help. The button sounds an alarm that brings most of the Secret Service contingent of thirty-five agents running. Almost every president has pushed the button by mistake.

"You brush it with the knee," an agent said. "It's on the left side. As many agents as possible come in. When that buzzer is pushed, guns are drawn. We assume there is a bad situation there, and it is going to be neutralized right now. It is a loud, buzzer-like alarm."

Compared with the Prussian-like staff surrounding Nixon, Ford's staff came as a relief.

"Ford's was a different operation," said Louis Lawrence, an *Air Force One* steward. "It was more relaxed. Ford talked to the crew members. There wasn't as much tension. When Mr.

Nixon was on the plane, everyone knew where he or she was supposed to be."

"I particularly liked President Ford," said Jimmy Bull, the chief communicator. "He and Betty were beautiful people. I really enjoyed flying with them. . . . I thought the Fords were real people."

Unlike the Nixons and the Johnsons, "The Fords slept together," said Nelson Pierce, the assistant White House usher. "They were the first of the ones I worked for, and every one after that did."

In contrast to Nixon's formality, "when I went to do President Ford [for the first time], he was in shirtsleeves, no tie," said Milton Pitts, the barber. "He said, 'Hi, Milton, how are you?' Nixon called me Mr. Pitts."

"Ford said, 'I need a little trim.' He said, 'You see my hair is thinning and light and if you cut my sideburns too thin, it looks like I have none. I'm using Vitalis.' I said, 'I know, Mr. President, everything you are doing is wrong.' "

At that, David Hume Kennerly, the White House photographer who was also in the barbershop, began to laugh.

"I said, 'Excuse me, Mr. President. I'm talking about your hair.' "[68]

"I took the Vitalis out and razor cut his hair, left his sideburns fuller, left hair lower on the back, and by blowing drying it, I fluffed that light hair up," Pitts said.

A Pulitzer Prize–winning former *Time* magazine photographer, Kennerly provided a reality check in the White House.

"Few people, with the possible exception of his wife, will ever tell a president that he is a fool," Ford wrote in his book *A Time to Heal.* "There's a majesty to the office that inhibits even your closest friends from saying what is really on their minds. They won't tell you that you just made a lousy speech or bungled a chance to get your point across. Instead, they'll say they liked the speech you gave last week a little better or that an even finer opportunity to get your point across will come very soon. You can tell them you want the blunt truth; you can leave instructions on every bulletin board, but the guarded response you get never varies."[69]

But Kennerly had no hesitation about telling Ford what he thought. In May 1975, a crisis developed over the Cambodians' seizure of the American merchant ship SS *Mayaguez*. Ford convened a meeting of the National Security Council to try to formulate his response. Henry Kissinger said the United States must respond firmly. Just then, Kennerly, who had been snapping photos, asked, "Has anyone considered that this might be the act of a local Cambodian commander who had just taken it into his own hands to halt any ship that comes by?"

"For several seconds," Ford recalled, "there was silence in the Cabinet room. Everyone seemed stunned that this brash photographer who was not yet 30 years old would have the guts to offer an unsolicited opinion to the president, the vice president, the secretaries of State and Defense, the director of the CIA, and the chairman of the Joint Chiefs of Staff."

Ford decided that what Kennerly said made a lot of sense. Having just been to Cambodia to take photos, Kennerly had an appreciation of the chaotic conditions there. Based in part on Kennerly's advice, instead of ordering massive air strikes, Ford ordered more limited, surgical strikes.[70]

When Ford lost to Jimmy Carter, he was devastated.

"I was worried about him the night he lost," a Secret Service agent said. "I've seen that look before. . . . We thought he could become suicidal."

On the trip back to Washington after the election, Ford's staff showed its displeasure by throwing peanuts around *Air Force One.*

"After Ford found out that he had lost, they [his staff] would eat anything in the mixed-nuts bowl but the peanuts. Then they threw them all over the place," said Gerald Pisha, another *Air Force One* steward.[71]

"The president was very upset about losing," said Russ Reid, an *Air Force One* steward. When referring to Jimmy Carter, Reid said, Ford "used some profanity like 'stupid SOB.' "

Now living in Rancho Mirage, California, Ford—like former Vice President Dan Quayle—has shocked Secret Service agents with how cheap they are.

"You go to a golf course, and it's an exclusive country club, and the normal tip for a caddy is twenty-five to fifty dollars. Ford and Quayle tipped a dollar, if at all," said William Bell, the former Secret Service agent.

Bell said Ford and his wife took some of their grandchildren to a McDonald's in Palm Springs and were amazed to see the cash register dispenser that automatically deposited their change in a steel cup.

"They were both sort of flabbergasted," Bell said.

Bell compared the incident with Bush's amazement when he saw a price scanner at a grocery store checkout.

"You have your suits pressed for you, you have all this stuff done for you, and you become very isolated," Bell said. "I think these people have the best intentions, but then they are in politics so long that they become isolated and forget where they came from. They don't know what the problems of ordinary American citizens are."

4

A Theft from the Presidential Suite

THE WHITE HOUSE OFTEN ASKS THE SECRET SERVICE TO PERFORM DELI-
cate missions, but rarely has the agency been asked to perform
one as sensitive as in the case of the missing heirlooms.

When Carter was president, the White House found out that
approximately half a million dollars in White House antiques
had been stolen from the presidential suite at Bethesda Naval
Hospital. Like other presidents before him, Jimmy Carter came
to Washington claiming he would cut government spending. It
would not look good if it ever got out that thieves had made off
with incredibly valuable White House furniture. So the Secret
Service was told to keep the theft hush-hush. Even within the
Secret Service, few agents were to know, and no reports were
to be written.

"Everyone was embarrassed," a Secret Service agent said.

Clement Conger, the White House curator, had the job of telling
the Secret Service about the theft so the agency could investigate.

"He said it's all American antiques, everything is original, Chippendale. It's from private donations, museums, archives," an agent said. "He [Conger] was extremely embarrassed. He was so concerned that nobody could know of this."

Based on Conger's report to the Secret Service and on the agency's own investigation, the Secret Service valued the missing items at $600,000.

Conger recently confirmed the theft—which has never come to light—but said he did not recall that the dollar figure was that high.

"It could be that one or two items ran the value up to $200,000 to $300,000 for two or three objects," said Conger, who could not recall which items they were. "But I can't imagine $600,000."[72]

Used only by the president, the suite of five rooms allows the president to meet with his staff and continue to direct the government from the hospital. Not even the vice president can use the suite. Its bullet-proof glass windows are fitted with shades that can make the rooms pitch black. Lyndon Johnson had insisted on the room darkeners to help him sleep.

The suite was under the control of the navy and the Naval Investigative Service (NIS). From the investigation of the security breaches at the American embassy in Moscow to the inquiry into the blast on board the battleship *Iowa* that took the lives of forty-seven sailors in 1989, the NIS had a reputation for incompetence.[73]

Sure enough, the Secret Service found that security in the presidential suite was laughable. Although the suite was kept locked, the key was in a glass box behind a guard's desk on the first floor of the hospital. When the key was needed for a presidential hospitalization, the guard used a nail clipper to remove a screw on the box. The key could then be removed without breaking the glass. There were no video cameras monitoring the entrance to the presidential suite.

In investigating the theft, the Secret Service found that only the most valuable items in the suite had been taken. Presumably, the thieves knew what they were doing and had simply carted the furniture off in a truck.

"Nobody saw anything, nobody knew anything," a Secret Service agent said.

"They had an NIS agent assigned to it [the hospital] full-time," a Secret Service agent said. "He was nowhere in sight. Half the time they [the hospital] didn't know where he was. It was obvious this guy was worthless. He didn't have a clue what a crime was."

"It [the theft] was $600,000 in the end," an agent said. "Chippendale icons over the fireplace. Two were valued at $250,000. A table, several chairs at $2,000 to $3,000. They even took the crystal chandelier out of the ceiling. That was worth $30,000 to $40,000. Eighteenth-century crystal. The cheap stuff they didn't touch."

The White House curator had photos of each stolen item, and serial numbers were imprinted on the furniture. The curator maintains a registry of everything owned by the White House. Items not immediately needed are stored in a humidity-controlled warehouse in Beltsville, Maryland. Presently, the warehouse holds 27,000 items, including 1,942 pieces of furniture, 338 paintings, and 3,145 items of glassware.

Despite checks with auction houses, the Secret Service never found the missing items. Normally, such unusual contraband is sold privately.

"They [customers] know exactly what they're buying," an agent said.

After the incident, the Secret Service made the suite as secure as the White House. Now TV monitors scan the suite twenty-four hours a day, and alarms have been installed at the entrance.

"Once you get inside, you trip pressure plates in the floors," an agent said. "Cipher locks were put in, and only the White House detail in room W-16 [the Secret Service command post a floor below the Oval Office] knows the numbers. The cipher locks record who comes in and when. We did it right."

During his campaign Carter had promised a cut in the White House staff of 30 percent, five points better than the cut later promised by Clinton. But the Carter administration used the usual manipulations—including detailees—to make it appear it was eliminating staff members and costs while actually increasing them. For example, Carter formed a new White House budget entity called the Office of Administration. The new Office of Administration was loaded with employees from the other White House entities so Carter could claim that the staff of the White House Office had been cut. Even with that artifice, Carter announced after only a few months in office that he would not be able to fulfill his campaign pledge of cutting the White House staff by 30 percent. The promise had been more hot air.[74]

If Nixon was known to the Secret Service as the strangest modern president, Carter was known as the least likable.

"Carter said, 'I'm in charge,' " a Secret Service agent said. " 'Everything is my way.' He tried to micromanage everything. You had to go to him about playing on the tennis court. It was ridiculous."

Carter—code named Deacon by the Secret Service—was moody and mistrustful.

"When he was in a bad mood, you didn't want to bring him anything," the agent said. "It was this hunkered-down attitude: 'I'm running the show.' It was as if he didn't trust anyone around him. He had that big smile, but when he was in the White House, it was a different story."

Carter denied in a press conference that White House aides had to ask him for permission to use the tennis court. But that was more dissembling. In fact, White House aides had to call Carter when he was traveling on *Air Force One* to get permission to play on the courts.[75]

"It is a true story about the tennis courts," said Charles Palmer, who was chief of the *Air Force One* stewards. Because other aides were afraid to give Carter the messages asking for permission, he often wound up doing it.

"He [Carter] approved who played from on the plane," Palmer said. "Mostly people used them when he was out of town. If the president was in a bad mood, the aides said, 'You carry the message in.' On the bad days when we were having problems, no one wanted to talk to the president. It was always, 'I have a note to deliver to the president. I don't want him hollering at me.' "

Palmer said Carter enjoyed the power. One time, Carter said, "I'll let them know," Palmer said. "Other times, he would look at me and smile and say, 'Tell them yes.' I felt he felt it was a big deal. I didn't understand why that had to happen."[76]

"Carter had the ability and didn't know how to use it," a Secret Service agent said. "His biggest problem was he had a chip on his shoulder. He was one of those guys who was small in stature and said, 'I'm in charge now, and I'm going to pay back everyone.' Plus his world view from Plains wasn't enough."

William Cuff, an assistant chief of the White House military office, said Carter one day noticed water gushing out of a grate outside the White House.

"It was the emergency generating system," Cuff said. "Carter got interested in that and micromanaged it. He would zoom in on an area and manage the hell out of it. He asked questions of the chief usher every day. 'How much does this cost?' 'Which part is needed?' 'When is it coming?' 'Which bolt ties to which flange?' "

If the true measure of a man is how he treats the little people, Carter flunked the test. Inside the White House, Carter was often abrupt and surly.

"When Carter first came there, he didn't want the police officers and agents looking at him or speaking to him when he went to the office," said Nelson Pierce, the assistant White House usher. "He didn't want them to pay attention to him going by. I never could understand why. He was not going to the Oval Office without shoes or a robe."

That was true even though Carter had a habit of jogging up and down the White House stairs, past a number of uniformed officers and Secret Service agents.

"Carter jogged a lot," Pierce said. "When it was raining hard outside, he would go from the basement to the third floor on the stairway outside our office and jog up and down the stairs. He would make five to seven trips at least."

"We never spoke unless spoken to," said Fred Walzel, who was chief of the White House branch of the Secret Service uniformed division. "Carter complained that he didn't want them [the officers] to say hello."[77]

"Carter came into the cockpit once in the two years I was on with him," said James A. Buzzelli, an *Air Force One* flight engineer. "But Reagan never got on or off without sticking his head in the cockpit and saying, 'Thanks, fellas,' or 'Have a nice day.' He [Reagan] was just as personable in person as he came across to the public."[78]

Meanwhile, Carter seemingly refused to carry out one of the most important responsibilities a president has—to be available to take swift action in case of nuclear attack. When he went on vacation, "Carter did not want the nuclear football at Plains," a Secret Service agent said. "There was no place to stay in Plains. The military wanted a trailer there. He [Carter] didn't want that. So the military aide who carries the football had to stay in Americus," ten miles away.

"He just didn't want the trailer on his property. It is shocking."

In the event of a nuclear attack, the agent said, Carter could not have launched a counterattack by calling the aide in Americus.

"He would have to drive ten miles," the agent said. "Carter didn't want anyone bothering him on his property. He wanted his privacy. He was really different."

"The guy with the football stayed in Americus, Georgia," confirmed Gulley, who, as director of the White House military office, was in charge of the operation. "We tried to put a trailer in Plains near the residence for the doctor [who travels with the president] and the aide with the football. But Carter wouldn't permit that. Carter didn't care at all."[79]

Through his lawyer, Terrence B. Adamson, Carter issued a blanket denial of nearly all the controversial items relating to him in this book, including whether he kept the nuclear football near him in Plains; whether items were stolen from the presidential suite at Bethesda Naval Hospital; whether he instructed uniformed officers not to say hello to him in the White House; and whether he approved who could play on the White House tennis court from *Air Force One*.

Like almost every presidential candidate, Carter claimed he would make government more efficient and cut the federal deficit. Indeed, Carter promised to balance the budget by the end of his term. He delivered on none of these promises.

As president, Carter pardoned draft evaders, deregulated the airline and trucking industries, and provided food stamps to those who are eligible. His greatest achievement was working to bring about peace in the Middle East, culminating with the Camp David Accords between Egyptian president Anwar Sadat and Israeli Prime Minister Menachem Begin.

Early in his presidency, Carter proclaimed that the White House would be "dry." Each time a state dinner was held, the White House made it a point to tell reporters that no liquor— only wine—was served.

"The Carters were the biggest liars in the world," Gulley said. "The word was passed to get rid of all the booze. There can't be any on *Air Force One,* in Camp David, or in the White House. This was coming from close associates of the Carter family. I said to our White House military people, 'Hide the booze, and let's find out what happens.' The first Sunday they are in the White House, I get a call from the mess saying, 'They want Bloody Marys before going to church. What should I do?' I said, 'Find some booze and take it up to them.'"

"We never cut out liquor under Carter," said Charlie Palmer, the chief of the *Air Force One* stewards. "Occasionally, Carter had a martini," Palmer said. He also had a Michelob Light. "Rosalynn may have had a drink. . . . She had a screwdriver."

"I have heard from the butlers he would have a cocktail once in a while. So would Rosalynn," said Nelson Pierce, the assistant usher in the White House.[80]

"They had champagne and liquor in the navy mess under Carter," said a General Services Administration building manager in charge of the west wing. "They partied all the time."

"That [the directive on liquor] was a joke," said a Secret Service agent. "The staff did what they wanted. They come up with rules, and the staff does what they want."

In denying the author's findings, Carter through Adamson said he and his wife occasionally had a drink but "that was hardly a secret and certainly not denied as implied." But that was a continuation of the show Carter and other presidents put on in the White House. Lillian Carter, Carter's own mother, contradicted her son's claim. In a 1977 interview with the *New York Times,* she said that, even though the White House was officially "dry," she managed to have a nip of bourbon every afternoon when he was there.[81]

"She said one evening to one of the butlers, 'I'm kind of used to having a little nip before going to bed. Do you think you could arrange to give me a little brandy each night?' " said Shirley Bender, the White House executive housekeeper.

"They [the Carters] put out the word they wouldn't drink," said Henry Haller, the executive chef.

The excessive drinking habits of Carter's brother Billy were well known, but what was not known was that Carter's younger sister, Ruth Carter Stapleton, who was married at the time, was secretly carrying on an affair with Willy Brandt, the West German chancellor, who was also married.

Stapleton, a Baptist evangelist and spiritual healer, was the last person anyone would suspect of having an illicit affair. Like her brother, Stapleton was a born-again Christian. She was active in Carter's campaigns and used her celebrity to establish a retreat center, known as Hovita. Slim and fashionably coiffed, she was a popular preacher at rallies of Christian evangelists, who shouted "amen" to her calls for the need to turn to Jesus.

"She at one point was deeply involved with Willy Brandt," said a member of the Carter staff. "Nobody ever found out about it ... it was a matter of concern [within the Carter White House]. It would not have harmed the government, but it would have been a hell of a story."

Stapleton died in 1983 at the age of fifty-four. Brandt died in 1992 at the age of seventy-eight. Her widower, Dr. Robert T. Stapleton, said recently he had no knowledge of such an affair.[82]

Of all the presidential children guarded by the Secret Service, Carter's second oldest son, James Earl (Chip) Carter III, was one of the least liked. Twenty-six when his father won the presidency, Chip had helped campaign for him in 1976 and again

91

gave speeches on his behalf when Carter ran for reelection in 1980.

"He was outrageous," said a Secret Service agent. "Chip, who was separated from his wife, was out of control. Marijuana, liquor, chasing women."

At one point, Rosalynn Carter told the press that all three of her sons had "experimented" with marijuana. Their oldest son, John William (Jack) Carter, had been discharged by the navy for smoking it.[83]

After he was forced to resign for using a fictitious name when writing a prescription, Dr. Peter G. Bourne, Carter's principal adviser on drugs and narcotics, said there was a "high incidence" of marijuana use among the Carter White House staff, as well as some use of cocaine.[84]

"I had to transfer twelve marines [from Camp David]," Gulley said. "They were participating in pot smoking parties with Carter's son."[85]

In August 1980, the press reported that in July 1977, Chip Carter had been advised to leave Panama City, Florida, because of a planned Customs Bureau drug raid there. Just who told him and why was unclear.[86]

What actually happened, a Secret Service agent said, was Customs told the Secret Service that Chip had been hanging out at the bar where the raid was to take place.

When asked to leave the city, "He said, 'I don't give a shit,' " the agent said. " 'I'll go where I want.' We actually called the president. He said, 'You get your ass out of there. You'll do what the Secret Service tells you to do.' He frequented the bar. I don't know if he bought marijuana there. We could not condone that. We make that clear to our protectees. You are not going to violate the law."

Half a block from the White House, the General Services Administration maintains a town house where former presidents may stay when in Washington. Located at 1716 Jackson Place NW, the town house faces Lafayette Park. After Chip Carter moved out of the White House, GSA—the government landlord—arranged for him to stay in the town house when visiting his parents.

"Chip Carter was coming here [to Washington] one time from Georgia," said Lucille B. Price, a GSA manager. "We had to get a key to him for 1716 Jackson Place. We got word to Chip and a friend named Earl through the state highway patrol to tell them how to get in."

After Chip and his friend had left, GSA managers went to inspect the town house.

"We went over there, and the kids had left the door open," Price said. "There was a note on the desk saying, 'Here is your key. Thanks. Earl.' . . . I don't know why the friend signed the note."

In the view of Shirley Bender, the White House executive housekeeper, children who are grown or have their own families should not be living at taxpayer expense in the White House. The atmosphere is seductive. "They enjoy the life at the White House," she said. "If you wanted it, you got it."[87]

Like others who knew her in the White House, Bender said Amy Carter was almost as "bratty" as Chip.

"You name it, and Amy Carter would mess up the plane," Charlie Palmer said of the president's daughter, who was ten when Carter became president. "She put crackers all over the floor. She was a little on the spoiled side. . . . I imagine it was a rough time for her."

"Amy Carter was a mess," said Brad Wells, another *Air Force One* steward. "She would look at me and pick up a package of [open] soda crackers and crush them and throw them on the floor. She did it purposely. We had to clean it up. That was our job."[88]

"Amy Carter crushed the crackers purposely," said Pisha, a third *Air Force One* steward. "She thought it was fun."

Carter denied that Amy purposely crumbled crackers on the floor.

"These are the human things that go on all the time," a Secret Service agent observed. "They like to think of themselves as being bigger than that. That it didn't happen. But it did."

The new Boeing 747 has a stateroom that sleeps the president and his wife in a double bed. But in the Boeing 707 the Carters used, the president and his wife had to sleep in separate staterooms. At times, Charlie Palmer said, Amy would insist on playing taped rock music in her mother's stateroom, where she slept on a foldout couch. To accommodate her wish to play music, Rosalynn Carter would sleep on the floor of the president's stateroom.

"Amy Carter was spoiled rotten," a Secret Service agent said. "Most kids become spoiled. They know they are somebody and have special privileges. It's the White House aura. It takes a real good kid to be able to handle himself. Most of them can't."

As the Secret Service now does with Chelsea Clinton, agents stayed with Amy while she attended the Stevens and later the Hardy public schools in Washington. At Stevens, "We took a little office across from her classroom," an agent said. "We were in there while she was in class. When the bell rang, an agent walked her to the next class. Then we went back to the office."

The Secret Service cruised the area as well in discreet, four-door sedans. Like FBI cars, the Secret Service cars have short aerials for two-way radios. They usually also have flashing front grille lights.

As happened at Stevens, occasionally a suspicious-looking man would show up in the area two days in a row. The roving car would stop the individual.

" 'Excuse me?' we would ask. 'Who are you and what are you doing here?' They might say, 'I can do anything I want.' Now we are going to ask you some more questions," an agent said. "We took a couple of people off the streets. We just take them. I can question you for two to three hours [without making an arrest]."

Through Adamson, Carter denied that his sister had had an affair with Brandt or that this had caused consternation in the White House.

Carter's effort to show he was a man of the people extended to carrying his own luggage when traveling. But like announcing that the White House was "dry," it was all for show.

"It was true that Carter wanted to carry his own bags," said Charlie Palmer. "On the first overseas trip, he just brought a carry-on and a briefcase. He carried it. He had one suit, three shirts. It was a five- or six-day trip. We had no valets. I had to open it. For five days, he had two suits."

Because Carter came so unprepared for trips, Palmer said the air force bought him a suit to keep on *Air Force One.*

"Down the road, he occasionally carried his own luggage for photo ops, but generally he stopped doing it," Palmer said.

"Carter and I had a run-in once," said Palmer. "He thought I lost his bag, and I didn't." Even though Palmer explained to Carter that the bag had been misplaced while being transferred from one helicopter to another, Carter continued to hold a grudge days later.

On their next trip, "When he got on the plane, he said, 'I'll keep it [his luggage].' A day or two later [on another trip], he said, 'Just make sure you get the bag on the right chopper.' I said, 'I never lost your bag.' He said, 'It's over and done with now.'

"I'm not sure if the Carters realized where they were," Palmer said, meaning Carter did not act like a president. "I'm from Georgia. I wanted them to succeed. But there were some trying times on board the airplane."

As another show at cost cutting, Carter decided that instead of flying Secret Service cars around the country, they should be trucked. It ended up costing taxpayers far more than flying them.

"The Secret Service had to accompany the cars that were trucked under Carter," a Secret Service agent said. "It went on for a year and a half. A mechanic was assigned to the cars. They had the responsibility of guarding the cars. . . . You could fly them in two hours, and it took a day and a half to truck them. With the per diem, overnight costs, transportation costs, it was much more expensive to truck them."

While Rosalynn Carter was extremely bright, she did not deal well with people.

"It took a year and a half for Rosalynn Carter to realize we were there for them and were not against them," Charlie Palmer said. "I think at first she thought we were the enemy. Maybe she felt a little inferior, a little insecure."

"Rosalynn was charming and fun to be around," a Secret

Service agent said. "She changed for the worst. She became disillusioned and felt used. She is right where she belongs now. Washington was too vicious for her. These people were too quick for her."

"Rosalynn was a bitch. Very unfriendly," said Gulley, the chief of the White House military office. "She was very disliked by everyone I knew except for a couple of those Georgia cracker women she brought with them."

Unlike the Nixons, "They [the Carters] were very affectionate and would kiss," Charlie Palmer, the chief of the *Air Force One* stewards, said. "Ford was always a gentleman with Mrs. Ford and would escort her. With the Fords, I didn't see the degree of affection the Reagans and Carters showed in their staterooms. I never witnessed affection with the Nixons. They talked to each other, but not as much as the others.

"The Carters sometimes got mad at each other over Amy," Palmer said. "It depended on what she was doing. There was a spanking or two. She needed it. Maybe thirty or forty minutes from landing, she was told to get ready and change clothes. She would listen to her music. She [Rosalynn] slapped her hand. Maybe they were meeting a foreign head of state. There are a lot of tensions involved in those things. It was not an everyday occurrence. I never witnessed Jimmy spank her. Sometimes there was control, sometimes they let her go. It was inconsistent.

"You never knew where you stood with him," Palmer said. "One day he wanted to be the president; the next he wanted to be a good old boy. You had to be on your guard. As a crew member, you never lowered yourself to calling him Jimmy. It was always 'Mr. President.' Sometimes he wanted to talk to you. A lot of days he closed the door and you didn't hear from him until you had to deliver something."

"Carter was totally decent," said Lloyd N. Cutler, who was White House counsel under Carter and later became Clinton's White House counsel. "He was an approachable person. . . . He read everything. Any memo you sent him, you would get back almost immediately. He had physical characteristics that got in his way, a high voice, short stature. He just didn't look presidential. But inside he was."[89]

"In terms of pure IQ, Jimmy Carter was probably the smartest president since Jefferson or Wilson," said Robert M. Gates, who dealt directly with each president from Nixon on, either on the staff of the National Security Council at the White House or as an official of the CIA. "But in terms of political intelligence and how you grasp complex problems and create successful public policy, Reagan may have been the smartest. When it came to foreign policy, both Bush and Nixon were very smart. In terms of understanding his moment in history and how to deal with it, Ford was."

But Gates said Carter made his job much more difficult than it needed to be.

"Carter probably was the most diligent president, but in many ways in my experience, he spent a lot of time on unnecessary trivia that he did not need to spend time on," Gates said. "Zbigniew Brzezinski [the national security adviser] would often send him papers with fat annexes and say, 'You don't have to read any of these annexes. They are there for form, or they don't have any information not in the summary.' Not only would he read them, but he would correct typos."

Gates said Carter also spent more time working in his office than any president before Clinton.

"Carter probably kept the longest hours in the office," Gates said. "Brzezinski briefed him at six-thirty every morning. The others all started their day at a more civilized hour."

At times, Gates said, Carter displayed a human side. For example, when the husband of a secretary to Brzezinski died of a terminal illness, "President Carter walked down the hall, sat in her office, and held and comforted her," Gates said. "He said, 'If there is anything I can do, please let me know.' "

But most of the time, Carter was remote.

"Carter was not an outgoing, friendly person," Gates said. "He was uncomfortable enough that he wasn't inclined to engage in small talk. . . . The others had a playful streak. In fact, I've always thought one of the things Presidents Carter and

97

Nixon had in common was a not very well developed sense of humor."

In the White House, the Carters liked lentil-and-franks soup, country ham with redeye gravy, fried apples, and corn bread and corn fritters. For dessert, they liked Georgia peach cobbler, pineapple upside-down cake, black cherry cheesecake, peanut brittle, and rich pecan cookies.

"Under Carter, there was no white bread," Palmer said. "They had rye or whole wheat and skim milk. They liked southern foods like fried chicken. For breakfast, they had grits. Most lunches were light sandwiches."

While presidents are supposed to pay out of their own pockets for personal items in the White House, Rosalynn Carter kept herself supplied with free cans of her favorite hairspray by taking the ones provided on *Air Force One*.

"We sent someone to pick that up," Palmer said. "We went direct to the shop to pick it up. We got two cans. It would suffice for a month. But after each trip, it was gone. We always had to get it for the next trip. It would have been paid for by them, in the White House. It was charged to the airplane, which was air force."

After the president leaves a hotel, the White House Communications Agency sweeps the suite for classified material that might have been left behind. Even bathrooms are checked. The aides who did the review were always amazed at how many tissues Rosalynn discarded with smeared makeup on them.

"I remember that everyone in Carter's staff wanted to do something his way," said Pisha, an *Air Force One* steward. "We knew what the president liked. Every staff member wanted to do what he liked. They would change things, change our menus."

During one trip to Georgia, the *Air Force One* crew had planned to purchase barbecue from Carter's favorite barbecue establishment for the trip back.

"They [the staff] said no, they don't feel like having it, let's go with the Reuben sandwich. We had everything prepared. We had these beautiful Reuben sandwiches made up. In the motorcade we went by this barbecue place, and he [Carter] wanted it. Everyone jumped off and said, 'We want this.' So we had to stop everything and prepare barbecue sandwiches for half the plane. They [the staff] would take the credit. Most of the Reubens had to go to waste."

On a trip to Florida, Phil Wise, a Carter assistant, asked the *Air Force One* crew to prepare a seafood buffet for the trip back. Since Wise had made the request late on Saturday, and the flight was leaving early Sunday morning, the crew did not have time to buy the items in Washington. A hotel in Florida charged $2,200 for the oysters, snow crab claws, and cherrystone clams, Palmer said. The crew finally got the tab down to $1,200—still outrageous for a president who claimed he was saving taxpayer money.

The buffet was served that Sunday night.

"It didn't go over very well on the plane," Palmer said. "Half the people ate it, and half didn't."

"There was so much confusion in the Carter White House," Pisha said. "Everybody and their brother wanted to manage. We would have four or five people come on the airplane at different times and say, 'I'm going to be in charge of this,' 'I'm going to be in charge of that.' Some of them were power hungry. Hugh Carter [Carter's cousin] would come on and act like, I'm in charge. Others would come on and say, 'Whose decision was this? He had no business doing that.' They weren't very professional compared with the other administrations. It was a joke on the airplane."

Pisha contrasted the Carter staff with Henry Kissinger.

"He didn't put up with any bullshit," Pisha said. "He got the job done. He was tireless when it came to working on the Middle East."

But with the Carter staff, he said, "It was a lot of fun and games."[90]

Carter ordered the heat in the White House turned down from seventy-two to sixty-eight degrees and delayed maintenance on the White House, which began to deteriorate.

"I think with Rosalynn Carter things swung the other way," said Shirley Bender, the executive housekeeper. "The dignity went down the drain. It got very casual. I think you have to look up to the first family."

"They came in and arbitrarily cut everything," said William Cuff, who worked for Gulley in the White House military office. "Camp David is not a bunch of rustic Boy Scout cabins. It's a nice mountain retreat. They would not spend any money, but buildings like that require maintenance. They have hard winters, and the roads take a beating. Under Carter, unless something was falling down, you did nothing about it."

Cuff said Carter had solar panels installed on the roof of the White House to save energy by heating hot water.

"It would not generate enough hot water to run the dishwasher in the staff mess," Cuff said. "It was a fiasco. The staff mess had to go out and buy new equipment to keep the water hot enough. That blew any savings."

Carter also got rid of the *Sequoia,* the presidential yacht that had originally been used by the White House in the twenties and then again had been used by presidents since Johnson. Cuff said Carter even tried to cut the crew on *Air Force One.*

"*Air Force One* is an airplane, and you need a minimum number of people to fly it," Cuff said. "You have to have a pilot, copilot, and others. They never understood that. The presidential pilot and the vice chief of staff of the air force had to argue with them."

"He wanted the stewards on *Air Force One* cut from seven to five because American Airlines had five flight attendants on the Boeing 707," Gulley said. "But the stewards had to help with the maintenance of the aircraft. The American Airlines attendants just went to a hotel. These guys had to work. We never did change it."

"Carter came in to get rid of perks in the White House," said an aide who works in the Situation Room. "He took 180 TV's out of the White House, so no one knew what was going on in the news."

Gulley said Carter became so involved in micromanaging the White House that he would veto replacements of carpets or polishing of doorknobs to save money.

"He wouldn't allow them to change the carpeting where the

public went through the White House," Gulley said. "The White House looked like a peanut warehouse when I left. Thousands of people pass through there, and it requires a high degree of maintenance. Carter himself got involved in that. It [the carpeting] was worn and dirty."[91]

Nor would Carter allow the residence staff to shine the doorknobs in the White House. "It was just ridiculous," Gulley said.

In fact, while the Executive Office of the President had 1,796 employees when Carter took over, it had 2,013 employees when Carter left.[92]

"My personal opinion of the Carter administration was it was a wasted four years," said Jimmy Bull, the *Air Force One* communicator. "I don't think he ever found out what he needed to do to be president."

Toward the end of his term, Carter became suspicious that people were stealing things and listening to his conversations in the Oval Office.

"They were becoming very paranoid," said a General Services Administration building manager in charge of the west wing. "They thought GSA or the Secret Service were listening in."

One afternoon, Susan Clough, Carter's secretary, insisted that some of the crude oil in a vial an Arab leader gave Carter had been stolen from the Oval Office.

"Susan Clough swore up and down that someone poured some of it out," a GSA manager said. "There was a big fuss over it. The Secret Service photographs everything in the president's suite. They photographed it [again], and it hadn't been touched. It shows the paranoia. It was sealed."

"Carter complained about mice in the Oval Office," said Price, a GSA manager. "He said, 'If Orkin can take care of mice in Georgia, why can't they take care of them here?' "

Carter called a meeting of a dozen GSA and White House aides to discuss the problem.

"That was when the Metro subway was being built," Price said. "Rats and mice were all over."

At five one afternoon, Price got a call from Clough.

"She said, 'The Olympic team is on the south lawn waiting

101

to see the president, and what should appear but a rat staggering around.' I had to call my boss at home and Rex W. Scouten [then the chief usher] to tell them there was a rat."

Since the Park Service is in charge of the White House grounds, the rat was not a GSA rat, Price said.

"I wanted to tell her [Clough], 'It wasn't our rat, it was the Park Service's rat.' But you can't say that. We found out the Park Service had put out pellets that make them want water. The rat was staggering around looking for water. I'm sure the rat didn't go to meet the president."

After Ronald Reagan was inaugurated, GSA found the Carter staff had left garbage in the White House and had trashed furniture in the old Executive Office Building.

"A couple of weeks after the inauguration, we saw furniture, desks, and file cabinets turned over," a GSA building manager said. "They tried to destroy the EOB where the staff was," he said. "They shoved over desks. We had to straighten it out. It was fifteen or twenty desks in one area. It was enough to look like a cyclone had hit. . . . They were mean-spirited people. That flowed over and hurt Carter."

Rotting food turned up in the west wing in what became the office of John F. W. Rogers, the Reagan aide over White House administration.

"They left chicken bones and White House mess dishes," a GSA manager said. "It smelled."

"We moved a table against the wall in the press office, and behind it was chicken bones," Larry Speakes, Reagan's press secretary, said.

After he was voted out of office, Carter occasionally stayed in the town house GSA maintains for former presidents at 1716 Jackson Place. Like other presidents, Carter also stayed in the town house on the evening of his successor's inauguration.

On the walls of the town house are photos of former presidents. Because GSA managers had to check on the premises while Carter was there, they found that Carter would temporarily remove the photos of Republican presidents Ford and Nixon and decorate the town house with another half-dozen sixteen-by-twenty-four-inch photos of himself. Charles B. (Buddy) Respass, then the GSA manager over the White House, became irate each time because GSA had to find the old photos and hang them up again.

Carter, through Adamson, denied this. He also denied that Carter thought people were listening to his conversations in the Oval Office.

But Price, the GSA manager, said, "Carter changed the photos. . . . He didn't like them [Ford and Nixon] looking down at him. We would find out he would put photos of himself up," Price said. "Then he would take the photos of himself back with him," she said.

"He was a wimp."[93]

5

"Don't You Ever Point a Finger at My Dog"

If Nancy Reagan's wealthy California friends reported getting their copies of *Vogue* and *Mademoiselle* before her, she flew into a rage. For that reason, Nelson C. Pierce, Jr., an assistant usher in the White House, always dreaded bringing Nancy Reagan her mail.

"She would get mad at me," Pierce recalled. "If her subscription was late or one of her friends in California had gotten the magazine and she hadn't, she would ask why she hadn't gotten hers."

The ushers would then have to search for the errant magazine at Washington newsstands, which invariably had not received their copies either. On those occasions when the magazine had arrived at newsstands, the anxious staff would buy copies with their own money so Nancy would not complain that her friends had already received theirs.

Pierce remembers one sunny afternoon when he brought

some mail to Nancy in the first family's west sitting room on the second floor of the White House. Nancy's dog Rex, a King Charles spaniel, was lying on the floor beside her. Pierce was old friends with Rex, Ronald Reagan's Christmas gift to her. During the day, the usher's office—just inside the front entrance on the first floor of the mansion—is often the repository for White House pets. For example, Chelsea Clinton's cat, Socks, often presides there on a cat bed under a chair. During such visits, Rex and the assistant usher had always hit it off.

But for some reason, Rex was not happy to see Pierce this time. Perhaps he sensed that Nancy Reagan was not big on Pierce. Appearances were everything to Nancy Reagan. While Pierce was immaculately groomed, the assistant usher was an older, portly man with white hair. He did not have the lean young California look Nancy preferred.

In any case, as Pierce turned around to leave, Rex bit his ankle. He pointed his finger at the dog, a gesture to get the dog to let go of his leg.

"She said, 'Don't you ever point a finger at my dog,' " Pierce recalled. "I said, 'Yes, ma'am.' "[94]

It is, of course, the job of the White House staff to be invisible. Consisting of ninety-seven people, the staff includes chefs, maids, housemen, butlers, painters, florists, calligraphers, engineers, assistant curators and assistant ushers, stewards, carpenters, electricians, plumbers, a maître d', and a doorman. The chief usher runs the staff and is in charge of the $7.9 million annual budget. The figure does not include the contribution of the National Park Service, which spends at least $2.8 million a year to maintain the grounds and the exterior of the White House. Nor does the expenditure include contracts to renovate or paint the White House or replace the mechanical systems. For example, $4.7 million is currently being spent to remove thirty-two coats of paint from the White House exterior. Once the coats are removed, a new coat of paint will go on the Virginia sandstone. These contracts are on top of the regular annual outlays.

"The term 'usher' goes back to when the house was much smaller, prior to the east and west wings," explained Gary Walters, the chief usher. "In 1902, when the west wing was added, all the presidential offices were on the second floor in the east end, although in earlier times some presidents like Thomas Jefferson used part of what is now the state dining room as his office. People literally came to the north portico [the front entrance] and were ushered from there to a room upstairs."[95]

"You do a little bit of everything," Pierce said of the usher's job. "I helped move the East Room piano for a special program Mrs. Johnson had. I took an upright piano off a dolly. I have set up chairs. J. B. West [the former White House usher who hired Pierce as an assistant] described it at my interview by saying, 'One day you'll be an electrical expert, the next day a plumbing expert, and God only knows what you'll do the day after.' That pretty much sums up the job of the ushers. You get involved in every detail."

But allowing a dog to bite one's leg is not one of those details. A kindly man, Pierce tried later to make light of the encounter.

"He grabbed my ankle with his teeth," he said. "He didn't bite hard, but you knew he was there. He let loose right away when I pointed at him."

But Pierce, one of three assistant ushers in the White House, was offended by Nancy Reagan's rebuke.

"I was a little upset," he said. "I didn't understand it."

If the incident gives insight into Nancy Reagan's character, it also helps explain why the presidency of Ronald Reagan was so successful. Reagan the actor played the good guy, mouthing his lines, charming the press, and making people feel good about the country and themselves. It was difficult to believe that Reagan would preside over illegal activity like the Iran-contra affair, yet the final report of special prosecutor Lawrence Walsh said Reagan "set the stage" for the scandal and created a climate where "some of the government officers assigned to implement his policies felt emboldened" to break the law.

Nancy Reagan, who was the real power behind Reagan, played the bad guy. She made sure Reagan fired aides who were incompetent, pressured him into softening his truculent approach to the Soviet Union, and kept him focused.

The oldest president in U.S. history, Ronald Wilson Reagan was almost seventy-eight when he left office. Ever since an actor fired a pistol near his head during the production of a movie, he has been hard of hearing. Reagan began wearing a hearing aid in his right ear in 1983 and in his left ear in 1985. Nearsighted since childhood, he wears contact lenses.[96]

In his first campaign, Reagan promised to promote conservative measures like increased defense spending, an antiabortion amendment to the Constitution, and supply-side economics. But Reagan's easygoing, confident personality and his ability as a communicator were the deciding factors. When Carter lashed out at Reagan in a televised debate as a threat to world peace, Reagan brushed aside the charge with a smile, a shake of his head, and a look of dismay. "There you go again," he said.[97]

From the start of his political life, Reagan was stage-managed by his wife, Nancy.

"Did I ever give Ronnie advice? You bet I did," Nancy Reagan wrote in *My Turn: The Memoirs of Nancy Reagan.* "I'm the one who knows him best, and I was the only person in the White House who had absolutely no agenda of her own—except helping him."[98]

As it happened, most of Nancy's advice was sound. As she explained it, "As much as I love Ronnie, I'll admit he does have at least one fault: He can be naive about the people around him. Ronnie only tends to think well of people. While that's a fine quality in a friend, it can get you into trouble in politics."

So when people like Raymond J. Donovan, Reagan's labor secretary, were investigated over alleged bribery schemes, it was Nancy who tried to get her husband to fire him. Donovan finally resigned after he was indicted; he was later cleared of any wrongdoing. When Donald Regan, Reagan's chief of staff, became a liability because of his abrasiveness, Nancy persuaded Reagan to let him go. Nancy tried, without success, to get Reagan to fire William Casey after he came under attack for his role in the Iran-contra affair. And she ordered that, because of his highly conservative views, Pat Buchanan, the White House director of communications, have nothing to do with writing Reagan's speeches.[99]

"All the presidents found it very difficult to fire people," Robert Gates said. "To a man, it was the worst thing they could do. These guys come across as tough and firm and ready to take on the Russians, and yet they absolutely cringe at the thought of firing someone."[100]

Nancy Reagan attributed her good calls to being a good judge of character. While that may have been true, it was also true that much of her advice about such matters as trip scheduling and the timing of her husband's medical operations came from her astrologer, Joan Quigley. Nancy Reagan was not the first wife of a president to rely on mystics. Mary Todd Lincoln relied on Madame Laurie of Georgetown, who told her that "the Cabinet were all enemies of the president, working for themselves." Julia Tyler said she received messages "from the other side" through her dreams.

But Nancy Reagan had far more clout with her husband than did most other first ladies. Nancy's judgments were often tied to physical appearance. She banished Lyn Nofziger, Reagan's longtime aide, because she thought he looked "scruffy," according to a Secret Service agent. As her comment about her own role suggests, her interest was narrowly focused on promoting her husband. In that equation, the interests of the American people did not figure.

"Mrs. Reagan was a precise and demanding woman," said John F. W. Rogers, the Reagan aide over administration of the White House. "Her sole interest was the advancement of her husband's agenda."

Even the impetus for her adoption of the "Just Say No" campaign against drugs was her desire to improve her image. It was Quigley, her astrologer, who recommended the drug abuse program after Nancy told her she wanted to be "loved."[101]

Rather than having the interests of the country at heart, Nancy Reagan was interested in clothes and a few wealthy friends. She treated even her own children with contempt.

"She was very cold," a Secret Service agent said of Nancy Reagan. "She had her circle of four friends in Los Angeles, and that was it. Nothing changed when she was with her kids. She made it clear to her kids that if they wanted to see their father, they had to check with her first. It was a standing rule. Not that they could not see him. 'I will let you know if it is advisable and when you can see him.' She was something else."

The agent said Nancy Reagan was so controlling that she objected when her husband—whose code name was Rawhide—kibitzed with Secret Service agents.

"Reagan was such a down-to-earth individual, easy to talk to," an agent said. "He was the great communicator. He wanted to be on friendly terms. He accepted people for what they were. His wife was just the opposite. If she saw that he was having a conversation with the agents, and it looked like they were good old boys, and he was laughing, she would call him away and remind him. She called the shots."

"Nancy was not liked by many of us," said Bell, the former Secret Service agent. "I think she was way over her head. Another person on her detail said she was about the dumbest female he had ever met, but she was really good at protecting Ronald's flank, I guess."

Reagan projected a macho image that he burnished whenever he chopped wood or rode horses on his 668-acre Ranch del Cielo in the mountains above Santa Barbara. In reality, Reagan was ruled by his wife. Calling Nancy a "manipulator," a Secret Service agent said she would often whisper in Reagan's ear and, like an automaton, he would do what she said.

"You had to be close to hear Nancy's instructions," the agent said. "He always went along with it. He let her make the decisions. You never saw a nasty side to him."

On the day Reagan left office, he flew to Los Angeles on *Air Force One*. Near a hangar, bleachers had been set up, and a wildly cheering crowd welcomed him while the University of Southern California band played.

"As he was standing there, one of the USC guys took his Trojan helmet off," a Secret Service agent said. "He said, 'Mr. President!' and threw his helmet to him. He saw it and caught it and put it on. The crowd went wild."

The Secret Service agent said, "Nancy Reagan leaned over to him and said, 'Take that damn helmet off right now. You look like a fool.' He reached up. You saw a mood change. And he took it off. That went on all the time."

James A. Buzzelli, an *Air Force One* flight engineer, recalled that when the Reagans were about to get off the plane after a trip, "Mrs. Reagan said to him, 'Where is your coat?' He said he didn't need his coat."

Charles Palmer, the chief of the *Air Force One* stewards, was standing nearby.

"She said, 'Charlie, get his coat,' " Buzzelli said. "He said, 'Charlie, I don't need it.'

"He walked out of the plane with his coat on," Buzzelli said.[102]

"Nancy Reagan was very protective of that guy," said Jimmy R. Bull, the chief communicator on *Air Force Once*. "The president would need forty hours a day to do all the things people wanted him to do. You can run him into the ground in a hurry, mentally and physically. The chief of staff and others wanted him to do things that he couldn't handle. His health was up and down in the White House."

"No one looked out for his welfare more or was more concerned about him as a human being," said James F. Kuhn, Nixon's administrative assistant during his second term. "Everyone said she was demanding. I remember her saying some things to me about things that should be done. But she never asked for anything for herself. It was always for her 'roommate,' as she called him."

"Reagan was very jovial," said Joseph A. Jaworski, who became chief communicator on *Air Force One* later in the Reagan administration. "He always had something nice to say. He was easy to fly with. His flying schedule was managed very well."[103]

"With Carter, if we had a function in Japan, they might leave Washington at 8 P.M. so they could be in Japan the following morning," said Robert A. Lazaro, an *Air Force One* pilot for Carter and Reagan. "They would plan it so he would have an hour to get ready for a function. With the Reagan administration, they seemed to plan a little further ahead. He would get there a day ahead to acclimate himself. I think that was good planning."[104]

Reagan's ability to remember names amazed the crew.

"Reagan would look at a list of names of people who were

meeting him on the ground," said James R. Saddler, an *Air Force One* steward. "He would memorize the names in less than a minute. Then he would get off and say, 'Hello, Sally, Dick, Joe,' which was pretty impressive."

"I think Reagan was probably the president who was affected least by the White House," George Reedy, Johnson's press secretary, said. "If you're an actor—and I'm not being derogatory here—you cannot have a really strong personality. You have to be Attila the Hun Tuesday night and on Friday night, Julius Caesar in Shakespeare's play. You go from character to character, and you can't have a strong personality of your own."

For all the spin from the Carter White House about not drinking, it was the Reagans who drank the least.

"I may have served the Reagans four drinks, maybe, with the exception of a glass of wine," said Palmer.[105]

"Mrs. Reagan was a very light eater," Palmer said. "We had fresh squeezed orange juice. It was a must. She would pick at her food. Sometimes she ate well, and sometimes she took three or four bites, and that was it."

Nancy Reagan tried to restrict her husband's diet to healthy foods, but whenever she was not there, he reverted to his favorites.

"She was protective about what he ate," Palmer said. "When she was not there, he ate differently. One of his favorite foods was macaroni and cheese. That was a no-no for her. If it was on the menu, she said, 'You're not eating that.' "

While other presidents liked their steak medium rare, Reagan liked his well done. He also liked hamburger soup—made with ground beef, tomatoes, and carrots—roast beef hash, beef and kidney pie, and osso buco. Nancy Reagan liked paella à la Valenciana, salmon mousse, and chicken pot pie. For dessert, the Reagans liked Apple Brown Betty, prune whip, fruit with Cointreau, and plum pudding.

"He liked simple foods, but Nancy Reagan liked fancy food," Henry Haller, the executive chef, said.

For breakfast, the Reagans often had scrambled eggs and sausages. On weekdays, they had only a piece of toast or an English muffin.

"Mrs. Reagan more than anyone was involved with food," Haller said. When an important dignitary was expected, "I would have her try the menu out for ten people. She would give her critique. Sometimes she made changes. Sometimes she said she didn't care for this meal. She was particular about the color combinations. She wanted small portions, but very pretty."

Both in the White House and on *Air Force One*, Nancy Reagan was constantly asking that thermostats be turned up. Before landing, "Nancy Reagan would always ask for the temperature," Palmer said. "She would be freezing," he said.

"They were very affectionate and would kiss," Palmer said of the Reagans. But they also got mad at each other over what to eat and other small issues. Moreover, Palmer said Nancy could push the president only so far.

"We were going into Alaska. She had put on everything she could put on," Palmer said. "She turned around and said, 'Where are your gloves?' He said, 'I'm not wearing my gloves.' She said, 'Oh, yes, you are.' He said he was not."

Palmer said Reagan finally took the gloves but said he could not shake hands with them on, and would not wear them. And he didn't.

William Bell, the former Secret Service agent, said he was guarding the Reagans at their ranch when Reagan displayed a rare streak of temper directed at his wife.

"He was waiting for Nancy to get off the telephone so they could go horseback riding together," the former agent said. "He was outside waiting for a long time, and when she didn't get off, he went in and ripped the phone off the wall. He pulled the cord out of the wall. He threw the telephone on the floor. That was one of the few times he displayed that kind of emotion."

The White House press corps liked to think it knew the whereabouts of the president and first lady at all times. But Nancy Reagan would sneak out of the White House at least once a month for unpublicized trips.

"She traveled at least once a month somewhere," said Glenn A. Quigg, a steward on *Air Force One* who flew with her on a

112

DC-9. "It was to get outfits in New York or to Los Angeles or to see her friends. She went to Phoenix to see her mother."[106]

"She made a trip once a month to see her mother in a nursing home in Phoenix," a Secret Service agent said. "Then she came to Los Angeles. For the most part it was off the record. She stayed in Steve McQueen's suite at the Beverly Wilshire. She would stay there and pamper herself," he said.

Nancy's routine was always the same, the agent said. With the Secret Service driving, "She made her way down Rodeo Drive. She went to Chanel, Van Cleef's," he said. "That woman had ice in her veins. She was really in love with her husband. Nobody else mattered, not even her children. She had four or five friends in Los Angeles. She saw the same people each time—Betsy Bloomingdale. She always got her hair done. She was upper crust."

Going back to Dolley Madison, first ladies had accepted free designer dresses. John Jacob Astor sent Dolley Madison free clothing from his American Fur Co. from what he called "motives of patriotism." But Nancy Reagan turned the practice into a small industry. She received free dresses from Galanos, Adolfo, Bill Blass, and David Hayes, among others. When she encountered criticism, she donated thirteen of the dresses to the Smithsonian and other museums, saying she had been trying to help the American design industry by publicizing its fashions.

Meanwhile, Reagan was so passive that he never mentioned to anyone that the desk he was using in the Oval Office was too low for him. Queen Victoria of England had given the desk to President Rutherford B. Hayes. Made of oak timbers from the HMS *Resolute,* which had been salvaged in the Arctic by American whalers, the desk was used by John F. Kennedy and most presidents since. Bush liked it, so he had it placed in his personal study on the second floor of the White House. David C. Fischer, Reagan's executive assistant during his first term, asked Reagan why he sat sideways behind the desk.

"He said he couldn't get his knees under the desk," said Kuhn, Fischer's successor. "But he never thought of asking for a raised desk. He thought that was the way it was."

Fischer had the desk raised so Reagan could fit his legs under it.

Quite often, Reagan quietly wrote personal checks to people who had written with hard-luck stories.

"Reagan was famous for firing up air force jets on behalf of children who needed transport for kidney operations," said Frank J. Kelly, who drafted presidential messages. "These are things you never knew about. He never bragged about it. I hand-carried checks for $4,000 or $5,000 to people who had written him. He would say, 'Don't tell people. I was poor myself.' "[107]

White House aides noticed that the Reagans invariably returned from trips well before dinner, but it was not until later that they realized it was because Nancy's astrologer had told her it was unsafe to be out at night.

"I knew nothing about the astrologer," said Kuhn, who scheduled Reagan's time. "It never entered my mind that she was giving us any direction."

Unlike Clinton, Reagan tried hard to be punctual and not keep people waiting.

"We had a schedule, and the Reagans liked to follow that schedule," Kuhn said. "When he knew someone was waiting for him, he raced. He never wanted to inconvenience anyone. He used to drive me crazy, because he would say, 'Jim, we have to get over there [to another appointment].' I would say, 'I know, Mr. President, but we have to finish what we're doing here, too.' I would say, 'I'll send word over, and they'll be fine. Someone will serve them coffee.' "[108]

In the Reagan administration, as in others, there was a pecking order based on proximity to the president. No matter how important an aide's position might be, if his office was in the old Executive Office Building, he was considered an outsider.

"Despite their shortcomings, offices in the west wing were hungrily coveted," Don Regan wrote in his book, *For the Record: From Wall Street to Washington.* "One high-ranking official, relegated to a beautiful and spacious vaulted office in the executive office building, pleaded with me with tears in his eyes for space, any space, in the west wing."

"It is a rabbit warren," said Lloyd Cutler, Carter's White

House counsel, of the west wing. "I had the same office Bernie Nussbaum [Clinton's counsel] has. It is a little room on the southwest corner. There is a parapet that goes above the eye level of the window, so when you see out, you can see the sky, but you can't see anything else. It's like living in a dungeon, and that's considered one of the better offices."

Kenneth L. Khachigian, Reagan's chief speechwriter, recalled that because he was trying to finish writing one of Reagan's speeches, he did not return the calls of a twenty-five-year-old aide in the west wing.

"He kept trying to get ahold of me," said Khachigian, whose office was in the old Executive Office Building. "I was writing a speech. He told my secretary, 'Tell him this is so-and-so calling from the west wing.' I said to tell that impertinent twit that this is Ken Khachigian from the EOB, and the EOB is not taking his calls.

"It can be a very unreal atmosphere," said Khachigian, who had worked in the Nixon White House before returning under Reagan. "The second time around under Reagan, I was older, wiser, more secure. I felt I had grown above the intrigue and mystique that one can attach to oneself working in the White House. I found myself lecturing some of the younger men and women on the staff not to get too full of themselves. You saw that all the time."[109]

Like everything else in the White House, the job of speechwriter is fraught with turmoil.

"Controlling the president's words is control of the agenda and the game," Khachigian said. "There is often an enormous tug of war over that process."

In drafting Reagan's first state of the union address, for example, Treasury, the Office of Management and Budget, and the President's Council of Economic Advisers all wanted to go in different directions.

"I was getting competitive updates from all those agencies until an hour before the speech," Khachigian said. "Don Regan was changing it after that on the TelePrompTer. The president hated that. He wanted to deal with one person at the end. One time I brought in some changes and he said, 'Damn it, did the committee get ahold of this again?' He made a big sigh. Quite often I faked the authority to filter out what I thought were the unimportant changes. You try to be as neutral as possible. But juggling the various turfs was often quite difficult."

Despite the infighting, Reagan's staff overall operated smoothly.

"There is an operating premise that the president of the United States should never be embarrassed," Mark D. Weinberg, a press spokesman under Reagan, said. "And that the most valuable commodity there is the time and attention of the president. How it is used and where it is focused is the single most important consideration of the staff. That is an important operating principle, at least it was for us."[110]

As the great communicator, Reagan tended to operate by conveying symbolic messages rather than by issuing directives.

"To this day I have never had so much as one minute alone with Ronald Reagan," Donald Regan wrote in a note to himself two months after he became Treasury secretary. "Never has he, or anyone else, sat down in private to explain to me what is expected of me, what goals he would like to see accomplished, what results he wants."

Regan concluded that when it came to economic policy, Reagan expected his public statements to be all the guidance needed.

"For a while, I struggled against a certain anxiety that this method of running the world's greatest economy might wreck the new presidency. Happily, I was wrong," Regan said. "In fact, Reagan's openness created an atmosphere of confidence and political dynamism that produced the longest period of recovery and the highest levels of employment in the history of the United States."

That is, until the bill came due. By the time Reagan left office, the deficit, adjusted for inflation, had grown by 50 percent, from $101 billion to $150 billion. The nation then plunged into the greatest recession since the Great Depression.

"Reaganites say that Reagan has lifted our 'spirits'—correct if they mean he led the nation in a drunken world-record spending binge while leaving millions of American workers, consumers, and pollution victims defenseless," Ralph Nader said.

According to George Reedy, "The presidents who go down as being great presidents came along when the country was united. Everyone knew what they wanted. The poor presidents came along when society was changing."

Reagan had the good fortune to become president when the country faced few divisive issues.

"Almost everyone was in agreement they had to reduce programs," Reedy said. "Reagan was in a period where there were no really great political issues facing the country. He actually did very little as president."

During the Reagan presidency, the Secret Service succeeded in fortifying the White House to an unprecedented degree, beginning with dump trucks loaded with sand and concrete barriers temporarily erected around the area. The fortifications culminated with steel-reinforced concrete posts that now encircle 1600 Pennsylvania Avenue. Under Reagan, East Executive Avenue, which borders the White House on the east, was closed to traffic, as West Executive Avenue had been closed in 1951. A $771,000 "garden pavilion" was added to the east wing to give the Secret Service more room to check tourists for weapons.

"The Secret Service has a huge institutional presence," John Rogers, who was in charge of administration for Reagan, said. "They outlive presidents and staff people, and they do what they want. The posts were supposed to be lower and based on a Parisian design with more space between them. The Secret Service wanted higher ones with steel I-beams inside. I overruled them. You can go and see my effect. They outlive you."

For all the precautions, Reagan became the first president since Kennedy to have been hit by an assassin's bullet. At 2:35 P.M. on March 30, 1981, John W. Hinckley, Jr., a twenty-five-year-old drifter, fired a .22 Röhm RG-14 revolver at Reagan as he left a speech at the Washington Hilton Hotel.

"I remember three quick shots and four more," said Jerry S. Parr, the agent who was in charge of Reagan's detail. "With Agent Ray Shattuck, I pushed the president down behind another agent who was holding the car door open. Agent Dennis McCarthy got ahold of Hinckley by leaping through the air. He got his hand. I got the president in the car, and the other agent slammed the door, and we drove off."[111]

The Secret Service car began speeding toward the White House.

"I checked him over and found no blood," Parr said. "After fifteen or twenty seconds, we were under Dupont Circle moving fast. President Reagan had a napkin from the speech and dabbed his mouth with it. He said, 'I think I cut the inside of my mouth.'"

Parr noticed that the blood was bright red and frothy. He ordered the driver to head toward George Washington Hospital Center, the hospital that had been preselected in the event medical assistance was needed.

"I didn't know he was shot until we got to the hospital," Parr said. "He collapsed as we walked in."

The surgeons found a bullet that had punctured and collapsed a lung and lodged an inch from Reagan's heart. If the car had not gone to the hospital, Reagan would likely have died.

"I forgot to duck," Reagan said.

In the White House, Alexander M. Haig, Jr., who was secretary of state, appeared on television saying, "I am in control here." In fact, under the line of succession, Vice President George Bush was. Meanwhile, the FBI had confiscated Reagan's authentication card for launching nuclear weapons, saying all of Reagan's effects were needed as evidence. Despite a demand by James V. Hickey, Jr., then the director of the White House military office, the FBI would not return it for two weeks.

Because no guidelines had been worked out for such a situation, it was not clear who could launch a nuclear strike. Bush could have taken it upon himself to launch a strike by communicating with the defense secretary over a secure line, but it was questionable whether he had the legal authority to do so. In the event a president is disabled, the Twenty-fifth Amendment to the Constitution allows the vice president to act for the president only if the president has declared in writing to the Senate and the House that he is disabled and cannot discharge his duties. If the vice president and a majority of the Cabinet decide the president may not discharge his duties, they may make the vice president acting president. But that would require time.

When Bush became president, his administration drafted a highly detailed, classified plan for immediately transferring power in case of serious presidential illness.

As the executive clerk in the White House, Ron Geisler is the institutional memory who keeps track of such papers. In his files on the ground floor of the old Executive Office Building, Geisler keeps form letters and messages to be used for almost any occasion. If a president dies, for example, Geisler has a sample statement to be read by the vice president expressing the nation's grief. Minutes after Clinton was sworn in, Geisler was meeting with him at the Capitol to have him sign an executive order on ethics and Cabinet nominations. Any law requiring the president to act is sent to Geisler. He makes sure it is followed.

"Executive clerk is the oldest career office in the White House," Geisler said. "Every president since Washington had a clerk. Most of the time they were secretary to the president. Many times they were relatives. Then in 1857, the secretary of interior felt sorry for the president and got an appropriation from Congress for executive clerks. We do all executive orders and proclamations. We're experts in that sort of thing," he said.

Having worked in the office twenty-nine years, Geisler is one of those invisible career employees who continue through different administrations. He prides himself on being apolitical.

"These are all career people," he said, pointing out his staff of half a dozen employees. "Even if your mother or father is involved in politics, we would not bring them in. We don't go to parties at people's houses. That is the line drawn by all my predecessors. You have to know how to work in this environment," he said. "It's a very sensitive place to be. If you cross the line [into partisanship], you are not going to last."[112]

According to Parr, after Hinckley had been taken to St. Elizabeth's Hospital, he told the Secret Service that he had planned on shooting Carter at a speech in 1980, but the Secret Service contingent around him discouraged him. Sure enough, the Secret Service went back and spotted Hinckley near Carter in photographs taken at the time.

On at least two occasions, Reagan, like Ford, became separated from the nuclear football—once in South America and once in the White House when an elevator got stuck with him in it.

"The president was going up to the State Dining Room for a luncheon," said Larry Speakes, who was Reagan's press secretary. "Normally, the lead agent gets on and maybe a staff guy. The rest—including the person with the nuclear football—run up the stairs. We waited and waited. No elevator. The Secret Service agent was with him. They were stuck. They had to wait for a guy to come [to fix it]."[113]

Of all the presidential children guarded by the Secret Service, Michael Reagan was the least liked. In his book, *Michael Reagan: On the Outside Looking In,* the adopted son of Ronald Reagan and his first wife, Jane Wyman, wrote that the Secret Service had accused him of shoplifting.

" 'You are a thief, Mike,' " he quoted an agent as saying. " 'We have the evidence, but we know that you don't know what you are doing, and we want to help you.' "[114]

Denying the charge, Michael related that Ronald Reagan suggested he see a psychiatrist. But what never came out is that while Reagan was president, the Royal Canadian Mounted Police (RCMP) reported allegations to the Secret Service that Michael Reagan physically abused his son.

"He had an incident in Vancouver where he spanked his child, and the RCMP said, 'If you ever do that again, you will be arrested,' " a Secret Service agent said. "It never came out because it was discreetly done. . . . Because he was the president's son, they felt a warning would be sufficient. We told them that if they felt they had grounds to arrest him for child abuse, they should do what they have to do. Somebody had seen him and told the RCMP. It was slapping and spanking. He treated his kid that way all the time.

"He was jealous of the agents," the agent said of Michael Reagan, who was thirty-six when his father became president.

120

"He had a bit part in a movie. His role was a used-car salesman. On the lot the extras were more interested in the Secret Service agents than in him. He said, 'What are you talking to them for?' He would say, 'I'm having trouble getting free tickets to a show tonight. Can you guys get me free tickets?' He was always panhandling. He got very insulted that the RCMP would tell him something like that. They were dead serious. They came to us and told us."

Michael Reagan confirmed that the RCMP had met with him and his wife and warned him that if he abused his then eight-year-old son, Cameron, again, the RCMP would arrest him. He said that on two occasions, Cameron needed to be hit. Because the Secret Service was in foreign territory, the RCMP accompanied the agents on the protective detail and saw Reagan hit his son.

"I took him behind a tree and gave him a swat," Michael Regan said. "At a shopping center, I took him to a men's room and gave him a swat. The RCMP said they would arrest me if I did it again."

Reagan said the Secret Service told him the reason the RCMP was upset is that in Canada, spanking a child in public is considered child abuse. But the RCMP, the Secret Service, and one of Canada's leading lawyers said there is no such law.

"We have the same laws in Canada as anywhere else," said Dr. Morris C. Shumiatcher, who has litigated Canadian cases involving child abuse. "If it is done by a loving father to correct an erring child, it is justified."[115]

Asked if he could cite the law, Reagan said he could not. Asked how many times he hit his son, Reagan said, "I wasn't counting."

"You're a fuckin' asshole," Reagan said at one point during a telephone interview, hanging up. He then called back and apologized.[116]

Michael Reagan had well-publicized flare-ups with the first family and his own siblings. In one incident, he attacked his stepmother, Nancy Reagan, after she said he had been estranged from the family for three years.

Describing himself as "shocked" and "hurt" by her remarks,

Michael Reagan said, "Maybe it's Nancy's way of justifying why she and Dad have never seen our daughter, Ashley. She's nineteen months old, and they've never laid eyes on her."[117]

Maureen Reagan, the former president's eldest daughter, then attacked Michael Reagan for waging a "vendetta" against Nancy Reagan that had left the president and his wife "just agonized."

While these exchanges were publicized, the allegations of child abuse and other problems the Secret Service had with Michael Reagan were not. The Secret Service confronted Michael Reagan over his alleged shoplifting, telling him that when he was in the presence of agents, he would have to pay for everything he had taken in stores.

Michael Reagan's temper tantrums infuriated his Secret Service detail.

"He would stop the car in the middle of the freeway, trying to lose the Secret Service," an agent said. "If he got mad, he would stop the car and leave the kids in the car and walk away because he was upset and didn't like the way they were acting. After ten minutes, he came back. We would be there watching the children."

"He was a loser big time," an agent said.

In every administration, the job of trying to keep errant family members straight falls to the White House counsel. Under Carter, it was Lloyd Cutler who dealt with Billy Carter over his receipt of a $220,000 loan from the Libyan government. Under Reagan, Fred F. Fielding was charged with baby-sitting Michael Reagan.

Without offending him, Fielding had to confront Michael Reagan over the report of child abuse from the RCMP. It was an impossible task. But in the end Michael Reagan, like other presidential children, did not mind having Secret Service protection.

"The positive side of having agency protection while traveling overseas was that we were on and off planes quickly," he wrote. "We never had to go through Customs, cars were provided and our rooms were often upgraded to suites. Also, our bags were never lost and were waiting for us when we reached our hotel. Not bad perks," he noted. "Ones I will definitely miss."

Of all the perks, none is more seductive than living in the 132-room White House. Servants are always on call to take care of the slightest whim. Laundry, cleaning, and shopping are provided for. From three kitchens, White House chefs prepare meals that are exquisitely presented and of the quality of the finest French restaurants. If members of the first family want breakfast in bed every day—as Johnson did—they can have it. A pastry chef makes everything from Christmas cookies to chocolate éclairs. If the first family wants, it can have a dinner party every night, all paid for out of government funds. Invitations, hand-lettered by five calligraphers, are rarely turned down. From Pablo Casals to Beverly Sills, from Mikhail Baryshnikov to the Beach Boys, musicians, singers, and dancers are delighted to perform at the White House. In choosing what to eat on, the first family has its choice of nineteen-piece place settings of china ordered by the first families. They may choose, for example, the Reagans' pattern of a gold band around a red border, or the Johnsons', which features delicate wildflowers and the presidential seal.

Fresh flowers decorate every room, and lovely landscaping—including the Rose Garden and Jacqueline Kennedy Garden—adorns the grounds.

Besides the jogging track that Clinton commissioned just after he took office, the White House has a tennis court, built in 1902 and moved to the south grounds in 1911; an outdoor swimming pool built south of the west wing in 1975; a one-lane bowling alley built in 1973; a movie theater built in the east colonnade in 1942; and an artificial putting green installed on the south grounds in 1991. It also has a basketball court, a horseshoe pit, and—in the new and old Executive Office Buildings—gym facilities.[118]

While the first family pays for the incremental cost of food—the grocer's bill for a lamb chop—it does not pay for the far higher cost of preparation. Nor does the first family pay for personal telephone calls, which come out of the annual appropriation for the Executive Residence, or the flowers, which cost $252,000 a year.

"As a place to live, the White House was far more pleasant than I had ever expected it to be," Ford wrote in *A Time to Heal*. Ford ticked off some of the creature comforts, including having a bowl of strawberries always available and a tobacco tin for his pipe always full.

For all the conveniences, members of the first family sometimes have requests that are difficult to fill. On the evening he was inaugurated, Nixon asked for a steak dinner, but Pat Nixon wanted a bowl of cottage cheese in her bedroom in the suite at the southwest corner of the second floor usually chosen by presidents as their sleeping quarters.

"Steaks we had—juicy, fresh prime fillets carefully selected by the meat wholesaler, waiting in the White House kitchen for a family who, we'd heard, loved steak. But cottage cheese?" J. B. West, the White House chief usher, said.[119]

For two weeks, the White House chefs had been stocking up on every food imaginable to accommodate whatever the Nixons desired. But something so simple as cottage cheese had escaped their attention. Now most of the stores would be closed, so the head butler jumped in a White House limousine and sped off to a delicatessen that had a good supply.

"The kitchen never ran out after that," West said.

For all the luxuries, most first families have complained about the lack of privacy in the White House. Edith Roosevelt, wife of Theodore Roosevelt, observed that security agents watched her closely, as if she was "about to hatch anarchists." Jacqueline Kennedy, who tried to protect her children from photographers, taught Caroline, at the age of five, to hold up a hand and say, "No photographs."

Some first ladies became virtual recluses. Margaret Taylor, wife of Zachary Taylor, rarely left the second floor. She was plagued by false rumors that she smoked a pipe.[120]

Only Jacqueline Kennedy required White House staff members to sign a pledge that they would not talk about their experiences once they left. But the professionals who work in the mansion usually keep quiet regardless. As civil servants, they generally spend their entire careers working for the presidents. After they leave, they are invited back for Christmas parties and other events. They do not want to be cut out.

"Even if you leave the White House, you never leave it completely," said Haller, the White House chef.

The greatest enforcer of White House secrecy has been Rex W. Scouten, a former Secret Service agent who became chief usher under Nixon and curator under Reagan. The prototypical unctuous White House servant, Scouten calls former White House staff to berate them if he thinks their quotes in the press reveal too much.

"After I left the White House, the *National Enquirer* misquoted me on the Carters," said Shirley Bender, who was the White House executive housekeeper. "Rex Scouten didn't appreciate it too much. It was after I had left. He wasn't my boss. He said, 'Shirley, did you say these things?' "[121]

Scouten gave interviews only if he thought the reporter would confine himself to the history of the White House and its art collection. During the Reagan administration, he created unfavorable press by giving an exclusive on Nancy Reagan's renovation of the second floor of the White House to *Architectural Digest,* then refusing to let other publications use the photos after the magazine had used them.

"Nancy Reagan's aides have refused to permit the press and television to distribute photographs of her $1 million White House redecoration after allowing an architectural magazine to present a broad treatment of it," an Associated Press story said. The story noted that *Architectural Digest* featured twenty-seven color photos and eighteen pages of description of the redecoration.

"Although the work was financed largely by tax-deductible donations and a good part of it involves public rooms, Mrs. Reagan's press secretary, Sheila Tate, said that 'the White House has decided not to release the pictures at this time.' "[122]

Clem Conger, who had been White House curator since the Nixon administration, said he had objected to Scouten's plan.

"The White House press corps was not invited [to the opening]," Conger said. "It was to get publicity for him [Scouten].

Their [*Architectural Digest's*] circulation is small. I said to Scouten, 'Why isn't this open to the media? This is insane.' He said, 'Helen Thomas, the dean of the White House press corps, always writes a nasty story.' "

Conger said he could get Thomas to take a positive slant by giving her additional information that the other reporters did not have.

"He wants to control everything," Conger said of Scouten. "He thinks of the White House as his private fiefdom."

"I have never known Scouten to talk to anyone unless it was a publication you wouldn't be interested in reading," said Gulley, the chief of the White House military office.

That is not entirely true. Scouten did give a quote during the Reagan years to Barbara Gamarekian of the *New York Times*. Asked by Gamarekian if any glitches had occurred during the time he ran the White House staff for the Reagans, Scouten replied, "I've scoured my mind, and I can't come up with anything."

According to Conger, in a classic power play, Scouten ultimately edged him out of the White House. As Conger recalled it, Scouten would tell Rosalynn Carter and later Nancy Reagan that Conger was busy and could not see them. He would then escort them around the White House himself.[123]

So skillfully had Scouten ingratiated himself with the Reagans that Nancy named her dog Rex after him. While Reagan was president, Scouten retired as chief usher, but six months later, Scouten said he was bored and wanted to be curator. He then persuaded the Reagans to replace Conger with him in June 1986.

"Heaven only knows why she [Nancy] agreed to it," Conger said. "Who knows what Mrs. Reagan thinks about anything? I tried hard to help that lady. I was always cut off at the pass by Rex Scouten. . . . He was jealous of my success and complained that the press likes me. I said to him, 'In this work, you don't operate in a vacuum. This is how I have raised millions of dollars.' "

In a classic example of the byzantine nature of White House finances, Scouten was put on the payroll of the White House

Historical Association. That way, he could continue to receive his pension as a former Secret Service agent and chief usher.

"That was money that was supposed to go for acquisitions," Conger said of the funds of the association, which has an endowment of $6.2 million.

Scouten had no background for the job, which Conger had held since the Nixon administration. In that capacity, Conger helped raise some $40 million to augment the White House and State Department collections.

"Don Regan called me and said, 'Clem, I'm mortified,' " Conger recalled. "He said, 'Everyone knows what a wonderful job you have done with the State Department and White House and all the millions you raised. But Mrs. Reagan wants to give Scouten a less stressful job, like yours.'

"I explained this was a career position, and Scouten was not qualified," Conger said. "He [Scouten] does not have a background in art and antiques and decoration of the late eighteenth and early nineteenth century, which was the golden era of the White House," Conger said.

"I was very happy to leave the White House. I was overworked. I had been looking for the proper person and had not found him or her."

Ultimately, Conger talked with Reagan about the situation, to no avail. Conger told Reagan that for the past sixteen years, he had raised $2 to $3 million a year at State and $2 to $3 million at the White House.

During Conger's last years, more restoration work was done on the White House than under any president since Truman.

"The second and third floors were completely redone," said John Rogers, who was over administration. "The first floor had a major restoration. The removal of the thirty-two layers of paint outside was started. It was the first two-term presidency, so you were able to do a lot."

It was while Scouten was chief usher that a doorman was caught stealing petty cash from the usher's office.

"Most of the butlers and maids were older black folk that you never had any problem with," said Fred Walzel, who was chief of the White House branch of the Secret Service uniformed division. "There was one person stealing out of Rex Scouten's office. A video camera surveillance was set up. Nothing happened for a month. Sure enough, it was a doorman who was young."

Like Scouten, Gary Walters, Scouten's replacement as chief usher, tended to think of the White House as his personal empire.

"The personal habits of the families we don't talk about," he said smugly during a rare interview. "That would have to come through the families or their press offices. We protect their privacy. They have so precious little of it here. We feel a little fortunate to be behind the scenes. But also to protect that and the families, we don't talk about what they are like."[124]

Like Clinton, Carter had spurned Milton Pitts, the barber who had been cutting presidential hair since Nixon. Instead, he used Yves and Nancy Graux, a Washington team who called themselves hair stylists. Reagan returned Pitts to his rightful place in the White House barbershop, but only after Nancy had given her approval. Before Reagan's inauguration, Michael Deaver, one of Pitts's customers, had arranged for Pitts to cut Reagan's hair in a house where the future president was staying in Virginia.

"I cut it, and Nancy came in and said to Reagan, 'Don't you look great?'" Pitts said.

At first, Pitts and the Graux team coexisted in the White House, alternating days in the west wing barbershop. Both Pitts and the Grauxes cut the hair of senior White House aides and Cabinet secretaries, and both had their respective fans. Budget Director David Stockman, White House spokesman Larry Speakes, and Barbara Bush, when her husband was vice president, liked the Grauxes. But Chief of Staff James A. Baker III, Attorney General William French Smith, and Treasury Secretary Donald Regan, who found the White House barbershop convenient, liked Pitts.

Saying Pitts and the Grauxes were engaged in a "raging dispute" over their territory, Baker proposed building an additional unisex shop in the old Executive Office Building. But the Grauxes, unhappy about being ousted from the White

House, wrote a letter to a senator questioning the legality of spending $9,000 on the new salon. The hairsplitting ended when Baker shelved the plan and had Rogers fire the Grauxes. Temporarily, Baker barred anyone but the president from using Pitts's services in the White House barbershop.

"The barbershop is the president's barbershop and should remain the president's," Baker told the National Press Club.

Nancy Graux was shaken by the decision. "I feel so upset," she said. But Yves Graux said, "In a way I'm glad it's over, because the last eighteen months have been just a series of insults and aggravations. They treated us terribly."

"I'm completely happy," said Pitts, who insisted he was a stylist, too. "I am not a barber," he said. "I style everyone's hair."

Pitts found that Reagan's hair needed reshaping.

"Reagan had a high pompadour," he said. "His hair needed the oval look. He needed it rounded out. I took two inches of that pompadour off and left his hair two inches longer."[125]

Pitts also told Reagan to stop using Brylcreem.

"I don't think he dyed it," he said. "I never detected it. I think he used a little rinse. It tones your hair if it is graying. You shampoo it tomorrow, and it's out."

As his hair was being cut, Reagan liked to watch old movies on TV.

"He would always say, 'Did I tell you the story of so-and-so?' I loved Reagan," Pitts said. "He was a wonderful man to work on."

6

A Rat in the Pool

PRESIDENT BUSH'S TWELVE-YEAR-OLD GRANDSON, GEORGE PRESCOTT Bush, was hitting tennis balls off the back of the White House tennis court when J. Bonnie Newman, assistant to the president for management and administration, and Joseph W. Hagin, deputy assistant to the president for scheduling, approached the court to play. Seeing the president's grandson, the two White House aides, who had earlier reserved the court, turned away and began walking back toward the White House.

Just then, Barbara Bush came along and told George, son of John E. "Jeb" Bush, to get off the court.

"When we went down and saw the president's grandson, there was no question he should be the one playing on the court," Newman said. "Mrs. Bush saw it and just plucked him off. She really sent the message not only to staff but to family as well that you remember your manners."[126]

Because of his policies and the way he projected himself, Bush—code named Timber Wolf—came across as the rich man's president. Flinty-eyed and imperious, he seemed to have little regard for the common man. Bush's amazement at seeing an electronic price scanner at a supermarket checkout counter symbolized how far removed he was from everyday America. His campaign themes betrayed insensitivity if not nastiness. Bush injected race into his 1988 campaign by citing the case of Willie Horton, a black convict who raped a woman and stabbed a man while on furlough from a Massachusetts prison, as representing his opponent Michael Dukakis's policies. In his 1992 campaign, Bush excluded minorities, gays, and working women. But as Barbara Bush's removal of her grandson from the White House tennis court suggests, Bush and his family rejected the imperial presidency. In fact, Bush was an anomaly among modern presidents, a man who was in actuality nicer and more decent than his public image. While the trappings of the presidency grew under Bush, he and his wife remained genuinely unaffected, perhaps because they had come from privilege and were therefore less corrupted by the White House atmosphere.

"George was a straight shooter," a Secret Service agent said. "Barbara Bush was a sweetheart. She was one of the nicest first ladies we have ever had. She was very personal and caring. Even Jimmy Carter's wife, Rosalynn, picked up on the life. Mrs. Bush remained the same."

The Secret Service's only complaint about Bush was that he was hyperactive.

"He can't sit still," an agent said. "He is in perpetual motion."

In every hotel, the Secret Service had to make sure Bush had an exercise bike in his suite. If the hotel did not have one, the Secret Service rented one.

"He can't read a book," the agent said. "He has to be on a treadmill or StairMaster. It's go, go, go. For the Secret Service, that meant more work. The tennis court, horseshoes, the golf course, the boat. Always something."

Bush was elected president in 1988, winning 54 percent of the popular vote. During his highly negative campaign, Bush implied that his opponent Michael Dukakis was unpatriotic for vetoing as governor of Massachusetts a bill that would have required all public school students in Massachusetts to lead their classes in the pledge of allegiance. He denounced Dukakis as soft on crime and called for execution of major drug traffickers. Bush vowed never to raise taxes under any circumstances— a pledge he ultimately broke.[127]

One of Bush's worst decisions was selecting as his vice president Dan Quayle, apparently because he thought his good looks would attract women voters. In fact, the choice later contributed to Bush's defeat when he ran for a second term. Besides his poor academic record, avoidance of the draft, and lackluster performance as a congressman, Quayle came across as a dunce. Quayle's twisted syntax and misspellings quickly became a favorite butt of jokes and cartoonists.

"May our nation continue to be the beakon [sic] of hope to the world," Quayle wrote on a 1989 Christmas card.

"Marilyn Quayle was the brains," a Secret Service agent said. "She knew what was going on. She accepted Dan for what he is. She took this liability on and stayed with it. The assessment was at first she is refreshing, straightforward, and honest and brainy. Over the years, the assessment became she is as bad as he is. Arrogant. 'We are what is good for America. Our thinking is the majority thinking.' Out to lunch. When the whole country makes a joke of you, and you don't acknowledge it, there is something wrong."

The agent said Marilyn Quayle would tell her Secret Service detail, " 'You're going to have us for twelve years.' She was out of her mind. If [Dan Quayle] had stepped down, Bush might have won."

Fred Walzel, who headed the White House contingent of the Secret Service uniformed division, said that when Bush was vice president, he invited Walzel and his wife, Rena, to a picnic at the vice president's home on the grounds of the U.S. Naval Observatory. After the Bushes had greeted everyone and it was time to eat, "They both sat with us," Walzel said.[128]

Later, when Bush was president, Barbara Bush saw Walzel and his wife at a reception given by the Vatican's representative to the United States.

"Mrs. Bush headed me off," Walzel said. "She said, 'I'm so

glad there is someone here I know.' She called George. He said, 'Let's go get a picture taken.' "

Lewis Hubbard, who often played tennis or paddleball with Bush, said the president in private was entirely different from his public persona.

"He [Bush] came across cold on TV, but if you shook his hand, he was fantastic," said Hubbard, the assistant director of the House of Representatives gym. "Bush gave me a brand-new tennis racket. He said get rid of that old wood one. It was a fiberglass Yamaha."

"To Bush, giving a speech was anathema," said Don Penny, who coached Bush on public speaking. "He didn't like it. He didn't want to rehearse for it or learn the techniques for giving one. Bush doesn't dislike people. He just doesn't like them in large groups. He's not a social animal."[129]

Like John Rogers, her predecessor in charge of administration under Reagan, Bonnie Newman had no particular experience in running a large organization like the White House. She previously had been dean of students at the University of New Hampshire, then was administrative assistant to Judd Gregg, a Republican congressman from New Hampshire. But Newman, like Rogers, was highly capable—a decisive manager with good judgment.

"As with any other environment, it's a matter of knowing where to obtain the information you need and being open to obtaining the information, whether it's setting up your budgets or computer systems or security," Newman said.[130]

When Newman first began working in the White House, her secretary gave her a schedule that said she was to attend a reception with POTUS.

"I said, 'I haven't heard of this group,' " Newman said. "My secretary hadn't either, but it turned out POTUS was president of the United States."

An electronic Secret Service box in key offices in the White House displays the present location of the president, listing him as POTUS. It also shows the location of the first lady, vice president, secretary of state, and speaker of the House. If they are not in Washington, the box displays the city where they are at the time.

When she took charge of administration and management for Bush, Newman found the complexity of White House funding overwhelming.

"There are so many sources of funds, and there are so many different functions," she said. "Some expenses are personal, some political, and others are official. There are inaugural funds paid by the inaugural committee. Other funds are raised privately. The president and first lady are billed for their meals unless they are official. They are billed for actual consumption. If they are dining by themselves, that is billed personally. If they are entertaining people considered politically related, they are billed, in our case, to the Republican National Committee. If it was a visiting head of state, then there are federal funds available from the State Department."

"After working there two and a half years, I'm not sure I understand how the White House works," said Lieutenant General Richard G. Trefry, who directed the White House military office under Bush.[131]

Despite the refurbishing done during the Reagan years, Newman found many areas of the White House in poor condition.

"It was in unfortunate if not deplorable repair," Newman said. "We had to do a great deal of window and roof, heating and ventilation, and plumbing repair."

One weekend, the sewer backed up in the west wing.

"It was not pleasant," she said. "There was a backup in the catch basin in the plumbing system from the White House mess on the ground floor of the west wing. It was a lot more than a Roto-Rooter job."

As in previous administrations, the White House had a problem with rats. Barbara Bush was sunning herself at the outdoor swimming pool behind the Oval Office when she saw a rat floating in the pool.

"She screamed, and the president got the rat out," Newman said. "He got him out with a broom. I'm not sure what condition it was in. It was stunned at least."

Newman created what she believed was the first organizational chart of the White House. According to the chart, more than a dozen assistants to the president reported to Bush through the chief of staff. Each assistant to the president was over a different office, such as communications, economic and domestic policy, legislative affairs, personnel, the counsel's office, and management and administration. Each of the offices was headed by a special assistant to the president and was further subdivided. Newman's office of management and administration had three main components—the military office, the office of administration, and operations. Operations included an administrative office, personnel office, telephone service office, travel and telegraph office, and visitors' office. Administration included facilities management, financial management, information resources, library and information services, and personnel management. The military office included airlift operations, Camp David, Marine Helicopter Squadron One, military aides, the office of emergency operations, the presidential pilot's office, a security adviser, the White House communications agency, the White House garage, the White House medical unit, the White House staff mess, and the White House television unit, which films activities within the White House.

While the chart was impressive, Bush's aides, like those in every administration, tried to deal directly with the president if possible. According to the chart, the chief usher in the residence reported to Newman through Rose M. Zamaria in her office. But that was news to chief usher Gary Walters.

"The chief usher has always reported directly to the family," he said smugly but correctly.

In contrast to Carter's childish insistence on scheduling use of the White House tennis court himself, Bush had an aide in Zamaria's office do the scheduling.

Bush was meticulous about responding to mail. He often had notes hand delivered around Washington. When the fifteen-year-old son of Larry Branscum, a communicator on the vice president's staff, died suddenly of previously undiagnosed leukemia, Bush called him at home to express his condolences.

"Someone who works with my wife answered the call,"

Branscum said. Because Branscum had said he did not want to talk with anyone, the woman said Branscum would call Bush back. Bush then identified himself as the president and said he would call again. By then, it was too late to put him on the line with Branscum.

"Her jaw dropped, and she said, 'That was the president,'" Branscum said. "He [Bush] sat down at his desk and wrote me a two-page letter saying he was sorry about Carl. The president asked the vice president's driver to take it. So two hours later, here comes a driver from the vice president's staff. I placed [the letter] on the casket."

The White House letter-writing unit is on the ground floor of the old Executive Office Building. Under the direction of Shirley M. Green, a special assistant to Bush, the unit had 138 staff members and 350 volunteers. The unit analyzes letters to determine how they should be answered and who should sign the response.

"Is it something we should answer with a form letter over my signature, or should it be answered by the president, or should it go into a policy office?" Green said. "Then we had the presidential messages unit, which determined if it would be appropriate to send a presidential message. We had a million guidelines on that. The majority were nonprofit organizations. We would not endorse anything commercially. A large part of our obligation was to protect the president. We did not want to send something out that would embarrass him."[132]

Green tabulated the letters and calls Bush received and presented him with the results.

"Once a week, I sent him a report which listed the mail to him, the staff, and to Barbara," Green said. "He saw the number on each issue and the pro and con. I always put a large representative sample in so he could see how people felt on each side. We sent those with a suggested response if he wanted to send one."

The Bush White House received an average of 40,000 to 50,000 pieces of mail a week. In addition, the White House received 12,000 pieces of mail from children each week. In his first year in office, Bush received 5.3 million pieces of mail, compared with only 2.5 million in his last full year in the White House. Reagan received as many as 6.8 million pieces of mail in 1985, but by his last year, he was receiving only 3.2 million letters a year. On average, Carter received 3.5 million pieces of mail a year, Ford received 2.4 million pieces, Nixon 2.7 million, and Johnson 1.7 million.

"Bush signed more mail personally than any other president," Green said. "I sent him fifteen to forty-five to sign every day. He was signing other mail as well. Brent Scowcroft would prepare letters that did not come through me."

Each year, Bush sent out 160,000 Christmas cards as well.

Like presidents before him, Bush found he could get more work done on *Air Force One* than any place else. Although a Boeing 747 was supposed to replace the old Boeing 707 as the presidential plane during Reagan's administration, it was not delivered until August 1990 during Bush's administration. With a top speed of 640 miles per hour, the new jumbo jet has ninety-three seats and can fly more than 7,140 miles without refueling. For years, *Air Force One* has had a backup that goes wherever *Air Force One* goes. The cost of both 747's was $410 million.

While the average 747 has 485,000 feet of electrical wire, the presidential plane has 1.2 million feet, all shielded from the electromagnetic pulses that would be emitted during a nuclear blast. Near the front of the plane, the president has an executive suite with a stateroom, dressing room, and bathroom. The president also has a private office near the stateroom and a combination dining room and conference room with enough telephones for everyone. Toward the rear are areas for the staff, Secret Service, guests, and the press. The plane can serve up to a hundred meals at a time. The plane can fire red hot flares from its engines to divert heat-seeking missiles launched to destroy it.

Before the Air Force accepted delivery of the new plane, Bonnie Newman, who was over administration, and other White House aides took a test flight. After leaving Wichita at 6 A.M., they flew to New Jersey, then to Atlanta, then to Albuquerque, before dropping the plane off in Seattle.

"We tried every system on board," Newman said. "Communications, computers, and the shower. I was the person selected to take the first shower."

Under Bush, smoking on *Air Force One* was banned for the first time. Pork rinds dipped in hot sauce replaced Reagan's jelly beans as snacks.

"Broccoli was not even allowed on board the plane under Bush," said Craig J. Spence, an *Air Force One* steward. "It was not allowed even for passengers. It was just understood. We were told by Bush aides, 'Don't even have it on the plane.'"

Besides barbecue, fried chicken, and hot dogs, Bush liked vanilla yogurt, white grapes, and strawberries.

"He had Grape-Nuts sprinkled on top of the yogurt for breakfast," Spence said.

"Besides Carter, Bush was the only president I knew who drank a beer," said Charles Palmer, the chief *Air Force One* steward. "He drank Michelob Light."

"We cut out free cigarettes under Carter and Reagan," said Joseph A. Jaworski, a communicator on *Air Force One*. "They were donated by the tobacco companies. Bush and Clinton did not have them. There was no smoking aboard the airplane under Bush and Clinton."

Nor were there any landing-strip haircuts. Even before he became president, Bush had gotten his haircuts from Milton Pitts. Once in the White House, he continued to have Pitts come to the White House barbershop. Initially, Pitts said, "I blocked his hair in the back instead of tapering it. I continued to give him a layer cut."

Unlike Reagan, who liked to watch old movies on TV, and Nixon, who would not watch TV, Bush liked to watch the news while having his hair cut. Bush was a channel cruiser, telling Pitts before he switched channels he was going to "gong" the show he was watching.

"He was very personable," Pitts said. "He seldom read. He would tell a joke, or I would tell him one."

In a television interview in New York, Pitts made the mistake of giving the interviewer what the barber said was presidential hair. He later claimed it was sweepings from the heads of presidents of several companies who had had their hair cut at Pitts's regular shop in the basement of the Carlton Hotel in Washington.

"I got a letter from Boyden Gray asking why I was showing the president's hair on TV," Pitts said. Pitts told Gray, the White House counsel, that the hair in question was not Bush's.

"I said, 'If this is going to interfere with me making money and going on TV, I don't want the job,' " Pitts said.

Throughout his presidency, Bush was plagued with rumors that he was having an affair with Jennifer Fitzgerald, his long-time assistant. The rumors finally saw print when Susan B. Trento, in a book about lobbyist Robert Gray, quoted her husband, journalist Joe Trento, as saying he had been told by a U.S. representative to U.S. control talks in Switzerland that he arranged for then vice president Bush and Fitzgerald to share a guest house in Geneva in 1984. The representative, Louis Fields, had since died.[133]

After the *New York Post* ran a story on the Trento allegation, Mary Tillotson, a CNN reporter, asked Bush on the air about the rumor. Visibly angry, Bush denounced the story as "a lie."

During her husband's campaign, Hillary Clinton kept the story alive by telling an interviewer for *Vanity Fair* that "the establishment" had shielded Bush from questions about the allegation. In fact, several news organizations, including the *Washington Post, Los Angeles Times,* and Gannett News Service, had investigated the rumor over the years and found no basis for it.

Charles G. (Chase) Untermeyer, an aide to Bush when he was vice president and later president, said he was with Bush and Fitzgerald constantly on trips and saw no indication they were having an affair.

"I never believed there was an affair between the two of them," he said. "They were in China when Bush was ambassador and at the CIA when he was director. She served an important role of bringing him unvarnished and candid advice." But as scheduler, Untermeyer said, Fitzgerald alienated people who wanted more access to Bush.

"The job of scheduler is the most crucial job for the vice

president," he said. "The only valuable commodity the vice president has is his time. Presidents have limited time, but they can assign others like ambassadors to work on issues. That made her a valuable commodity. I think that led to a lot of disgruntlement and rumors about her. Jennifer brought him down to earth with a thud. She is very non–star struck. She would decide what trips he would take. The fact that she rankled an awful lot of staff members made people look at the relationship with a more skeptical eye than they otherwise would have."[134]

In 1989, Bush named Fitzgerald deputy chief of protocol in the State Department, where she was said to have felt angry at him for not denying the rumors more aggressively.

In any case, it would be virtually impossible for a president to have an affair without the Secret Service's knowing. According to an agent, the rumors about the affair were "bullshit."

"It's not in him," the agent said. "The Secret Service would know. We had him eight years as vice president and four as president. No one saw that."

In fact, the Secret Service dogged Bush so closely that when Bush visited then Director of Central Intelligence William Webster at the agency for a top secret briefing, agents insisted on sitting in.

"Even Webster assistants who were cleared to receive the highest levels of intelligence were not allowed at the meeting," one amazed Webster aide said.

Bush repeatedly questioned the level of security protection he received but usually went along with what the Secret Service wanted. Despite his avowed wish to minimize the number of people who accompanied him on foreign trips, the number mushroomed. On one overseas trip, 695 government officials went along.

"Bush was always very frustrated at the numbers of people," Bonnie Newman said. "We got to the point where we had every agency in government report to us before a foreign trip. It was like assigning a White House office. People would rather have a closet across from the Oval Office than a spacious office with a fireplace in the old EOB. On a presidential trip, almost every agency of government, if they felt there was any relevant reason to go there, wanted to be seen on the trip. Bush asked why they needed to be there."

Newman set up a system for clearing requests to accompany the president, but the numbers who went overseas remained astronomical.

According to Newman, the Bushes wanted to avoid setting an imperial tone.

"They made it very clear that they did not want people associated with the White House thinking they were regal in any sense of the word," Newman said. "I think they tried to tone down everything while maintaining a sense of dignity that should surround the presidency itself."

But many on Bush's staff ignored that message. As the then chairman of a House Post Office and Civil Service subcommittee with jurisdiction over the White House, Representative Paul E. Kanjorski, a Pennsylvania Democrat, tried to obtain answers to simple financial questions about the White House. The Bush White House treated him with contempt.

"They would never return calls," Kanjorski said. "They almost took the approach that we have no right to know it."[135]

Kanjorski objected both to the air of secrecy about White House finances and the way the numbers are juggled.

"The White House has no responsibility to be honest with people," he said. "When you look at the budget for travel for the president, it's a joke. It's $100,000 or something. They said they only spent $29,000 of it. It's $185 million a year, at least."

Another sham is the president's $50,000 annual expense account. Bush reported spending only $24,000 of it in 1991 for stationery, official gifts, and working lunches. The appropriation serves to mislead the public by suggesting that that is the extent of the president's expenses. In fact, no one knows the full extent of presidential expenses, except that they total well over $1 billion a year.

Kanjorski also questioned the level of Secret Service protection.

"They have the attitude, 'We are in a state of war, and there is a hit team around the corner,' " Kanjorski said. "The vice president is probably getting as much protection as the president used to. It grows like Topsy."

Kanjorski said that shortly after becoming president, Clinton met with the speaker of the House and the majority leader in the Capitol. Bottles of Coca-Cola were passed around, and Clinton began to drink one.

"The agents grabbed it," Kanjorski said. "They gave him their own. Can you imagine? They had to open it for him."

After investigating for more than a year and holding hearings, "We still didn't know how much it costs to run the White House," said Mary E. Weaver, who was in charge of the Kanjorski probe. Because of the detailees and other categories of temporary employees, "We don't know how many work there," she said. "In our General Accounting Office investigation, we ran across a rather intriguing category of people called nondetailees," she said. "This is very interesting," she said, as if she were an entomologist discovering a new species of ant. "We had never heard of that term before. When we asked them to define the term, the White House gave a definition similar to another category called nonreimbursable detailees. It went around like that."[136]

As it turned out, the White House staff never asked Bush what approach to take toward disclosing costs to the Kanjorski committee. Paul W. Bateman, who succeeded Newman as the Bush assistant over administration and dealt with Kanjorski, said he thought the investigation was politically motivated. Without consulting Bush, the White House made things difficult for the committee.

"He [Kanjorski] was out to make news," Bateman said. "It was just bomb throwing."

In a classic example of the kind of imperiousness the White House fosters, Bateman added: "They didn't know what questions to ask. We weren't going to roll over and play dead. The imprecision of the questions made it easy to not play the victim. I don't think they had a clear idea of the scope of the executive office of the president. They had no idea. If they had done their homework, they would have been more potent."[137]

Of course, the entire purpose of the Kanjorski probe was to

From left: Luci Johnson Nugent holding son Patrick Lyndon
Nugent; her husband, Patrick John Nugent; President Johnson; Lady
Bird Johnson; and daughter Lynda Bird Johnson. NATIONAL ARCHIVES

From left: David Eisenhower, husband of Julie Nixon; Julie Nixon; President Nixon; Pat Nixon; and Tricia Nixon. THE WHITE HOUSE

Betty Ford with
President Ford.
NATIONAL ARCHIVES

President Carter in
the Oval Office.
THE WHITE HOUSE

President Reagan
and Nancy Reagan
in the Oval Office.
THE WHITE HOUSE

President Bush waves from the new Boeing 747 acquired during his term to serve as *Air Force One*. AP/WIDE WORLD PHOTOS

President and Mrs. Clinton stride through the Rose Garden. AP/WIDE WORLD PHOTOS

Former presidents Ford, Nixon, Reagan, and Carter gather in the
Oval Office with President Bush (center).

From left: Lady Bird Johnson, Pat Nixon, Nancy Reagan, Barbara
Bush, Rosalynn Carter, and Betty Ford attending the dedication of
the Ronald Reagan Presidential Library in Simi Valley, California.

The south portico was added to the rear of the White House in 1824. THE WHITE HOUSE

The north portico was added to the front of the White House in 1829. THE WHITE HOUSE

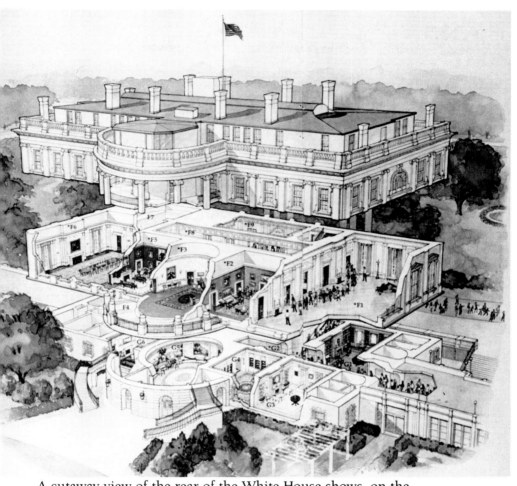

A cutaway view of the rear of the White House shows, on the ground floor: G1—the Library; G2—Ground Floor Corridor; G3—Vermeil Room; G4—China Room; G5—Diplomatic Reception Room; G6—Map Room. On the first floor are: F1—East Room; F2—Green Room; F3—Blue Room; F4—South Portico; F5—Red Room; F6—State Dining Room; F7—Family Dining Room; F8—Cross Hall; F9—Entrance Hall. COPYRIGHTED BY WHITE HOUSE HISTORICAL ASSOCIATION; PHOTOGRAPH BY THE NATIONAL GEOGRAPHIC SOCIETY

The old Executive Office Building with the White House in the
upper left corner. The White House

The seal of the president of the United States. The White House

determine the scope of the executive office of the president. If the scope had been known, there would have been no need for hearings. Yet his committee had more difficulty obtaining information about what the White House spends than the Senate Select Committee on Intelligence has finding out about CIA expenditures.

The bewildering nature of the White House's finances occasionally has its origin in historical happenstance. The reason navy stewards run the White House mess, for example, is that during World War II, the *Sequoia,* the presidential yacht, had been put in dry dock because the Secret Service believed the boat would be an easy target for the Nazis. Since navy stewards were already detailed to the White House to cook meals on the yacht, they were assigned instead to the White House staff mess, which had just started as a place where employees could grab a quick bowl of soup and a sandwich. Eventually, the mess became one of the premier status symbols. Because it was so small, only a limited number of White House staff members could eat there.

But most of the bizarre ways the White House is financed are purposeful obfuscations, designed to conceal the true cost of the White House. By charging costs to other agencies, the White House manages to hide what it really costs to run the institution. Even after leaving the White House, Lieutenant General Trefry, who headed the White House military office under Bush, said he would not reveal how much the Defense Department spent for White House operations. Asked for the figure, Trefry waxed eloquent about the awe people feel toward the White House and Americans' need to have a president who acts presidential.

"People lined up at half past six in the summer to take the White House tour that starts at 8 A.M.," Trefry said. "They chatter away. The minute they hit the door, all you hear is shuffling feet. The institution of the presidency is what they respect." He said they "want the White House to look like the White House."

But how much does it cost?

"I'm not going to tell you how much it was," Trefry said.

143

"That's my secret. I probably know more than anybody how much it costs. That's why I never told anybody. It's mental masturbation. They [the press or Congress] would do anything to make it sound big."[138]

Asked again for the figure, Trefry said, "Let me put it this way. It's not as much as you think it is. It's not $1 billion. I could count $2 billion or $100 million [in spending]. I didn't tell anybody. I didn't think it was any of their goddamned business."

This is the American version of Marie Antoinette's "let them eat cake": the taxpayers who pay the bill do not deserve to know, are not entitled to know, what the White House costs. In part, the attitude stems from the ambivalence Americans feel toward the presidency. From the founding of the country, Americans have never been quite sure whether they want their president to act more like royalty or a democratically elected chief executive.

"When human beings started to organize into societies, the ruler was always a god," George Reedy, Johnson's spokesman, said. "The pharaoh of Egypt was a god. If you delve into primitive groups, the rulers were always god. It wasn't until a few hundred years ago that we got the idea the people were god, that they make the decisions."

In part, the attitude stems from a universal need for a father figure—for divinity, Reedy said. "People impart divinity to the ruler because you have to have some reason for obeying order," he said. "In England, even though the monarchy no longer runs anything, every Englishman still raises his glass in a toast to the queen."

But the Founding Fathers of the United States firmly rejected that model. Selected by George Washington to plan the White House, Pierre L'Enfant came up with a plan for a royal "president's palace" five times larger than the structure eventually built. Congress balked at the idea, and Thomas Jefferson, who was secretary of state, fired L'Enfant. Even the White House as built has had its detractors, such as Pennsylvania congressman Charles Ogle, who, in 1840, called the White House "a royal establishment at the cost of the nation." He questioned whether

President Martin Van Buren should be allowed to use "knives, forks, and spoons of gold that he may dine in the style of the monarchs of Europe."

While that kind of tension has continued, the concept of an executive mansion as the people's house is well established and symbolized by the fact that the White House is the only home of a chief of state open to public tour free of charge. Unless it would genuinely jeopardize the national security, the government is required by the Constitution to account to the public for its expenditures.

"No money shall be drawn from the Treasury but in consequence of appropriations made by law," says Article I, "and a regular statement and account of the receipts and expenditures of all public money shall be published from time to time."

The notion that taxpayers should not know how much it costs to run the White House is but another example of White House–bred arrogance. Even though the funds go to buy such mundane items as toilet paper and jet fuel, many of the details of White House spending by the Defense Department are classified, as is the Secret Service budget for guarding the president.

"The Secret Service budget was classified, which was all bullshit," said Bill Gulley, who headed the White House military office. "We [in the military] never cared because it allowed me to classify a good portion of our budget."

Even when the accounts are not classified, Freedom of Information Act requests for data on White House spending are routinely denied. In response to one such request, Gary Walters, chief usher of the White House, said the residence portion of the White House is not even subject to the Freedom of Information Act.

In 1982, as a reporter for the *Washington Post,* the author barraged the White House and other agencies with Freedom of Information Act requests for data on White House spending. William F. Cuff, then executive assistant to the director of the White House military office, recalled sitting in on meetings with Chief of Staff James Baker, White House Counsel Fred Fielding, White House Military Director Edward Hickey, and

Communications Director Michael Deaver to decide how to handle the requests.

"Obviously, you had done a lot of in-depth research," Cuff said. "You skewered us very well." While the White House initially was agreeable to complying with the requests, after several internal meetings the staff began to realize the size of the costs that had been hidden from the public.

"I think there was a sense that it is early in this administration, and this is what we inherited," Cuff said. "Why should we take the heat for this? There was a lot of discussion of how it would appear in the press and how it would sound on a forty-five-second sound bite."[139]

In the end, citing any number of exceptions in the act, the White House denied the requests. Americans are entitled to know only what the White House wants them to know.

To further the cover-up, almost any cost figure disclosed by the White House is likely to be understated. For example, the Reagan administration told the press the cost of removing the layers of paint from the White House and repairing some of the stonework would be $384,200. In later budget hearings not covered by the press, it turned out that the true cost was $4.7 million.[140]

"There certainly is a sensitivity to being the first president to spend so much," Bonnie Newman, Bush's assistant over administration, said. "The numbers get manipulated. It's like lying with statistics. You can present the numbers either in a beneficial or nonbeneficial way, depending on whether you want to support or detract from the person in office."

After holding hearings on White House costs, Representative Kanjorski took the position that, whatever the true cost of the presidency, it should be disclosed.

"I think disclosure would make people more frugal," he said. "Seventy percent of the White House costs are not disclosed. The first thing a business needs is cost accounting. You can't get accurate figures on the White House."

When Bush was president, Kanjorski—a Democrat—introduced a bill that would consolidate spending for the White House by all the agencies, thus disclosing for the first time what the true costs are. But as soon as Clinton became president, Kanjorski seemed to lose interest in pushing the bill. Previously eager to promote honesty in the White House, his staff suddenly became slow to return calls on the subject. While under Bush, Kanjorski never saw a White House expenditure that he approved of, he now complained that the White House itself is "threadbare."

"I've never seen it look so poor in my life," he said after Clinton became president.

Given the fact that Bush wanted to avoid an imperial tone, it was amazing how many staff members ignored his direction. Besides Paul Bateman, another of Bush's staff members who did not hear Bush's message was John H. Sununu, his chief of staff. When people in the White House let the atmosphere get to them, insiders say they have White House–itis. They could just as aptly refer to such people as having Sununu Syndrome. Sununu came to symbolize the kind of imperiousness that the White House, more than any other institution, can breed. Sununu acted as if the presidency were a monarchy. His frequent use of military aircraft for personal trips, his subsequent improper solicitation of rides on corporate jets, and his defiance when criticized by the press for his extravagance finally did him in.

On a trip to Iowa, Sununu mocked those who questioned his travel and dismissed their complaints as unrelated to concerns of the real world outside Washington. Asked in a CNN interview if the controversy had been a learning experience for him, Sununu said no.[141]

C. Boyden Gray, the White House counsel under Bush, said many White House aides used government aircraft for personal trips, but Sununu's trips at government expense were far more frequent.

"They were appearance problems," Gray said of the trips. "They created the appearance of abusing government largesse. Was there any illegality in what he did? No. Scowcroft or [Robert M.] Gates were doing much the same thing, but not with the same frequency. The question became, when is it too much? How do you draw a line? Fifteen trips? Twenty-five trips? They would take military planes because they needed to be in communication. In the end, I think they started taking commercial flights. But Sununu is the only one who had a weakness for this."[142]

"Being in the White House goes to people's heads very easily," said Bradley H. Patterson, Jr., a former White House aide under three presidents and author of *The Ring of Power: The White House Staff and Its Expanding Role in Government*. "You are never off duty. If you are very senior, you are in the public eye. If your kids or wife do something stupid, that gets in the paper. Some White House people don't realize that. Sununu was an example of that, flying to collect stamps."[143]

"There are two kinds of people who are attracted to working in the White House," said William P. Barr, who worked in the Reagan White House before becoming attorney general under Bush. "One is the person who is caught up in the superficial aspects of it—the pomp and circumstance and the perks. They tend to become absorbed over time with who is going to ride on *Air Force One,* who has mess privileges, and who is going to sit in which car in the motorcade. That unfortunately is usually a very large number of people at any White House. Even people going in initially who think they are going to change the world somehow get seduced by that atmosphere. Then there are people who really care about policy or people and who are interested in substance."[144]

"Every administration has people in it who get White House–itis," said Robert Gates. "It got to the point where it got to be fun to pick the people out early on who would have a problem. The first giveaway is when a relatively junior staffer has his secretary place calls saying, 'The White House is calling' instead of 'Joe Schmo from the National Security Council is calling.' "

Dr. Burton J. Lee III, Bush's physician, came down with his own version of White House–itis. While President Buchanan was the first president to invite a physician friend to live in the White House, William McKinley was the first to appoint an official White House physician. At the White House Correspondents' dinner in the spring of 1991, Lee grabbed *Washington*

Post reporter Donna Britt around her thighs and yanked her backward across his lap and onto a dinner table, according to her subsequent *Post* column on the incident.[145]

Britt later recalled the anger she felt at finding herself first chatting with a colleague and then "sitting—in my Hanes Ultra-Sheers and strapless dress—atop a dinner table surrounded by strangers." Because she was so stunned, a friend had to lift her off the table as Lee gazed at her with a "delighted smile." Britt became even more outraged when Lee, who is married, told *USA Today* the incident was "no big deal" and had "barely registered" on him.

Gray dismissed the Lee incident as the type of thing that can happen in any organization.

"Dr. Lee got a little touchy-feely on the dance floor," Gray said. "It was totally public. That was minor. That's nothing. You have people in every operation who at some point are going to have more to drink than they should."

While that may be true, working in the White House exacerbates any existing tendency to go beyond appropriate behavior.

"There are those in the White House who are intoxicated by it and who are almost in a perpetual orgasmic state," said Dr. Brown, the psychiatrist who has been consulted by many White House aides. "One symptom is overaggressiveness. Impatience gets out of control. It was very prevalent in the Nixon White House. Others just do their work because they have an inner tranquillity."

Brown recalled the exhilaration he felt when, as an aide to Kennedy, he first experienced the power of the White House. A taxi had slammed into his car in Washington, and he was having trouble collecting for the damage. The taxi company had taken the position that the driver would have to pay Brown for the damage, and the driver would not pay because his policy had a large deductible. When nothing worked, Brown called the taxi company and said he wanted a check delivered to him at the White House.

"That afternoon, the check arrived," said Brown, who continues to consult for the Secret Service through Academy Group Inc. in Manassas, Virginia. "I was just shocked when the check arrived. That's when I realized the power of the place. The lesson was being at the White House carried power beyond my comprehension."

Looking back, Mark Weinberg, a press spokesman for Reagan, realized that the White House atmosphere had made him haughty.

"I could be curt and arrogant and sarcastic and demanding," Weinberg said. "I wish I had been a little bit more patient. We were under pressure, and the press was sometimes adversarial, and if you screwed up, the stakes were high. It was all true. They all help to mitigate. But I could have been as efficient and successful as I was—if I was—and not be as difficult as I often was, especially early on."

Boyden Gray came to view the White House as a cauldron of turf battles and leaks, a place where envy plays a major role.

"You start with an organization that you put together very fast," he said. "No successful organization in our culture is put together that quickly. It is just very hard to expect that to operate. The second problem is there is no way to reward people there other than through some bureaucratic advantage. The pay for senior staff is within a small band. There is no differentiation," said Gray, whose $125,100 annual White House salary would not cover the taxes he now pays on his income as a partner of the Washington law firm of Wilmer, Cutler & Pickering. "Probably envy is the strongest human urge," Gray said. "How does it find its expression? You do it through bureaucratic advantage, through leakings and knifings."

In this equation, the press plays a large part, Gray said. White House aides have tremendous power and responsibility. They feel strongly about what they are doing. And they have different views about how to approach issues.

"They become frantic to vindicate their points of view," he said. "You have the press trying to worm its way in to develop sources. They are playing the game of taking people apart. That becomes a perk or gratification. You can't have the perk of good office space or a view, but you can get good press. That is corrupting. The ultimate Faustian pact is, 'I will give you good press if you will leak.' "

Ultimately, said Untermeyer, one of Bush's assistants, a White House aide is just an aide—an invisible cog in a wheel.

"I believe the agencies are the more satisfying places to be because you can do things there," he said. "There is a sense of accomplishment and seeing a finished product. Whereas in the White House, for all its glamour and being close to the center of things, it is staff work; it's holding meetings and pushing paper. That happens at the agencies too, but at least in the agencies you have a chance to get things done."

Untermeyer is one of the few White House aides who opted to work in an agency, leaving the White House to become an associate director for broadcasting at the U.S. Information Agency. Few people take that option. While the money is a fraction of what the private sector would pay and aides constantly step on one another, the perks of working in the White House are beyond compare—being waved through the gate at the southwest entrance to one's own free parking space or being picked up by a White House car and driver, being able to hand out presidential cuff links and *Air Force One* matches, attending White House dinners, or sitting in one of the president's boxes at the John F. Kennedy Center for the Performing Arts.

"If I looked back on twenty-seven years in the White House, the one general observation I have is that the White House staff was interchangeable," said William Cuff, who was assistant chief of the White House military office. "Democratic, Republican, liberal, conservative, it didn't make a damn bit of difference. Once they got in, there were half a dozen people who had the president's best interests at heart. But after a few months, everyone was strictly personally motivated. They were sharpening up the resume, trying to get a ride on *Air Force One,* looking for car privileges, mess privileges—whatever they could get for themselves. When beepers came in, everyone had to have one as a status symbol. Then it was cellular phones. The ones who were loyal to the president had been with the individual for a long time."

One of the greatest perquisites is the ability to give friends and relatives special tours of the White House, including the

Oval Office, which is not on any scheduled tour. Each year, 1.2 million people take the White House's public tours. Scheduled from 10 A.M. to noon Tuesday through Saturday, the public tours do not include the west wing or the residence portion of the White House. During the Gulf War, the White House canceled the tours for security reasons.

Besides these tours, the White House visitors' office distributes tickets to members of Congress for constituents who request them. These VIP tours take smaller groups of forty to seventy-five people beginning at 8 A.M. They do not require waiting in line for tickets. While the VIP tours cover virtually the same ground as the public tours—a few extra rooms may be added—they are highly coveted.

"A member of Congress may say, 'I'm not going along with that budget request because I could not get enough tickets,'" said Bonnie Newman, Bush's aide over administration. "It gets as petty as that. A tour turndown can really haunt you when you get into more substantive matters. You can't give all of them what they want all of the time. The best you can do is be consistent. If you start trading off, whether it's for tickets or presidential cuff links, you are bound to lose. Then the people who supported you originally will pull out."

Indeed, a highly public spat broke out between the Reagan White House and Representative Thomas J. Downey over tour privileges. Congressmen are limited to ten VIP tickets a week, but they may also request tours for groups of fifty people if space is available. Downey's office asked the White House for permission to take a group of a hundred Boy Scouts on a tour and was turned down. In a newspaper interview, the Long Island Democrat claimed the White House had told his staff the reason for the turndown was that Nancy Reagan was discouraging tours by children on the grounds they do not "appreciate the art work and rugs, and they should be able to take public tours."

Carol McCain, the director of the visitors' office, admitted saying that the hundred Boy Scouts could not be accommodated because priority was being given to senior citizens and the handicapped.

"I did say I thought it was easier for Boy Scouts to stand in line than it was for senior citizens and handicapped people," McCain said. But she denied discouraging children or saying Nancy Reagan thought children would not appreciate the art.

When Nancy Reagan saw Downey's comment, she became enraged. As a result, Downey's tour privileges were cut off. Delicate negotiations ensued. Each side wanted an apology. No one budged. Finally, Downey's tour privileges were restored, but no apologies were made.

"Downey was going out of his way to perpetuate a falsehood," Michael K. Deaver, Reagan's deputy chief of staff, said at the time, adding that hundreds of children take the VIP tours each week.

"I wanted a letter from them saying the tours were reinstated, and that my constituents who were unable to take the tours could do so now," Downey said. "A gracious and intelligent White House would have given me a letter," he said, adding that it showed the White House could engage in "pettiness and breathtaking stupidity."

Of all the perks, dinner at the White House is one of the most stellar. For many, it is the achievement of a lifetime. Just being able to say "I had dinner at the White House the other night" carries a cachet impossible to surpass.

"When the president issues a dinner invitation to you, that means divinity is looking at you with favor," George Reedy, Johnson's spokesman, said. "I spent three or four years at the White House, where I didn't do anything I consider particularly great except write a book about it. I spent a good deal more time in the Senate, where I think I did a great deal that was more important. Most people don't know I was in the Senate. That is because it is not divine. It is divinity that counts."[146]

For Richard A. Snyder, president of In-N-Out Burger Inc. in Baldwin Park, California, being invited to a dinner at the White House fulfilled a ten-year dream. A Republican campaign contributor, Snyder peppered every politician he knew with requests for an invitation. Finally, in June 1992, Bush invited him to dinner. After dinner, Bush and his wife danced, and the president asked Snyder and his wife to join in.

"My wife felt a little shy," said Snyder, who called the dinner the best party he had ever attended. "But when the president orders you to do something, you do it. There we were, dancing with the president and Mrs. Bush, the only ones on the dance floor."

Jessica Lee, a *USA Today* reporter, described with awe attending a White House dinner given by Bush for Brazilian President Fernando Collor de Mello. In an electronic memo to her colleagues, she said, "Going to a state dinner at the White House is unbelievably seductive. It was like being Cinderella at the prince's ball. . . . Driving through those big iron White House gates and up to the circular drive was awesome."

Opening her car door and escorting her into the White House was one of the military social aides who volunteer to help at official functions. While Lee was impressed by her aide, she did not know that his function included performing what is known as the turkey trot.

"It's how we got rid of guests," said Stephen M. Bauer, an army colonel who was a White House military social aide in five administrations. "We never had to do it after a state dinner because then it's already late and guests are ready to go. But after a 5:30 P.M. reception, who wants to leave the food and booze to go out into Washington traffic."[147]

That is when the military aides go into action, forming what appears to be a casual picket fence that gradually moves hangers-on forward, much the way turkeys might be herded across a barnyard. Soon, the guests are on their way home.

Occasionally, when a guest does not get the hint, a social aide, pretending to be engaged deep in conversation with somebody, will back up slowly until he bumps into the guest. While the aide apologizes, he never budges. Reception lines are kept moving by a pull-off aide, who uses eye contact to signal that a guest should keep moving, then motions to indicate in what direction the guest should migrate.

At the dinner for the Brazilian president, Lee described meeting Dan and Marilyn Quayle, Supreme Court Justice Anthony Kennedy, ABC's Sam Donaldson, Detroit Pistons center Bill

Laimbeer, and Commerce Secretary Robert Mosbacher and his wife, Georgette.

"The food was wonderful," she gushed. "Mrs. Bush served tomatoes stuffed with crabmeat, loin of lamb with peppers . . . summer salad with Trappist cheese . . . mocha bombe with Tia Maria sauce. The tables were decked out in peach and white damask and the Johnson china."[148]

The job of drawing up the guest lists falls to the White House social secretary.

"The most difficult aspect of the job is the pressure you get from the west wing and Congress and the State Department to put all their friends at each dinner," said Letitia Baldrige, who did the job during the Kennedy administration and helped out during the Reagan administration.

"I saw the seductiveness of the place," Jerry Parr, a former Secret Service official, said. "In Washington, there is an addiction to power, to control. To the extent you are mature and have a sense of perspective, you are able to handle it better. If you are looking for sheer raw power, you find it in the White House."

While Bush set the correct tone in the White House, he did not deal forcefully with aides like Sununu and Lee when they got out of line, suggesting that he was a poor leader. Bush aggressively pursued foreign policy and military goals, successfully turning back Iraq's invasion of Kuwait, but he wore kid gloves when managing the White House and its staff. Despite prodding, Bush refused to fire aides who got into trouble. The fact that, after he had left the White House, Bush took Sununu with him to a victory celebration in Kuwait suggests that their values, in the end, were not that different.

Thus Bush, like many presidents, remains a cipher. On a personal level, he was unaffected and sensitive to people's needs. On a policy level, he was the opposite, ignoring domestic concerns and willing to use racial issues to help retain power.

Like most recent presidents, Bush thought nothing of breaking his campaign promises. "Read my lips: No new taxes," he proclaimed repeatedly, then reneged by raising income taxes and federal taxes on gasoline, cigarettes, beer, and other items.

There are those who thought Bush was simply the victim of bad advice.

"I liked Bush," Kanjorski said. "I think he was mishandled and mismanaged." But a president is responsible for the selection and direction of his staff. While a president cannot be aware of every action taken on his behalf, he is aware of what his campaign themes and programs are. Bush described the Willie Horton ads as an attempt to "kick a little ass." If that was so, he bore the responsibility for the message of bigotry they conveyed.

Like most recent presidents, Bush thought nothing of lying if he thought it would help him politically. In running for re-election, Bush insisted he was "out of the loop" when the events leading up to the Iran-contra scandal were discussed. Yet the report of independent counsel Lawrence Walsh said that contrary to his claims, Bush was "regularly briefed, along with the president, on the Iran arms sales, and he participated in discussions to obtain third-country support for the contras."

After Clinton was inaugurated, the president's Boeing 747 flew Bush and some of his closest staff members and friends to Houston. Because Bush was no longer president, the plane was designated SAM 28000 instead of *Air Force One*. SAM 28000—for Special Air Mission No. 28000—is what the Boeing 747 is called when the president is not on board.

"As he stepped on board, some of us were teary-eyed," Untermeyer said. "He said, 'No tears today.' "

On the flight back, nineteen television monitors displayed a video prepared by J. Dorrance Smith, a former producer for ABC's "Nightline" who was Bush's assistant for media affairs. Called the "White House Home Video," it featured people like Boyden Gray telling embarrassing anecdotes. At one point, the video zoomed in on Bush's daughter Dorothy LeBlond greeting her children as they came home from school in Bethesda, Maryland. After offering them cookies and milk, she told the children they would have to eat their snacks sitting on the floor.

156

"Grampy took the dining room table to Texas," she explained dejectedly.

Not quite. As a former president, Bush was entitled to receive a lifetime pension equal to 71.5 percent of his former pay, indexed for inflation. That came to $153,269 in his first year out of office. For the rest of his life, Bush was also entitled to free office space and an annual payment for staff salaries ranging from $150,000 in the first two and a half years to $96,000 after that. To cover the expenses of his transition from office, he received another $1.5 million during his first six months out of the White House.

Beyond the presidential entitlements, because he had worked for the government for twenty-one years, Bush also received an annual pension of $44,000. He received income from his personal investment portfolio valued at $1.3 million. And he received additional income from speeches at $60,000 to $100,000 each, a $2.2 million book deal by his wife, and another book deal on foreign policy.[149]

On the trip back to Houston, the lunch menu featured "Texas-style barbecue." But like everything connected with the White House, that too was a charade. While delicious, the ribs and beef brisket were from Red, Hot and Blue, a Washington chain that makes Memphis-style barbecue.

7

Bimbo Eruptions

WHEN ONE FIRST FAMILY LEAVES THE WHITE HOUSE AND THE NEXT
one comes in, it is like anyone else's moving day—somewhat
melancholic for the family packing up its memories and moving out, and triumphant and exciting for the new family moving in.

But unlike ordinary households, the White House has the
staff of the residence and the resources of the General Services
Administration to coordinate the transition. Detailed floor plans
of the west wing are prepared so that the new staff can assign
offices there. During transition is when the outlines of the parking
spaces on West Executive Avenue get a new coat of paint. Desks
are emptied, stationery supplies distributed, walls touched up
or repainted.

While the president is being sworn in at the Capitol, GSA
removes the former president's flag in the Oval Office and replaces it with a new one. Glossy color photographs of the new
president replace the photos of the previous president. Combinations to safes are changed. New telephone lists are distributed. The Cabinet chair with the previous president's name on

it is shipped to him, to be replaced by a new chair bearing the new president's name.

When Bill Clinton was inaugurated, GSA performed these tasks or coordinated them as usual. But something was wrong. Unlike previous administrations, the Clinton staff provided very little help. It was not that the Clinton people did not want a smooth transition. Not at all. It was in their interest to have their offices assigned and parking passes issued as quickly as possible. Rather, it was an overwhelming lack of competence that prevented the Clinton people from doing what was necessary to carry out the tasks that every other administration in memory had performed.

"The Clinton administration was not set up to do anything," a GSA building manager said. "If they had any preplanning, no one was aware of it. It could have been a lot smoother if they had done their homework. The government shouldn't miss a heartbeat."

In contrast, when the Reagan administration took over, "They knew everything beforehand," the GSA official said. "They knew the parking. They knew the buildings. The telephone book was immediately put out. This administration is very disorganized. It is almost like, 'We haven't been there for twelve years, and we don't want to hear from you how to do it.' "

Even the Carter administration, known for sloppy staff work, was better organized and more skillful than the Clinton team, according to the GSA manager.

"These [Clinton] people are not organized. Very young, very rude," said Lucille Price, another GSA manager, whose office is in the old Executive Office Building.

Expressed just a month after the inauguration, these evaluations from the bowels of the White House soon became a metaphor for the Clinton administration. From Travelgate to HaircutGate, the Clinton administration distinguished itself for ineptitude and indifference.

By himself, the president can do very little except—in the words of Bradley Patterson, a former White House aide in three administrations—go to the bathroom. While the president sets basic policy, he needs a staff that will carry it out. As in any organization, that requires answering telephones, returning calls, opening and responding to mail, making decisions promptly, treating people with respect, and following the rules. The Clinton people simply did not know how or were not willing to perform those simple tasks. Behind it all was arrogance, confused thinking, and lack of judgment that began with the president and radiated throughout his staff.

While the White House atmosphere magnifies such tendencies, Clinton's arrogance was well developed before he moved to 1600 Pennsylvania Avenue. As evidence, one need look no further than his twelve-year affair while in public life with Gennifer Flowers. When the press revealed Gary Hart's brief affair with Donna Rice, he was forced to withdraw as a presidential contender. But through clever spin control, Clinton managed to overcome the Flowers incident, undermining her credibility to the point where her name now evokes guffaws. Yet the tapes she made of some of their telephone conversations—tapes authenticated by an independent audio expert—clearly establish that they had had an affair. Nor did Clinton ever explicitly deny having sex with Flowers, a question reporters never asked him.

When Clinton appeared with his wife, Hillary Rodham Clinton, on "60 Minutes," correspondent Steve Kroft said that Flowers "is alleging and has described in some detail . . . what she calls a twelve-year affair with you."

"That allegation is false," Clinton said, allowing for the possibility he had an affair with Flowers of shorter duration.[150]

"I'm assuming from your answer that you're categorically denying that you ever had an affair with Gennifer Flowers," Kroft said.

"I said that before. And so has she," Clinton said, failing to answer directly.

Clinton then danced around the question of whether he had ever had an extramarital affair, acknowledging that he had engaged in "wrongdoing" and caused "pain" in his marriage but saying he was not prepared to discuss the issue.

The fact that the Flowers affair was first detailed by a weekly tabloid—the *Star*—did not help her credibility. The *Star* had the story because it was the only paper that had seriously investigated widespread rumors of Clinton's womanizing. Once the tabloid prepared its story, the paper showed it to Flowers, offering her $175,000 if she could provide further evidence of the affair. She then gave to the paper the tapes she had made of some of her phone conversations with Clinton.

The Clinton camp made much of the fact that Anthony J. Pellicano, an expert on audio recording analysis, had told the press that a twelve-minute portion of the tape of conversations between Flowers and Clinton had been "selectively edited" at two points. But Pellicano, who later achieved celebrity status defending singer Michael Jackson against charges he molested a thirteen-year-old boy, stated at the time that without having the original tapes, he could not prove his suspicions. Pellicano had only a copy of the tape provided by a Los Angeles television station.

"Without having the original tape recorder and tape recordings, there is no way to ascertain authenticity either way," Pellicano told the author. "These were sound bites or snippets of conversations that may have been edited. The tape is suspect at best. That is why it has to be authenticated."[151]

On the other hand, the *Star* had an independent laboratory examine the original tapes. The lab—Truth Verification Laboratories Inc.—concluded that the tapes had not been tampered with in any way.[152] Even accepting Pellicano's unsupported suspicion that a twelve-minute portion of the tape had been edited in two places, the extensive conversations that are not in question provide ample evidence that Clinton and Flowers had been intimate. Moreover, Clinton's concern about the allegations went well beyond what might be expected if he were merely giving Flowers advice on how to deal with allegations that he knew to be untrue.

In the tapes, Clinton repeatedly expressed concern that reporters would obtain evidence of their affair, such as photographs. In the tradition of Richard Nixon, he advised her to stonewall reporters.

"I expect them to come look into it and interview you and everything, uh, but I just think that if everybody's on record denying it, you've got no problem," Clinton reassured Flowers.

". . . they're gonna try to goad people up, you know, if everybody kinda hangs tough, they're just not going to do anything. They can't."

"No, they can't," Flowers agreed.

"They can't run a story like this unless somebody said, 'Yeah, I did it with him,' " Clinton said.

Jokingly, Flowers reminded Clinton of a previous conversation when she had said that, if asked about Clinton, she would simply tell reporters that he "ate good pussy."[153]

"What?" Clinton asked.

"I'll just tell them you eat good pussy," she repeated. Clinton did not respond, and Flowers added, "I try to find the humor in things."

"God, I know it," Clinton said. Referring to his political career, he said, "There's no negative except this."

Clinton raised the possibility that reporters might obtain incriminating evidence, such as phone records.

"See, you've always called me," she said. "So that's not a . . ."

"I wouldn't care if they—you know, I, I— They must have my phone records on this computer here, but I don't think it— That doesn't prove anything," Clinton said, speaking from the governor's mansion in Little Rock.

"If they don't, if they don't have pictures—" Clinton said. "Which they [garbled], and no one says anything, then they don't have anything, and arguably, if someone says something, they don't have much."

Still, Clinton worried that he would be found out. Asked by Flowers if he would run for president, he said, "I want to. I wonder if I'm going to be blown out of the water with this."

Clinton made a remark about Mario Cuomo acting like a mafioso. After the transcript became public, Clinton apologized to the New York governor, which further confirmed the authenticity of the tapes. Flowers apologized for bothering Clinton with the latest news about efforts to prove that they had had an affair.

"No, I love that you've called," he said. At another point, he said, "I need to know every time—'cause it enables me to run the traffic, see what else is going on."

"But anyway," Flowers said, "I think we're okay for now."

"I really want to talk to you," he said at another point. "I really want to see you."

"How do you like holding [garbled] future in [garbled] hands? Do you like that?" he asked. Clinton advised her to remain on the alert. "We have to watch as we go along," Clinton said.

"All right, darling," Flowers said, "well, you just hang in there. I don't mean to worry you. I just—"

"I just want to know these things, and if I can help you, you let me know," Clinton said. "Good-bye, baby."

After the story appeared, Betsey Wright, Clinton's chief of staff when he was governor of Arkansas, referred to allegations made by Flowers and other women who claimed they had had affairs with Clinton as "bimbo eruptions." She and other Clinton staff members tried to suggest that Clinton was trying to calm Flowers even though they had not had an affair. Yet the level of his concern, his comment that the affair could not be established unless reporters had photographs, and the fact that they engaged in intimate talk are compelling evidence that the two had had an affair.

Nor was Flowers a bimbo, as the Clinton people portrayed her. She had worked as a television news reporter and a night-club singer. If she had been a man who had had an affair with a female politician, the press would have clamored to find out the nature of the relationship and what insights that person might have into the politician's character. Because of a double standard, the fact that Flowers was female and beautiful—with a shapely body and long dyed white-blond hair—worked against her.

"Some thirty women said they had a relationship with Bill," Flowers said. "Betsey Wright called it a 'bimbo eruption.' What a sexist statement to make. Some of those women may indeed be what we might perceive as bimbos. But you can bet your sweet ass I am not a bimbo. I might have a little bimbo in me on a good Saturday night. But overall, I am not a stupid, uninformed woman. I have made my way, and I haven't asked anybody for a damned thing. I resent being called a money-grubbing opportunist. I really thought in my heart of hearts I would be famous, but it would be for my talent as a singer. Why God has chosen me to be a player in this deal I'm not sure yet. I believe anyone who was not as strong as I am would have already done away with herself. It's been tough."

Flowers later appeared nude in the December 1992 issue of *Penthouse*. But that does not detract from the fact that for more than twelve years, Flowers had apparently asked for nothing more from Clinton than to continue their affair. Throughout that time, she had strenuously avoided confirming their romance, even threatening to file a lawsuit when a broadcaster alleged they had been intimate. Only when it appeared that the *Star* had nailed the story down did she finally confirm it. Although deluged with requests from the national media, she refused further requests for interviews.

To this day, Flowers is torn about Clinton. She said their affair began when he was attorney general and she was on assignment as a reporter for KARK-TV, NBC's Little Rock affiliate. He commented on her looks and asked her out. While she broke off their affair in 1989 because she hoped to marry a stockbroker she was seeing, she admits to getting a "twinge" when she hears about other women who might have been involved with Clinton. At other times, she becomes angry about his effort to put her down and distance himself from her.

"On one hand, I still want to defend him, and on the other I want to blast him," she said. "I have mixed emotions."[154]

While Flowers was pleased with Clinton as a lover—he enthusiastically gave her oral sex, she said—she said he also has an arrogant streak. In Flowers's view, Clinton is an insecure man who is not particularly competent as a manager.

"He thought he was bullet-proof in Arkansas," Flowers said. "He was so obvious when we were out in public that it would make me uncomfortable."

Flowers saw Clinton two to four times a month, usually in her apartment. Occasionally, he attended her performances. She called him "baby"; he called her "pookie." On one of Clinton's first visits to her apartment, the doorman watched as he went to her floor.

"Because there were already rumors about us, the doorman looked to see if he was going to see me, which he was," she said. "He [the doorman] told everyone in the building about it. At one point, I started putting a paper in the exit door. I was on the second floor and two doors from the exit. So he would get in and out without being seen and not go through the main lobby."

Neighbors noticed that Clinton's driver stayed outside the apartment building in his car for an hour or two each time Clinton visited the apartment. The Clinton people put out the word that some of his aides lived in the building.

"People noticed this guy was sitting outside," she said. "I think one night the security guy saw [Clinton] come out the side door. He could have had an aide in the building. He said he did. We never talked about it again.

"He couldn't deny it," Flowers said, referring to the fact that Clinton has hinged his denials on whether he had had a twelve-year affair with Flowers.

"If he had said, 'We had a relationship at one time and it's over'—and it was—'but our marriage is strong, and it's good, and we want to get on with our lives,' the issue would have been dead in the water. But Hillary wouldn't have sat still for it," she said.

Citing reports in the press that Clinton becomes enraged with aides over small incidents, Flowers said Clinton has a temper and feels threatened by highly competent advisers.

"It strokes his ego to have people who are not that competent tell him how good he is," she said.

Flowers said that in her view, Clinton is in over his head as president.

"You don't get the kind of experience that he needs by being the governor of a small state," she said. "Arkansas is pathetic. The per capita income is low, and the cost of living is almost as high as Dallas. I never did see that Bill did a lot for Arkansas," she said. Having worked for the Arkansas government for six months, Flowers came away with an impression of a bureaucracy that was adrift.

"The mentality was to have meetings to set up a task force

to have other meetings to review the findings of that meeting," she said.

From what she could learn from Clinton, Flowers said he and Hillary have a "cold" relationship.

"I can't imagine it's changed, unless they have established another facet to the relationship, but I doubt it," she said. "I know Bill has a lot of respect for Hillary. He respects her mind. He likes women who are independent, strong women. It was always my impression that there wasn't much to that relationship other than the general respect they had for each other. But I didn't encourage that kind of conversation. If he wanted to discuss in any detail his sex life with his wife, it would have ticked me off."

Flowers said she once raised with Clinton the fact that there were widespread rumors that Hillary Clinton was a lesbian—rumors that Hillary herself referred to and totally dismissed on at least one occasion during the presidential campaign, in a board meeting of the Children's Defense Fund.

Flowers said, "He was aware of it [the rumors]. There were rumors around Little Rock for years about that, and about a lover. I didn't ask if he knew of specific lovers. We didn't always have a lot of time with each other."

Somehow, Clinton managed to be on time for most of their assignations, Flowers said.

"I don't recall him being real late," she said. "I can recall things coming up, and he would call me. He would say he would call me later. He never did not show up."

But once Clinton became president, he developed a reputation for being perpetually and embarrassingly late for almost everything, suggesting both an arrogance and an inability to manage himself, let alone the government. Given his impressive educational credentials, Clinton's sloppiness was surprising.

Clinton graduated fourth in a class of 323 from public high school there, and he went on to Georgetown University, Oxford University as a Rhodes scholar, and Yale Law School, where he met his future wife, Hillary Rodham, a fellow student from suburban Chicago. They married in 1975.

After graduating from Yale in 1973, Clinton joined the faculty of the University of Arkansas as a law professor. By early the next year he was running for the U.S. Congress. Although he narrowly lost, he gained name recognition in Arkansas politics and two years later was elected state attorney general. While serving in that office, he was elected the youngest governor in Arkansas history in 1978, at the age of thirty-two. Defeated in a reelection bid in 1980 after raising the state gasoline tax to finance an ambitious highway-building program, he went on to win four consecutive terms as governor.

On October 3, 1991, Clinton became the sixth candidate to enter the race for the Democratic presidential nomination, after all of the party's leading national figures had declined to challenge President George Bush's commanding lead in the polls following the Persian Gulf War.

Clinton's poise and unrivaled command of the issues quickly propelled him to Democratic front-runner status, but long-standing questions about his personal life then surfaced. Clinton dropped seventeen points in the polls, but still came in second in New Hampshire. During the spring primaries he weathered other allegations concerning his marriage, his escape from the draft during the Vietnam War, and past marijuana use. By April he had recovered his front-runner place. He locked up the nomination in June and selected Senator Al Gore, Jr., as his running mate.

Saying it was time for a new generation of leadership in Washington, Clinton stressed domestic issues, particularly the stagnating U.S. economy, accusing Bush of neglecting problems at home. On November 3, 1993, Clinton won with 43 percent of the popular vote to 38 percent for Bush and 19 percent for Ross Perot.

Once he got in the White House, Clinton realized that everyone waited for him, not the other way around. Typically, he would show up for White House receptions an hour late, diminishing the goodwill that he hoped to generate by having them in the first place. At a $1,500-a-plate Democratic fundraiser, he stepped up to the podium at 11 P.M. By then, half the people had left. Supreme Court Chief Justice William H. Rehnquist had to cut short a meeting with Clinton after the president left him waiting for forty-five minutes. On Inauguration Day, George and Barbara Bush were kept waiting at the White House for coffee with the Clintons.

"Clinton is usually late," said James Saddler, an *Air Force One* steward. "It varies from half an hour to an hour to fifteen minutes. When he starts shaking hands with people, he forgets about time."[155]

While Bush or Reagan would notify the White House chef when running late, Clinton rudely ignored such niceties.

According to Jane Burka, coauthor of *Procrastination*, such behavior is often a tool of control. "In effect, they [tardy people] are saying, 'I'm in control. I run on my own schedule,'" she said. These people are "oblivious to the needs of others—they get so self-absorbed they literally lose track of time."[156]

Within hours of taking office, Clinton began complaining that the vaunted White House telephone system was archaic.

"I think the president was pretty stunned by the phone system," said John Podesta, an assistant to the president and staff secretary. "He groused about it a lot. He likes to shake hands. He seems to like nothing better than to jump out of a limo and start shaking hands. He listens hard to people and likes to relate to them. He picks information up that way. The phone system was symbolic of the isolation, of the disconnect, of the president's inability to be in contact directly with the public."[157]

In any White House, it's monkey-see, monkey-do. Following the president's lead, Clinton's staff began complaining about the computers. In fact, every recent administration has found the level of computerization in the White House to be inadequate, and each administration has upgraded the system. The Clinton people happened to be used to Apple Computer Inc. products, so nothing the White House offered met their expectations. In fact, *PC Magazine* has rated Apple products, which account for about 10 percent of the total government personal computer market, far below many IBM-based machines in reliability and customer satisfaction. *Computer Shopper* magazine even claimed that Macintosh computers are not as easy to learn or user-friendly as IBM-compatible machines. But contradicting that, *Consumer Reports* concluded that for those buying their first home computer, the Mac is easier to learn and use.[158]

Previous administrations quietly went about upgrading the existing White House computers. But like children who whine that their school is better than someone else's, the Clinton staff, as if they had nothing better to do, went out of their way to knock them. As for the telephones, both Bush and Reagan had liked the idea of being able to pick up the receiver in the Oval Office and in the residence and talk with a White House operator, who would connect them to anyone they wished. It was like having a secretary place calls for them. But Clinton, concerned about his privacy, liked to dial numbers himself, without going through the operator. It was a simple matter to give the president a dial tone instead of an operator. Still Clinton complained.

Clinton chose W. David Watkins to be the person in charge of such things. As assistant to the president for administration and management, Watkins occupied the spot previously held by Bonnie Newman in the Bush administration and John Rogers in the Reagan administration.

Watkins could not be described as an inexperienced kid. Like many other Clinton aides, Watkins had graduated from the University of Arkansas and its graduate school. In 1975, he started an advertising company, garnering an account of Wal-Mart Inc. In 1982, Watkins started a long-distance telephone company. That same year, he contributed advertising and public relations counsel to Clinton's campaign for governor. In 1983, for $2,014, he sold Hillary Clinton a 2.5 percent interest in a cellular phone company he had started. Five years later, she sold her interest for $48,000. In 1985, Watkins started a merchant banking firm. During Clinton's presidential campaign, Watkins was deputy campaign manager and chief financial officer.

But as he later demonstrated during the fiasco involving the White House travel office, Watkins was exactly the wrong kind of person to place in such a sensitive position. Lacking any real national experience, Watkins quickly became consumed with White House–itis, that combination of arrogance and lack of judgment that turns into a deadly malady when its victim is infected by power. It was Watkins who recommended firing all seven members of the White House travel office after Clinton's television-producer friend, Harry Thomason, had raised questions about its selection of charter companies to provide planes for the press. Thomason, in turn, appeared to be influenced by a friend and business partner who wanted the contract for a company in which both men had an interest. It was also Watkins, as Clinton's aide over administration, who placed Catherine A. Cornelius, a distant cousin of Clinton who desperately wanted to run the travel office, in the travel office to snoop around. After Thomason had raised questions based on hearsay that there might be corruption in the travel office, Watkins assigned Cornelius, who had no background in such matters, to check them out. Her snooping was so clumsy that the employees of the office quickly realized she was copying documents. They then locked up the financial files.

As the White House's own review later concluded, "Given Cornelius' personal interest in running the travel office, Watkins should not have placed her in the office to make recommendations on how the office should be structured. Watkins compounded the problem when, in response to Thomason's complaints, he asked Cornelius to be alert to possible wrongdoing or corruption. Cornelius lacked the experience or preparation for this role. Nor was she given any guidance."

In fact, according to the review, Watkins never spoke with the travel office employees himself, understood what they did, or realized how highly the press thought of the job the office did in handling the press's travel arrangements.

It was typical of the indolence of Clinton's staff. Watkins seemed to have little interest in finding out what the departments under him did. In an interview four months after he had accepted the job, he referred to the National Park Service as the "Park Foundation." When agreeing to let the White House chef be interviewed, he said the chief steward in the White House mess should be contacted.[159] In fact, the White House mess is a separate operation from the food operations in the residence.

After Cornelius's Keystone Kops approach had failed, Watkins hired KPMG Peat Marwick to audit the travel office's books. Watkins put as much effort into selecting the firm as he did into finding out what the travel office does. He chose the firm because an assistant recommended the company after he happened to attend a seminar given by Peat Marwick.

The accounting firm found "abysmal management" and lack of documentation for $18,000 in checks made out to cash. Watkins and William H. Kennedy III, a former law partner of Hillary Rodham Clinton who was associate White House counsel, then called in the FBI. When the FBI did not jump as quickly as he wanted, Kennedy threatened to take the matter to another agency, like the IRS, that would respond to the White House. He told the FBI the matter was being directed "at the highest levels" of the White House. This gave the appearance that the Clinton White House was operating the way the Nixon White House had operated, using the agencies of government to exact retribution against the administration's perceived enemies. However, unlike Nixon's aides, Clinton's aides were not maliciously motivated. Inexperienced and immature as they were, they sincerely thought they had uncovered a major scandal and hysterically tried to use their authority to make sure it was investigated.

Even before the accounting firm had done its review, Jeff Eller, a senior White House aide described as having a personal relationship with Cornelius, urged Chief of Staff Thomas F. (Mack) McLarty to fire the travel office employees on the spot. McLarty decided to wait until the review was finished. When the review determined that there was no record in the petty cash book of $18,000 in checks made out to cash, McLarty fired everyone in the office. As the White House's own review of the matter later concluded, the White House had failed to conduct "the kind of deliberate, careful planning that the reorganization of an office like this warrants and requires." It had failed to exclude people who had a personal interest in the outcome from evaluating the performance of the travel office. Finally, the review concluded, the White House had failed to treat the employees with enough "sensitivity." Indeed, it had tarnished their reputations unfairly.

Once the audit was complete, Watkins informed the travel office employees at 10 A.M. on May 19, 1993, that they were being dismissed. He ordered them to leave the White House that day. Yet five of the seven dismissed employees had had no access to money.

When the firings caused an uproar, George Stephanopoulos, then White House communications director, repeatedly issued statements that he later had to retract. He claimed it was merely coincidence that nearly all the changes Cornelius had proposed in a memo were made.

Deciding to put a better light on the matter, Stephanopoulos asked John E. Collingwood, head of the FBI's congressional and public affairs office, to meet with him in the White House. During the meeting, Stephanopoulos extracted from Collingwood the fact that the FBI believed, based on what the White House had alleged, that it had a basis for conducting a criminal investigation of the matter. Knowing that the White House would likely use that statement, Collingwood the next day strengthened the FBI's own statement to be used if reporters inquired about the investigation. That same day, the White House press office itself issued the FBI statement, which was a violation of normal FBI procedures. The White House actions created an appearance of trying to use the FBI for political purposes.

To make matters worse, Watkins tried to replace the travel office with World Wide Travel of Little Rock, which had handled travel arrangements for the Clinton campaign and for Watkins's advertising firm. World Wide had also used Watkins's firm for its advertising. Moreover, Watkins was a longtime friend of its owner. In yet another coincidence, within weeks after Clinton won the election, Steve Davison, World Wide's director of customer services, had told *Arkansas Business* that although nothing was definite, World Wide was studying the possibility of opening an office in Washington to handle travel arrangements for Clinton's White House staff. Only a dolt would think that he could enter the White House, terminate the travel staff, and replace it without competitive bidding with his friendly travel agency from Little Rock.[160]

Critics of the Clinton White House said it was populated with kids. But Watkins was fifty-one, so his performance had nothing to do with age. In contrast to Watkins, Reagan's aide over administration, John Rogers, was only twenty-four when he got the job. From GSA to the military, those who worked in the White House had nothing but praise for the professional way he did his job, demonstrating that in this case the problem with the Clinton staff was not youth but ineptitude.

Admitting it had erred, the Clinton White House eventually rehired in other jobs the five travel office employees who had had no access to cash. It also severed its tie to World Wide. But Watkins and others involved were only reprimanded, and Stephanopoulos was given a promotion that meant he advised Clinton daily on policy. After the hysteria in the White House had died down, the FBI found that only one travel office employee had engaged in conduct that could be considered even questionable.

In reporting the debacle, the press corps was in no mood to give the White House the benefit of a doubt. In a towering example of Clinton's lack of management skills, he came to the White House with the perverse idea that he would go around the national press, appealing directly to the people by appearing before "town meetings" or by answering the softball questions of local reporters. In part, this strategy was a result of his bruised feelings over the way the press had treated the Gennifer Flowers incident. While many thought the press had not pursued the story enough, Clinton understandably was unhappy that it had come out at all.

Bruce Lindsey, Clinton's close friend who had been placed over personnel, foreshadowed the new press policy in an interview two months before Clinton was sworn in. "You all have been asses ever since we started," he told reporters on Clinton's jet. "I think you still push up too close. I think he's entitled to some measure of privacy."

Lindsey said Clinton was examining the issue of press coverage and the possibility of experimenting with limiting the access given by the White House to the press.[161]

Once Clinton became president, the White House press office

banned White House reporters from the corridor outside the offices of the White House communications staff. This had been one of the few ways reporters could get enough access to ask questions and get behind what they were fed at press conferences. As it is, the White House beat is tightly circumscribed.

"The White House beat is the gilded cage of American journalism," Howard Kurtz, media reporter for the *Washington Post*, has written. "There is the heady sense of being close to the seat of power, of posing momentous questions at televised press conferences, of traveling around the globe with the world's most important newsmaker. There is no more automatic ticket to the front page."[162]

An adroit White House—such as Reagan's or Bush's—treats White House reporters with respect and inundates them with news calculated to make the president look good. By leaking tidbits and insights to reporters, the White House staff manipulates them, making them dependent on them and diminishing their desire to head off on their own into areas that might embarrass the president.

This is all standard operating procedure at any savvy press operation. In the case of the White House, there is the added benefit that the product being sold is the president. People identify the president with the country, and reporters often write about him as if he were a potentate. That cast makes it even less likely that reporters will probe deeply into such tawdry matters as presidential romances or the true cost of running the White House. It was not an accident that two reporters on the metropolitan staff of the *Washington Post* broke the Watergate scandal. As detailed in Bob Woodward and Carl Bernstein's *All the President's Men*, the newspaper's national staff tended to believe Nixon White House denials that the administration had any connection with the Watergate break-in.

Stephanopoulos compounded the Clinton White House's poor press relations by developing a reputation for failing to return reporters' calls. Yet that was what he was being paid to do. Many in the press office lazily followed his example or were simply rude. When the *Wall Street Journal* ran an incisive piece by Jeffrey H. Birnbaum on Clinton's deteriorating press relations, Stephanopoulos wrote a sophomoric rebuttal to Al Hunt, then Washington bureau chief. The story said Clinton not only becomes incensed about critical stories in the press, he tends to blame staff members like Stephanopoulos for allowing them to appear. As if Hunt were a member of the White House staff, Stephanopoulos drafted the peevish and un-supported reply in the form of a memo.

As journalist and author Sally Quinn put it, it was as if new neighbors had moved in and put out the word that they hated their neighbors. The reaction was predictable and highly dam-aging to the new administration. For much as the president may want to go over the head of the press, the fact is most people get their news from the national media. The president's image ultimately depends to a large degree on how the national media portray him.

A press corps that has been "avoided and ignored and treated in a way that is Nixonian is not going to cut [the president] any breaks," said George Condon, president of the White House Correspondents Association.

But the Clinton staff still did not get it. "For many of the 1,800 accredited White House reporters, phone calls went un-returned," *Newsweek* noted, adding, "White House staffers are not quite sure what to do about Clinton's poor press."

When it seemed things could not get worse, Lois Romano of the *Washington Post* reported in her gossip column that Clinton had gotten his hair cut by Cristophe Schatteman, a Beverly Hills stylist, on a runway at Los Angeles International Airport. That act, which shut down at least two runways for an hour, symbolized all the arrogance and inexperience demonstrated by the Clinton White House since inauguration day.

For weeks after Clinton took office, Milton Pitts had been patiently waiting for word from Watkins to return to the White House barbershop. On Bush's last day in office, Pitts had given him a haircut and had asked him what he should do. Bush had advised him to stay on until Clinton signaled whether he wanted Pitts to continue. But the attitude of the Clinton staff was that anyone having anything to do with a previous administration was suspect. Typically, no one in the White House would return Pitts's calls.

When no word was forthcoming, Pitts wrote a letter to McLarty. He pointed out that he had served four previous presidents and already had a clearance from the Secret Service.

"I didn't hear anything for three weeks," Pitts said. "I then got my things. The way they handled it was real stupid."

Indeed. History may record that Clinton's failure to continue using Pitts was one of the dumbest presidential decisions ever made. While the haircut on *Air Force One* did not seriously disrupt the airport because traffic was not heavy, it did mean shutting down runways and rerouting some landings and takeoffs.

"We flew out of San Diego to L.A. to pick him up," recalled James Saddler, a steward on the fateful trip. "Some guy came out and said he was supposed to cut the president's hair. Cristophe cut his hair, and we took off. We were on the ground for an hour. They closed the runways. That is a standard thing."[163]

When it came out that the price of the haircut was $200, people wondered what planet Clinton was on. To be sure, the government had not paid for the haircut. But a man who so outrageously wasted his own money did not inspire confidence. This was the same president who had claimed during the campaign that he would reduce the White House staff by 25 percent to demonstrate his commitment to cut the federal deficit? But in line with a long tradition of manipulating White House cost figures, Clinton's later announcement that he had indeed cut the staff by 25 percent was fiction, as credible as the denial of his affair with Gennifer Flowers and his claim that the runways at the Los Angeles airport had not been shut down.

First, to show that he had cut the staff by 25 percent, Clinton—on the advice of Watkins and McLarty—removed from the comparison the Office of Management and Budget and the U.S. Trade Representative, two departments that accounted for 38 percent of the Executive Office of the President's 1,814 employees. Then the Clinton White House counted as full-time employees people who had been temporarily detailed to the White House from other federal agencies during the Bush administration. Since Clinton cut back on the number of detailees, this inflated the base comparison by showing that people had been cut when they really had not been; they were still on the federal payroll. When all the offices are included and only full-time positions are counted, Clinton's reduction had cut the staff by only two hundred employees, a mere 11 percent.

But that was just the beginning. Having stacked the deck by changing the basis for comparison, Clinton then quietly asked Congress for additional appropriations for the White House beyond what the Bush White House had already requested for fiscal 1994. The additional $11.8 million was to hire temporary workers to do the work of the staff members being fired and to upgrade the computer and telephone systems.[164]

Letter writers whose expertise was needed to answer mail had been among those who had been fired early on. Soon, the Clinton White House, which received a record 700,000 letters a month, had a backlog of a million pieces of unanswered mail. The mail was put in storage until it could be answered, said Lorraine Voles, a White House spokesperson.

This came from the same White House that had gone out of its way to ridicule the slowness of the White House computer and telephone systems. Dee Dee Myers, Clinton's press secretary, had compared the state of technology in the White House with that in use during the Roosevelt and Truman administrations.

"The whiz kids were dismayed to discover a shortage of faxes, beepers, voice mail, laptops, and high-speed E-mail," *Time* said. "Given the equipment around here," a young aide was quoted as saying, "it's no wonder Bush lost."

Yet Bush knew how to do one thing that is a prerequisite for any well-run office: answer his mail. Clinton himself knew nothing about computers, preferring to draft letters on legal pads.

Even with savings from the minuscule reduction in staff, the total requested by Clinton was still $2.5 million more than what Bush had requested. Thus instead of saving taxpayers money, Clinton's campaign promise of a 25 percent staff reduction actually wound up costing taxpayers more.

In announcing the cut, Clinton said, "The government must do more but make do with less." As if the cut had already taken place, Clinton continued to cite the alleged reduction as an effort to "set an example" for the rest of the government. McLarty claimed it was the first time the White House staff had been cut.[165]

This was more hot air, as valid as the claim that for the first time in history, the Clinton White House would open the White House to visitors the morning after inauguration day. In fact, Bush had let four hundred visitors into the White House after he was inaugurated. Presidents William Taft and Andrew Jackson had done the same thing.

"Every president I have worked for has cut the staff," said Ron Geisler, who has been executive clerk for twenty-nine years. "They all announce they will have a lot smaller staffs than their predecessors. They always say they are the first to do it. But that is not true. They cut fifteen or sixteen people, and then staff is usually added back. But 25 percent is the biggest cut I have seen."

As it turned out, Clinton's cut was actually a *plan* to reduce the White House staff by October 1, 1993, the start of the next fiscal year. During that time, the White House staff actually *increased*. By May 1993, the White House Office had 559 employees, a 37 percent increase over the number during the Bush administration. The larger Executive Office of the President had 1,991 employees, a 10 percent increase over the Bush administration.

By October 1, 1993, when Clinton said he would fulfill his campaign promise to cut the staff by 25 percent, Clinton had actually reduced the staff by 11 percent, but many of the jobs and functions had been shifted to the budgets of other government agencies. The greatest portion of the cuts came in the Office of National Drug Policy, which meant efforts to fight drug trafficking were being reduced.

To further confuse the issue, the Clinton White House tried to include a reduction in funding for what is known as the drug forfeiture fund as part of its reduction in overall expenses. But the fund merely funnels money to agencies that enforce

178

the drug laws. It therefore has nothing to do with White House costs or staffing levels. Finally, Clinton moved many White House functions to the budgets of other agencies. For example, the Clinton White House moved a GSA unit that planned space allocation to GSA, even though the unit continued to report to the White House.

Thus Clinton's pledge of cutting the White House staff was a joke and his effort to show that he had carried it out a sham. When the smoke had cleared, the cost of running the White House had actually increased, in part because Clinton had hired part-time employees to replace full-time ones. Moreover, Clinton managed to focus attention only on the visible portion of the White House budget. The total appropriation of $167.4 million requested by Clinton represented only a tenth of the cost of running the White House. It did not include such additional contributions as $90.6 million from the Defense Department for the White House Communications Agency, $185 million from Defense for White House travel, and at least $356 million from the Secret Service. Anyone who walked through the Clinton White House could see that the number of employees had increased dramatically when compared with the Bush White House.

When Clinton first announced that the staff had been cut, the press was largely asleep. While White House reporters barraged White House press secretary Dee Dee Myers with questions about the planned staff cuts, they did no analysis of the budget figures themselves. The only mention of the possibility that the numbers were not what they seemed was a news item on a study by Citizens for a Sound Economy, a conservative think tank. Because the analysis came from an interested party, the item rated small play on page A-19 of the *Washington Post*.[166]

Then Ann Devroy of the *Washington Post* reported in August 1993 that rather than decreasing the White House staff, Clinton had actually increased it. Clinton's announcement of the planned cuts was the lead story in the *Post*; Devroy's story reporting what had actually happened was buried on page A-25. The *Post*'s lead story that day came straight out of the

White House's press office—an announcement by Clinton of a new wetlands policy.

Devroy's story made it sound as if cutting the White House staff was as hard as getting rid of the federal deficit. Instead of flatly showing that Clinton had lied, the story began by saying that the Clinton administration "has a lot of riffing, shuffling, and downright firing to do to get anywhere close to approximating its once vaunted pledge of a 25 percent staff cut by October 1." The story went on to note that "as the difficulty of the task has become clear, Clinton's references to the 25 percent cut virtually have disappeared." A more appropriate lead would have been, "Having announced that he would cut the White House staff by 25 percent, President Clinton has actually increased the White House staff by 10 percent since he made the announcement last February." If the original announcement was important enough to lead the paper, the fact that Clinton had misled the nation should have at least been the second lead in the paper.

Unlike many other decisions the president makes, reducing the White House staff requires no approval from Congress. He simply has to say the word to fulfill one of his major campaign promises. But having already gotten away with making it appear as if he were cutting the staff when he actually increased the total cost of running the White House, Clinton figured he might as well go all the way, increasing the staff, too.

While Devroy's story lacked punch, it had at least reported the facts, accompanied by a graph that showed clearly how Clinton's staff had increased when compared with Bush's. The rest of the press ignored the story entirely.

Devroy wrote a more hard-hitting story the day before the cuts were to become effective.

"Some Clinton aides acknowledge, on the deepest of background, that the staff cut had become 'the quintessential Washington game,' " Devroy wrote. "An unrealistic pledge, made by a candidate without knowledge of the White House operation, must now be kept because of its symbolism and because otherwise Republicans in Congress would make an issue out of it."[167]

But there was nothing unrealistic about Clinton's pledge to

cut the White House staff, any more than his plan to reform health care was unrealistic. Rather than being presented as an unavoidable slipup, the outcome of Clinton's pledge should have been presented as another broken campaign promise.

Still, the *Post* story signaled that Clinton had been less than truthful. The day it appeared, U.S. Representative Frank R. Wolf, a Virginia Republican who serves on the subcommittee that oversees the White House budget, took to the House floor to denounce Clinton's claim that he had cut the staff by 25 percent as a "lie" and "unethical." Besides using a false baseline for the number of White House employees during the Bush administration, he noted that most of the ousted employees were career workers rather than political appointees.

Clinton responded with an unfounded slur at career employees, saying it was the political appointees who work the hardest.

"The truth is that in the White House, at least, it's been my experience—not just for me, but for my Republican predecessors—that the so-called political appointees are the ones that have to work sixty to seventy hours a week and are making most of the decisions and doing most of the hard work," Clinton said.

To be sure, whether the staff is increased or decreased is largely symbolic. The costs have little impact on the federal budget.

"Cut the staff of the White House staff 25 percent? Why? Who cares really?" said Mark Weinberg, a press spokesman under Reagan. "The presidency is a big job. It doesn't matter if it takes 256 or 482 employees. It matters if the job is getting done. If you cut it, the mail may not get answered as quickly. Well, people are entitled to get timely responses."

What was important was that Clinton had broken his campaign promise and then deceived the public. If Clinton's figures about the White House staff could not be trusted, it was likely his figures on health care costs and funding—a far more complex subject—also could not be trusted.

Meanwhile, having helped McLarty work up the misleading figures on the bogus staff cut, Watkins got the bright idea that the White House would save money by getting computer hardware and software firms to contribute their wares free.

"We found the equipment in the White House to be user unfriendly," Watkins said. "A lot of the technology was early eighties." So Watkins said he asked himself, "Why couldn't the White House, which is the most prestigious address in the world, be a showplace for America's state-of-the-art technology?"[168]

In the White House, soliciting wealthy donors to help upgrade the perks is a long tradition. From Nancy Reagan's chinaware to Clinton's jogging track, the White House has used private and corporate donors to pay for items that might make presidents look rapacious if they charged them to taxpayers. But in recent memory, this was the first time the White House had gone begging for goods and services that are a staple of government procurement.

Watkins made the usual noises about not becoming obligated to the companies that would dispense the largesse. And he claimed the lucky donors would be selected by a task force on the basis of merit. But people do not contribute to the White House without expecting something in return. While the quid pro quo is usually difficult to trace, it eventually shows up in decisions that may favor the company. The idea that the White House would become a showplace for computer technology was, of course, pure advertising hype—something Watkins was schooled in. A secure building where access is limited to those with appointments, the White House is the last place that could serve as an exhibit area. Watkins's claim that the selection would be impartial was another ruse. Watkins and most of the White House staff were already partial to Apple products. Soon the White House was full of Macintoshes.[169]

While not illegal, the entire exercise was amateurish. People with no experience at the national level often try to reinvent the wheel. They declare that everything they do is so important and critical that existing rules and conventions must be waived. For example, Watkins decided that the government's procurement rules were cumbersome. Therefore, he bought software for storing resumes without going through the normal competitive process. The General Accounting Office, in a June 1993 report, found that, failing to follow normal procurement procedures, the White House under Watkins's direction had already leased the Resumix system before it had completed the required acquisition process.[170]

The same kind of arrogance led Watkins's office to disregard personnel rules that prohibit employees from receiving two salaries at once and from receiving retroactive appointments and pay increases. The GAO found that 25 employees of the Executive Office of the President for months at a time received pay both from the White House and the General Services Administration. Of the 611 people named to White House jobs in the three months after Clinton took over, 230 received retroactive appointments, meaning they received lump sum payments when they were hired, covering the months before they had started working for the White House. In addition, 22 new appointees received retroactive salary increases worth $1,000 to $25,000 a year.

Because the Clinton White House refused to turn over to the GAO its computer diskettes, the GAO had to laboriously hand-copy information on White House personnel from White House records.

The White House claimed the employees who received retroactive appointments or increases had been working at the required levels before the actions were taken. Even the law requiring White House employees to file financial disclosure reports seemed to be too burdensome for Watkins's office to comply with. The GAO found that 14 of 147 senior administration officials required to file such disclosure reports had failed to do so. The White House then asked for waivers of penalties for failing to file the reports on the grounds the employees did not know they were required. The White House also said it would not turn over computer diskettes to the GAO because of concerns about privacy.

"Every time we find one problem, they have the same answers," said Representative Jim Lightfoot of Iowa, the senior Republican on the committee that had asked for the GAO report. " 'It was a mistake, we are going to get it under control.'

183

It's more incompetence than anything else, and total disorganization."[171]

While that was true, the incompetence and disorganization were fed by arrogance. For the pattern was so pervasive and unprecedented that only arrogance could explain such widespread flouting of the laws and regulations.

In May 1994, Watkins finally self-destructed. The Frederick (Maryland) *News-Post* ran a photo of Watkins and two other aides, dressed in golfing clothes and carrying golf clubs, climbing into a marine helicopter as a marine in full dress uniform saluted them.

When the story hit the press, Clinton asked for and received Watkins's resignation. He pledged the taxpayers would be reimbursed for the $13,129.66 cost of the trip by the helicopter and an accompanying one. When Watkins—who lists a net worth of $1 million—refused to pay for the trip, White House aides said they would chip in to cover the cost. Still denying any wrongdoing, Watkins eventually agreed to pay for the regal trip.

Things were not much better in the rest of the White House. When the Clinton administration first came in, syrupy press stories noted that the staff ate pepperoni pizza in their offices late into the evening. This was supposed to mean that a youthful, new generation had taken over the government, one that was attuned to the ordinary needs of the people.

"Think ethnic food, think eclectic Adams-Morgan neighborhood, dark dives like Chief Ike's Mambo Room," cooed an early *New York Times* story on the Clinton White House. "Think renting over buying. Think movies. Most of all, for the moment, think work."

But while some staff members worked hard, the late hours often hid the fact that the Clinton staff was merely socializing or was not competent enough to get its work done during normal hours. There was a frenetic quality to the way the staff worked. Loose and disorganized, they preferred to make decisions on the run rather than by carefully considering memos. In fact, as if at a giant fraternity party, they spent much of their time gabbing.

"They are just goofing off—a lot of walking around and drinking Cokes and hanging around," said Lucille Price, the GSA manager, whose office is in the old Executive Office Building. "It's like a campus. Nothing is happening. They don't like to work. They don't return calls. They are rude. They are the most unprofessional people I've seen since I've been here, which is since Ford."[172]

When four young men demanded a table at the Bombay Club, an Indian restaurant in Washington that had just been visited by Clinton, the maître d' asked if they had a reservation. One of the men—who looked as if he was too young to shave—flashed his White House pass.

"I *said*, a table for four," a *Washington Post* story quoted him as saying. He got his table.

What was most baffling, Price said, was the Clinton staff's lack of interest in learning how to do things properly. For example, Price said, the Clinton people dragged their heels on designating a staff member to clear vehicles into the White House grounds.

"I think they just don't know that there is a need for these things to happen," Price said. "They won't ask. They didn't keep enough people from previous administrations to walk them through these problems. It's simple coordination."

In any White House, great stress is placed on getting names of dignitaries right. In the Clinton White House, less attention was paid to spelling than to ordering pizza toppings. When the Clinton staff sent invitations to a high-level jobs conference in Detroit in March 1994, the letters and briefing documents spelled the names of British Chancellor of the Exchequer Kenneth Clarke as "Clark"; German Labor Minister Norbert Bluem as "Bloehm"; and the first name of Italian Treasury Minister Piero Barucci as "Pietro."

Even putting the right speech in a TelePrompTer was too much to ask of Clinton's staff. When Clinton stepped up to the podium in the House chamber to announce his health care proposal on September 22, 1993, the TelePrompTer in front of him began to scroll the text of the February 17 address that Clinton had delivered the last time he had gone before a joint session of Congress.

As Clinton improvised for five to seven minutes, he enlisted the aid of Vice President Al Gore—virtually the only person on his staff who was organized—to rectify the problem. Gore had to leave to alert aides.

"It took five to seven minutes to fix while he was speaking," admitted David Dreyer, a communications staffer who helped write the speech.

This was the most important speech of Clinton's presidency. How could it happen? "We're trying to determine it," communications director Mark Gearan said.

Meanwhile, the White House counsel's office, when headed by Bernard W. Nussbaum, jumped from one gaffe to another. Having failed to vet properly the nominations of Zoë E. Baird and Kimba Wood for attorney general, Nussbaum then failed to read the patently antidemocratic and inconsistent writings of Lani Guinier. But Nussbaum had plenty of time to attend Washington parties, and he began most morning meetings by trying to impress staffers with tidbits from the dinner party or embassy reception he attended the night before.

Nussbaum's deputy, William Kennedy, was supposed to make sure everyone in the White House had been cleared by the FBI. But more than a year after Clinton had become president, roughly a hundred members of his staff had not complied with regulations that require them to answer questions about their finances and background in order to obtain a security clearance. The employees, including press secretary Dee Dee Myers, used temporary passes to enter the White House. In her job, Myers had daily access to classified information. Thus her refusal to comply was not only arrogant and sloppy, it most likely meant that the government's rules concerning access to classified information had been broken. Only when the case of accused spy Aldrich H. Ames broke did Myers finally agree to submit the required paperwork. The lapse not only illustrated the ineptitude of the White House counsel's office, it displayed the juvenile mind-set in the White House.

Bruce Lindsey, Clinton's childhood friend who was supposed to oversee the appointments process, was so disorganized that piles of resumes stacked helter-skelter on his desk kept spilling onto the floor. In intelligence circles, Anthony Lake, the national security adviser, was considered to be over his head and lacking in ideas or a coherent strategy. Clinton's wandering course in Somalia, Haiti, and Cuba represented but a few examples.

While Hillary Rodham Clinton was smart and professional, many of the problems—including the selection of Nussbaum and Kennedy as lawyers in the counsel's office—pointed back to her. Like Clinton's solution to gays in the military—they could serve as long as they did not admit to being gay—first ladies have usually influenced their husbands but rarely admitted to it. Dolley Madison got her husband to promote a War Department bookkeeper to chief accountant and to have Anthony Morris, a friend, sent to Spain on a diplomatic mission. She had another friend, Joel Barlow, named ambassador to France and managed to get the conscientious objector son of an old Quaker friend freed from prison. Millard Fillmore was said never to have taken an important step without running it by his wife, who was well read and informed on the topics of the day. Mary Todd Lincoln, even though she had no official role, liked to be addressed as "Mrs. President Lincoln." Frances Cleveland would sit in for her husband on speeches in the House, reporting back on what was said.[173]

As a public relations gesture, each first lady takes on a project that is usually forgotten as soon as she leaves the White House. Lady Bird Johnson promoted a campaign to improve America's landscape—the so-called Beautification Program. Pat Nixon talked up "volunteerism." Betty Ford spoke out in favor of liberalized abortion laws and promoted aid to the handicapped and retarded. Nancy Reagan supported a program against drug abuse among the young. Barbara Bush helped promote adult literacy programs.

Rosalynn Carter took a more active role, testifying before Congress on behalf of more funds for mental health programs and sitting in on Cabinet meetings. But only Hillary Clinton assumed an operational role, tackling reform of the health care system. Yet after her gaffe in saying that instead of becoming a professional woman she could have stayed home and baked cookies, Hillary Clinton decided to fade into the woodwork, mouthing nothing but banalities in public. In trying to promote the image of the helpful wife whose most controversial thought was that her husband should eat healthier food, Hillary Clinton was following a well-established White House tradition. Just as presidents are supposed to be decisive, in command, and upbeat, first ladies are supposed to be tenuous, adoring, and witless. As Mamie Eisenhower wrote when she turned eighty-two, every president and first lady "is an actor or actress. Nobody is completely himself. It isn't possible, especially in public life."

Briefly, Betty Ford broke that mold when "60 Minutes" asked her what she would say if her daughter, Susan Ford, came to her and said, "Mother, I'm having an affair." Betty Ford answered truthfully. "Well, I wouldn't be surprised," she said. "She's a perfectly normal human being . . . if she wanted to continue, I would certainly counsel and advise her on the subject."

The comment stirred tremendous controversy. The Los Angeles Police Department took issue with what she had said, a Texas minister denounced her for having a "gutter-type mentality," and the Women's Christian Temperance Union censured her. But support also poured into the White House. One woman wrote that Betty Ford kept "abreast of these changing times" and was aware that "what was once considered right and proper changes from generation to generation."[174]

Months later, Betty Ford's Harris poll rating had shot up from 50 percent before her statement to 75 percent.

But for the most part, first ladies prattle on about the history of the White House or the demands of being first lady. Barbara Bush was considered charmingly outspoken and independent because she said she would like to see Saddam Hussein hanged—he had, after all, called for her husband's death—and because she cooked her own spaghetti at their home in Kennebunkport and served it on paper plates.

Weeks after coming to the White House, Hillary Clinton had lunch with Jacqueline Kennedy. Through carefully orchestrated press appearances, Jackie had managed to develop an image as a culture maven—a charming intellectual with the perfect marriage. As it turned out, Camelot was pure fiction, a White House creation designed to conceal her desperately unhappy marriage, as illustrated by the president's compulsive womanizing. Despite marrying a man in public life, Jackie Kennedy devoted her life to dodging cameras.

During their lunch, Jackie Kennedy advised Hillary Clinton to keep Chelsea's life private. Hillary Clinton then issued orders that no one in the White House could disclose anything publicly about the first family's personal life, particularly about their daughter, Chelsea.

Despite the demands on their time, the Clintons have managed to devote themselves to Chelsea. Raymond Young, Clinton's former security director in Arkansas, said Clinton bawled him out when he delayed telling him that Chelsea's cocker spaniel, Zeck, had been run over by a car and killed.

"It happened about 10 P.M., and I didn't tell him until the next morning," Young said. "He and I were leaving to go to Georgia that morning. Hillary was in New York on business. Chelsea was in the governor's mansion. I said, 'I thought someone else would be there to take care of the problem.' He said, 'That isn't enough.' I didn't understand the emotion connected with it. I have never been close to a dog."

Hillary Clinton flew home early from New York to be with Chelsea, Young said.

But the idea that the president and his wife had a right to absolute privacy about their personal lives after seeking and obtaining the highest office in the land was another manifestation of the arrogance and inexperience of Clinton's immediate entourage.

"It shows naïveté," Reedy said. "After all, the first family is the United States. Americans personalize the president and his family. Hillary's situation is even more so because of the task force she has headed on health care problems. That means whatever claims she might have to privacy she has abdicated."

Belatedly, after the Whitewater affair had taken on the appearance of a full-blown scandal complete with the appointment of a special prosecutor, Hillary Clinton said she now realized that her desire to maintain privacy was unrealistic. In

189

a *Newsweek* interview in March 1994, she attributed her failure to respond more fully to Whitewater to not "understanding why [journalists] were pursuing what to me seems so insignificant" a matter. She said she regretted not focusing on it earlier "to try to deal with it."

Mrs. Clinton told the magazine that "I get my back up every so often" about having to answer questions she believes have no connection with her husband's public life. She suggested that also played a part in mistakes made in connection with responding to Whitewater.

"I really have been pulled kicking and screaming to the conclusion that if you choose to run for public office you give up any zone of privacy at all," she said—a realization most politicians come to long before they get to the White House.

But Hillary Clinton never did understand that if she and her husband wanted to achieve the highest office in the land, they would have to pay the price. She continued to resist any form of public disclosure, contributing to the appearance that the couple had something to hide in the Whitewater affair. Not until Lloyd Cutler temporarily took over the job of White House counsel after Nussbaum was forced out did Bill and Hillary Clinton begin to act like the national players they were supposed to be. Suddenly, both Clintons began responding to nasty press questions by saying, "I'm glad you asked that." And Hillary Clinton gave a press conference lasting more than an hour to respond to media questions about Whitewater.

While due in part to his own depression, the tragic suicide of White House Deputy Counsel Vincent Foster, Jr., was another symptom of the lack of sophistication of the White House staff. On the morning of July 20, 1993, Foster attended the announcement by Clinton of U.S. District Court Judge Louis J. Freeh to head the FBI. It appeared clear that Clinton's nomination of Judge Ruth Bader Ginsburg to the Supreme Court would encounter no difficulties in the Senate.

After the ceremony, Nussbaum, Clinton's counsel, was in his office switching television channels. On one channel, Ginsburg was sailing through her confirmation hearing. On the other, Freeh was drawing praise. Foster walked in.

190

"Take a look, Vince. Back-to-back homers," Nussbaum said.

"He didn't say anything," Nussbaum recalled. "I said, 'Vince, is something up?' He said, 'No, I just heard that you had the TV on. I wanted to see what you're watching.' "

After eating lunch at his desk, Foster told his colleagues in the White House at about 1 P.M. that he would be back later. A secretary offered him some M&M's. He said he would have them later.

What Foster did in the next several hours is not clear. But eventually he drove to Fort Marcy Park in McLean, Virginia. There, overlooking the Potomac River, he cocked a 1913 army Colt revolver and shot himself in the mouth. At 6 P.M., an unidentified man driving a white van notified the Park Police maintenance office at Turkey Run near Fort Marcy of a body in the park.

Since the fiascoes involving the White House travel office and a series of failed appointments, the staff had subjected itself to enormous pressure to avoid future blunders. Without the ability to deal on the national level, the staff became even more desperate as the strain increased. Despairing at the mistakes he had participated in, Foster, a former law partner of Hillary Clinton, blamed himself. Even though he was deputy counsel, Foster, as the Clintons' longtime friend and lawyer, had more clout than his boss, Bernard Nussbaum. He was considered the Clintons' "great protector" and the "Rock of Gibraltar," a wise counselor to the Clintons. Indeed, it was Foster who had instructed fellow Arkansan William Kennedy in the counsel's office to pressure the FBI to investigate the White House travel office by saying the White House would go to another agency if the FBI did not respond quickly. The fact that the *Wall Street Journal* had run silly editorials hinting at nonexistent conspiracies among Hillary Clinton's "legal cronies" from the Rose law firm in Little Rock added to the stress on Foster.

Anyone with Washington experience knows that such public attacks, whether justified or not, are part of the price one pays for accepting a job at the national level. Moreover, anyone who reads the *Wall Street Journal*, as Foster did, knows that the paper leads a schizophrenic existence. The news side is among the best in the country, with solid, incisive, honest reporting. The editorial side, run by Robert Bartley, espouses crackpot conservatism, a mixture of right-wing ideology, inaccurate reporting, and McCarthyism, as demonstrated by the editorials concocting conspiracy theories about Foster's former law partners.

With no evidence whatsoever, the *Journal* had accused Foster of cutting "some legal corners" in defending in court the closed meetings of Hillary Clinton's health care task force. By acting as a lawyer defending the government against a lawsuit charging that the closed meetings were illegal, the *Journal* claimed Foster had "struck a blow for separation of powers, executive authority, critics of the litigation explosion, and we dare say, even for the formulators of the Reagan White House's off-the-books Iran-contra operation." The paper went on acidly: "As for Iran-contra, we suspect that Vincent Foster and Ollie North might hit it off."

If one did not know better, one might suspect that the *Journal*'s editors had a third grader's appreciation of how the American legal system works. Following the paper's line of reasoning, lawyers defending any civil suit are engaging in improper conduct because they should know that they will lose and are therefore condoning illegal acts. In fact, the paper's editorialists are ideologues who found Oliver North's circumvention of congressional restrictions on the use of funds to support the contras perfectly acceptable if not laudable, while Foster's routine court defense of a client—in this case the Clinton administration—was contemptible.

Most people would shrug off such blathering, and several friends of Foster in the White House told him he should forget it. But foolish as the attacks were, they were mortal blows to Foster; he became obsessed with the idea that his reputation had been besmirched. The *Journal* ran two of its editorials during the week preceding Foster's death. On July 14, 1993, the paper complained that the "Rose clique from Little Rock" had shown a "willingness to cut many legal corners." A few days later, Foster asked Nussbaum whether the Rose lawyers were hurting the administration.

"He said it looks like we've become liabilities here," Nussbaum said. "I said that's crazy. He took it seriously, though, obviously."[175]

The *Journal* ran another inane attack the day before his death.

A month earlier, Foster gave the commencement address at the University of Arkansas Law School. His reputation was clearly on his mind.

"Treat every pleading, every brief, every contract, every letter, every daily task as if your career will be judged on it," he advised. "There is no victory, no advantage, no fee, no favor which is worth even a blemish on your reputation for intellect and integrity. Nothing travels faster than an accusation that another lawyer's word is no good. . . . Dents to the reputation in the legal profession are irreparable."

"He couldn't understand why the press was the way it was," said Walter Pincus, a *Washington Post* reporter to whom Foster confided his anxieties. "It was a sense that people would print something that was wrong, and that other people would repeat it. I'd say, 'You can't let the press run you, get your goat; you have to go on. This is how the game is played.' He'd say, 'Fine.' "[176]

In April 1993, Foster told a newspaper reporter from the *Arkansas Democrat-Gazette*, "I did not have a full appreciation of the variety of issues that the office would face, nor the time demands."

To be sure, the White House counsel's office, like the legal counsel for any large corporation or agency, deals with a wide range of issues. In the White House, Foster had dealt with such diverse matters as the impact of a new health care system on malpractice law, the legal policy on Haitian refugees, the legal implications of a deficit trust fund, and how committees on White House redecoration should be set up. He had worked on establishing blind trusts for the Clintons, sifting candidates for federal judgeships, and advising wives of government officials on which charities they could participate in.

"I've had meetings with the president that started at 10:30 P.M.," Foster complained to the Arkansas paper. "A normal day is not normal. There are day-to-day policy decisions that have to be made . . . that affect millions of Americans and sometimes billions of dollars. That's pretty heady stuff."

Foster told the interviewer the worst part of the job was the effect it had had on his family. His youngest son, Brugh, had wanted to finish high school in Little Rock, so Foster's wife, Lisa, had remained with him until the end of the school year. After visiting her husband in Washington, Lisa Foster had advised a friend: "Don't go up there."

Skip Rutherford, an aide to chief of staff McLarty, recalled Foster telling him a week before his death: "No one back in Little Rock could know how hard this is. You try to be at work by seven in the morning and sometimes it's ten at night when you walk out just dog-tired. About the time you're thinking, 'What a load,' you turn around and see the White House lit up, and the awe of where you are and what you're doing hits you. It makes you realize it's worth it."

Even the fact that Foster had had to give up his membership in the Country Club of Little Rock was too great a load for Foster to handle. The club is a gathering place for Little Rock's power elite. In March 1992, Bill Clinton, who was not a member, was photographed playing golf there with his friend Webster Hubbell. Clinton was then engaged in the primary race, and going to the all-white club caused a momentary flurry of criticism. Clinton said he was wrong to have played at a club that has no black members, and the controversy passed.

When the Senate Judiciary Committee quizzed Hubbell during his confirmation hearings as associate attorney general, his membership in the club became an issue. In the past, the committee had agreed that membership in all-white clubs was not grounds for disqualification from high office. But freshman Carol Moseley-Braun, the first African-American woman in the Senate, objected. Although Hubbell had a number of testimonials from blacks who supported him, he resigned from the club. Foster, whose position in the White House does not require Senate confirmation, then felt impelled to quit also. Foster had to telephone his wife to tell her to cancel a tennis match at the club that afternoon.

This minor inconvenience for the privilege of serving in gov-

194

ernment upset Foster still more, particularly since he and Hubbell had unsuccessfully tried to integrate the club.

"On the one hand, he couldn't understand why they, who had tried to integrate the club for the first time, had to give it up," a friend of Foster's said. "On the other hand, he blamed himself for not seeing it coming."

Foster did not come equipped with the mature perspective needed to balance the personal and professional aspects of his life. In Arkansas, Foster was one of the state's leading lawyers. He could do all his work, give it all the contemplation it deserved, and still be home for dinner with his family. He was making $300,000 a year. But in Washington, sterling a man as he was, Foster was another Clinton White House staffer over his head.

According to Dr. Brown, the psychiatrist who has been consulted by dozens of White House aides, the fact that Foster and most of Clinton's key aides are old buddies makes things even worse. Because of their personal loyalty, they become even more emotionally upset when they embarrass the president.

"You have a situation where the chief of staff [McLarty] is a close friend of the president, and the tragic flaw is he is an extension of Clinton," Brown said before McLarty was replaced. "He does not have the detachment of having served other politicians. That does not provide the kind of wisdom and separation that a person like Foster would have needed to go to if you accept that he overreacted to feeling responsible for things having not gone quite right. He feels responsible for the country and the president going to hell. He didn't have anyone he could talk to in that White House who would put his arm around his shoulder and say, 'It's all right. This will pass, the president will recover.' There is nobody there. They are all extensions of Clinton."

Clinton's staff compounded the tragedy by initially covering up the fact that Foster was known to have been depressed. After Foster's death, Clinton's press office said there had been no indication Foster had been depressed. A week later, the White House said he had taken to working in his bed with the shades drawn. A few days before his death, Foster had sought and received Desyrel, a medication for depression, from a physician in Little Rock. Desyrel is the brand name for the chemical compound trazodone hydrochloride, which boosts the level of serotonin in the brain. Low levels of the chemical have been linked to depression and incidents of suicide. According to the *Physicians' Desk Reference*, the drug may be taken if four of the following eight symptoms of depression are present: "change in appetite, change in sleep, psychomotor agitation or retardation, loss of interest in usual activities or decrease in sex drive, increased fatiguability, feelings of guilt or worthlessness, slowed thinking or impaired concentration, suicidal ideation or attempts."

According to friends, Foster had suffered from at least four of the signs of depression. His appetite had been off; since coming to Washington, he had lost fifteen pounds. He had had difficulty sleeping. He had had feelings of guilt and worthlessness. His concentration at work had been diminishing.

The night before his death, Foster had taken one fifty-milligram dose of the drug. Typically, the drug takes a week to two weeks to have any effect. Foster also had compiled a list of two psychiatrists in the Washington area, a list that he had in his pocket when he died. Having already undercut its own credibility during the Travelgate episode, Clinton's press office lost all believability by issuing conflicting statements about Foster's death.

The White House again committed a serious error by waiting for thirty hours before turning over to investigating authorities the remains of a note Foster had written to himself. Foster had written the note after his wife had urged him ten days before his death to write down what was troubling him. In the note, Foster expressed dismay at his life in Washington. Many of his complaints were unfounded or exaggerated.

In the note, Foster wrote, "The FBI lied in their report to the AG [Attorney General Janet Reno]."[177]

This was a reference to an FBI report that recounted the pressure the bureau had received from the White House to investigate the travel office. As might be expected, the White House had a different version of events, both in terms of the words used and the tone. While no one can be sure without a tape recording of the precise words used and the way they were conveyed, it is not every day that the FBI claims to have been pressured by the White House. Just how the message was conveyed is not of great consequence. It is clear that it happened and that it represented yet another instance of the unprofessionalism of the Clinton White House, in this case of its lawyers.

In his note, Foster went on to complain, "The press is covering up the illegal benefits they received from the travel office."

This was a reference to the fact that some members of the press have avoided paying Customs duties on gifts purchased overseas. However, there has been no evidence that the travel office participated in this evasion. Rather, a limited number of reporters acting on their own have failed to declare their gifts when asked to do so by Customs officers.

"The GOP has lied and misrepresented its knowledge and role and covered up a prior investigation," Foster went on. This was apparently a reference to the fact that when John Rogers was Reagan's aide for administration, he ordered an audit of the travel office and found—just as Clinton's White House did—that bookkeeping practices were sloppy.

"The usher's office plotted to have excessive costs incurred, taking advantage of Kaki and HRC [Little Rock interior designer Kaki Hockersmith and Hillary Rodham Clinton]," the note said.

This was a reference to a difference in estimated costs for the redecorating of the Oval Office, the Treaty Room, and portions of the White House residence ordered by the Clinton administration. For example, the rug in the Oval Office was replaced with one with a darker shade of blue. The new drapes are gold with blue trim instead of blue, and the fabric is heavier. The two white high-back armchairs near the fireplace have been re-covered in gold fabric, and the two cream couches were covered with burgundy-and-cream striped silk. The original estimate of the cost, which was to be raised privately, was $250,000. Because of deadlines imposed by Hockersmith and the addition of other items to be redecorated, the cost was raised to $337,000.

While these complaints were largely baseless, others had validity.

"The WSJ [*Wall Street Journal*] editors lie without consequence," Foster wrote. "The public will never believe the innocence of the Clintons and their loyal staff. . . . I was not meant for the job or the spotlight of public life in Washington. Here ruining people is considered sport."

Foster was right both about the *Wall Street Journal* editorialists, who for decades have been a concern of the reporters and editors on the news side of the paper, and the attitude in Washington toward ruining people. In Washington, the coin of the realm is power, not money. Going back to George Washington, who was criticized for acting royally, anyone with power is considered a fair target of politicians and the press, which feed off controversy for their existence. But that is also a fair description of how a democracy by its nature works. In return for the power they are given, politicians and the press recognize that they must remain above suspicion or they will become the hockey pucks in the latest controversy or scandal. Anyone who is not prepared to play by those rules does not deserve to serve in a position of power. For only by recognizing that anyone can become a target of public condemnation can people in power be held accountable.

If Foster was correct when he complained about the way Washington works, he was even more accurate when he acknowledged in the first paragraph of his note his own shortcomings.

"I made mistakes from ignorance, inexperience, and overwork," he said.

After writing the note, Foster apparently tore it up. A week after Foster's death, an aide to Nussbaum found the twenty-seven pieces of the note at the bottom of one of Foster's briefcases. A twenty-eighth piece was missing. The note obviously had a bearing on the circumstances of his death. One does not need to be a lawyer or a high-ranking government official to know that such evidence should be turned over immediately to investigators—in this case, the U.S. Park Police. The Park Police had jurisdiction because Foster's body had been found in his car in a park owned by the Park Service. Despite its relevance, Nussbaum and the rest of the counsel's office held off on turning it over to the police. Like ten-year-olds, they apparently had no idea what they should do with it.

In explaining the delay, Dee Dee Myers on July 29, 1993, said top White House officials had decided to show the note to Clinton and to Foster's family before sharing it with investigators. If in fact the counsel's office had planned this sequence of events, it was another example of the parochialism of the Clinton staff. In thinking that giving the note to the president and Foster's family was more important than giving it to investigators, the aides displayed a shocking lack of judgment. But given the record of the Clinton White House, it was more likely that they did not give the note initially to investigators because they had no idea what to do, thought the matter was their own personal business, and did not have the wit to understand that they were now working for the government and that their business was the public's business. That was confirmed when Clinton himself explained the delay to *Newsweek* by saying, "Most of us who make decisions around here are still grieving about this. We're not capable of calculating the ins and outs of this."[178]

That kind of explanation is the kind one might expect from a private, unsophisticated individual—not from a lawyer and the president of the United States. If the White House could not carry out its responsibilities properly when a staff member committed suicide, it was doubtful it could run the country properly. The difference was that the public rarely got a chance to see the way decisions were made when they involved weightier policy matters. The Foster suicide laid bare the amateurish nature of the White House staff for all to see.

When it seemed no more mistakes relating to the suicide could possibly be made, the White House made another one by failing to disclose the note's contents immediately to the press. This time the excuse was that the note was being investigated by the authorities. But nothing precluded the White House from deciding on its own to release it. By keeping it secret, Clinton's aides prolonged the controversy and deepened the mystery over

Foster's death. Almost every day, the media learned an additional detail about the letter and ran stories dredging up the matter all over again. Most of the stories exaggerated the note's contents, saying that, in effect, it was a letter of resignation.

" 'I can't believe I gave up a life to put up with this crap . . . I can't believe I left Little Rock for this bullshit,' " *Newsweek* quoted Clinton aides as paraphrasing Foster's note.

Instead of one story reporting the contents of the note, the White House action meant there were weeks of stories. These stories helped fuel rumors of vast conspiracies that Foster might have been engaged in, including that organized crime figures from Europe had knocked him off. But the Park Police firmly concluded that Foster had killed himself. According to the Park Police, the gunshot entered Foster's mouth and severely damaged his brain stem, which controls heartbeat and breathing. The gun was found in Foster's hand. Residue from firing the gunshot was found on the skin of his hand.

The report by Whitewater special counsel Robert B. Fiske, Jr., confirmed that Foster committed suicide after a depression that began before he had begun working in the White House.

After the White House finally turned Foster's note over to investigators, the Justice Department announced that because the note claimed the FBI had "lied" in its report recounting the pressure the White House had applied to the bureau, the FBI's Office of Professional Responsibility would investigate to see if the FBI's report had accurately conveyed the White House's message to the bureau. Besides that investigation, the FBI was looking into whether any travel office employees had, in fact, engaged in fraud and whether any White House officials had been guilty of conflict of interest in selecting World Wide to handle travel arrangements for the White House.

The FBI quickly established that, contrary to the belief of Clinton's aides, the White House travel office employees had not engaged in fraud. Rather, they had been guilty of sloppy bookkeeping.

"There was sloppiness, and the White House made it into a big event," an FBI official with knowledge of the investigation said. "You had mass hysteria."

As a result of the White House decision, five of the aides were paid while on leave, and Congress passed an amendment to a Transportation Department bill to provide them with $150,000 to pay their legal fees. Thus, instead of saving taxpayer funds, the decision to fire them actually wound up costing the government more money.

In the last days before his death, Foster had become traumatized by the prospect of new inquiries into the travel office episode. Besides the FBI investigations, Congressional Republicans were looking for blood, and Representative Jack Brooks, the chairman of the House Judiciary Committee, had been asking if reprimands of White House aides had been sufficient punishment. Foster had been looking into the possibility of hiring a lawyer to defend himself during these investigations.[179]

But unlike the Nixon White House, the Clinton White House was not mendacious. It was unlikely Clinton aides were trying to cover anything up. As Foster said in his note, "I did not knowingly violate any law or standard of conduct. No one in the White House, to my knowledge, violated any law or standard of conduct. . . . There was no intent to benefit any individual or specific group."

Rather, the delay in making public the note, not to mention the blundering that had led to the controversy in the first place, were examples of the sophomoric nature of Clinton's staff. It is not enough for those in the White House to obey the law and follow ethical standards. To function in that superheated atmosphere, one must also have common sense. Repeatedly, the Clinton staff demonstrated that it lacked that basic asset. Over time, the staff's lack of competence, when combined with the arrogance that the White House normally breeds, could be expected to result in far more serious problems.

Stephanopoulos illustrated the callowness of Clinton's staff when he remarked that he had not realized how much public attention the White House gets.

"The White House is even more of a fishbowl and a pressure cooker than I thought," he whined to the *New York Times*. "Every single gesture is scrutinized, which you know intellectually but you don't know in your bones. You can't know."

Having lived and worked in Washington, Stephanopoulos could not have been unaware of the kinds of pressures the White House generates. But because of arrested maturity or inherent shallowness, he never absorbed or appreciated its significance. Having previously achieved nothing more than being a congressional aide, Stephanopoulos lacked the kind of inner strength and wisdom needed to help guide a president.

"Nixon and Kennedy and Truman were not afraid of having superstrong people," said Dr. Brown, the psychiatrist who consults for the Secret Service. "Show me an Acheson or a Kissinger. You don't see them in the Clinton White House."

"Clinton has an awful lot to learn," George Reedy said. "I think he came to Washington with the feeling Washington was a larger Little Rock, but it's not. The German philosopher Hegel said differences in quantity make differences in quality. That's true in politics. Washington has been there for two hundred years now. It has developed certain ways of doing things. If you don't handle them that way, you aren't going to get anything done."

In the end, Clinton was to blame. Having selected a parochial staff, he did not know how to manage it or the rest of the government. That became evident almost immediately when he delayed replacing William S. Sessions as FBI director. Even though everyone in the White House said Sessions would have to go because of the string of abuses he had engaged in, Clinton let the process drag on for more than six months. As in the case of the White House travel office, no one in the White House would take the time to carefully study the issue, to read the Justice Department's report on Sessions's abuses, or to find out what effect the delay was having on the FBI. At the bureau, morale plummeted, and the administrative, personnel, budgetary, and policy sides of the agency became paralyzed. By dragging his feet, Clinton telegraphed a message that officials could abuse their position as long as they are high enough up in government and have some perceived political support. Clinton was as indifferent to the effects of his delay as he was to the need to be on time for appointments.

While he mastered issues and facts like the Rhodes Scholar

he was, Clinton tended to micromanage just as Carter had. A few weeks after he took office, Clinton was returning to the White House from a jog when he saw a GSA engineer walking toward the old Executive Office Building.

"Clinton came over and asked him his name and what he does," said Price, the GSA manager. "He said he was the chief engineer and takes care of heating and air-conditioning. He asked what he was going to do now. He said he was going to check on these chillers."

"Do you mind if I go with you?" the president asked, indicating he wished to watch how the engineer did his work.

Clinton then spent the next half hour learning about the intricacies of the White House heating and air-conditioning system. While Clinton's interest in what the little people do may be endearing, it is a luxury a president cannot afford. Instead of relying on his staff to filter proposals, Clinton liked to wade into the details of policy initiatives himself, asking for more information and scribbling nearly indecipherable notes in the margins of memos. Clinton routinely held White House meetings that went on for two hours and accomplished very little. Balancing the value of obtaining minute details against the harm from letting proposals languish, Clinton tended to make the wrong choices.

Raymond Young, a captain in the Arkansas State Police who was Clinton's director of security from 1983 to 1992, said Clinton was usually late because of a need to make contact.

"He wants to shake hands with everyone," Young said. "He would be the last man to leave a function and would then go through the kitchen and shake hands with the cook and people cleaning up. I've seen him stop and talk to people with health and financial problems. He tries to help them. He is probably late because he tries to see everyone."[180]

Young said Clinton delayed making decisions because, "He would want to talk to everyone involved and would try to please everyone. Sometimes you have to make a decision. You can't please everyone."

Clinton's own lack of discipline was reflected in his staff, which tended to put out the latest fires without focusing on the future.

In this ad hoc atmosphere, job titles meant very little. Health care policy was not decided by the Health and Human Services Department but by free-floating White House adviser Ira Magaziner. The president's management reform initiative was not run by the Office of Management and Budget but by an aide to Al Gore. The czar of Russian policy was not National Security Adviser Anthony Lake but Clinton's friend, former journalist Strobe Talbott.

"From what you see on the outside, it is a severely under-organized presidency; there is almost a contempt for routine," said Fred Greenstein, a Princeton political scientist. That, he said, is "what gave us the Bay of Pigs with Kennedy."

"They need a mechanism that disciplines him and his use of time, which is his most important resource, and forces the process to deal with issues that it needs to deal with," said Dick Cheney, who was Ford's chief of staff and later became Bush's secretary of defense. "Maybe there's a need for a couple wise old heads in there. There is something to be said for experience."

White House chiefs of staff usually focus the president and his staff, but as an amiable childhood friend of Clinton, McLarty was in no position to serve that role.

"The White House is usually populated by very brainy, hard-driving, aggressive men and women—some pragmatists and some ideologues, some young, some old, some military, some civilians, from different factions of the party," said Brad Patterson, a former White House aide in three administrations. "You have a lot of disagreement within the White House staff. Mix that in with their big egos, and you have an incendiary situation when it comes to formulating policy. To get issues focused for the president is the job of the chief of staff. The chief of staff has to be a real son of a bitch."

Because of McLarty's lack of administrative skills, Clinton kept propping him up with deputies who were supposed to "make the trains run on time," as the Clinton people liked to put it. But after fewer than six months in the job, Roy Neel, the first such deputy, ran screaming from the White House, confiding that his job of bringing discipline to the staff was hopeless.

Eighteen months after he took office, Clinton finally replaced McLarty with Leon E. Panetta, his budget director. While Panetta had more savvy than McLarty, it was doubtful he could do much to change the chaotic and confused way the president made decisions.

There was no question that Clinton worked hard. Raymond Young, his former chief of security in Arkansas, recalled him starting work at 6 A.M. and working until 9 P.M. or midnight seven days a week. In the White House, Clinton often stayed up until 2 A.M. working in his office. He then took a nap in the residence for half an hour to an hour around 3 P.M. every day. Rather than not working hard enough, the problem was what he did with his time.

"What has become clear is that Clinton isn't focused and is passive," Dr. Brown said. "He is reactive as opposed to having that inner center. He gets kicks out of interacting with people on the talk shows. He clearly is intoxicated and overwhelmed as anybody might be by the thrills of the presidency—the fame, the excitement, the importance. He is not doing the hard work of being a CEO, of thinking, planning, and strategizing. He is a mediocre guy getting his kicks out of being the top politician in the land."[181]

Even Clinton's abilities as a lawyer left something to be desired. When he informed Sessions that he was fired, Clinton neglected to say when the termination would take effect— something any competent lawyer would be sure to include. When the president learned that Sessions had remained in his office after receiving his call, Clinton embarrassingly had to call him a second time to tell him his termination was effective "immediately."

By June 1993, Clinton had become the butt of more jokes on the late-night television shows than even Dan Quayle. His popularity had dipped to 38 percent. In true Nixon style, he began trying to plug leaks, deciding that the media and disloyal staffers were at the root of his problems.

"Presidents, like any politicians, are warriors," Reedy said. "They don't use guns, not in our country, but they substitute votes and arguments for those guns and bombs. Like a general, they see the world as those who are for them and those who are against them. They have to maintain secrecy about their operations. If they are engaged in a battle, they'll distort things to the enemy so the enemy will make mistakes. That's the way presidents are."

Like other Clinton staffers, Vincent Foster had fallen victim to the paranoia that so often overtakes the White House, and he helped to spread it. He and other Clinton loyalists believed that a cabal of career White House employees—from Secret Service agents to maids and butlers to the fired travel office employees—were out to do them in. Whenever a leak occurred or a critical story appeared, Foster and other aides blamed the professional staff. For example, when the *Wall Street Journal* obtained a computer listing of the then secret members of Clinton's health care task force, health czar Ira Magaziner immediately concluded—without a shred of evidence—that the Secret Service had done it.

"Vince had the sense that there were these permanent occupants, they were fat and lazy, and they hated the Clintons," *Newsweek* quoted a White House aide as saying. Displaying his own paranoia, the aide added, "These are not the ravings of a madman."[182]

The truth is that White House leaks usually come from high-level political appointees who use the press to try to manipulate policy decisions or bolster their own positions.

"This paranoia about leaks happens in any White House," Reedy said. "I'm doubtful that the permanent staff of the White House is the major source of the leaks. The major sources of leaks really are people that are battling for better positions in the White House. You can leak stories that put others in a bad light or put you in a good light or that will irritate the president against someone. For example, if Johnson was considering anyone for a high job in the government and the story leaked, he would call off the appointment. I'm pretty certain a couple of people got queered that way."

Leaks are but a manifestation of power struggles within the White House.

"The leaks are from the palace infighting in which people use the press as one of the weapons in the battle," Reedy said.

Like staffers from previous administrations, the Clinton staff entered the White House with a hostile attitude toward anyone who had not been in the trenches with them during the campaign. Much of the bungling of the Clinton White House could be traced back to that attitude. For example, the White House fired the travel office employees in part because they were seen as being, as a White House memo put it, "overly pro-press." Foster then urged associate counsel Kennedy to pressure the FBI into investigating. In his note, Foster spoke of the Clinton staff's "loyalty" and said the FBI had "lied" about the contact. He surmised that the White House usher's office had allowed costs for redecorating to escalate in order to embarrass Clinton.

"It was sort of a setup to embarrass us," agreed another Clinton staffer.

The paranoia began with Clinton himself, who called his former Arkansas security chief Raymond Young to complain that the White House domestic staff had leaked the story that Hillary Clinton had thrown a lamp at him—a story Clinton denied.

"He was pretty upset," said Young, who now works for the federal government. "He called me concerned about what the Secret Service was saying. He said he traced it to some domestic help. He said it didn't occur." In fact, Young said, "He didn't know who leaked it."[183]

The truth was that Gary Walters, the chief usher, was so obsequious toward any president that if Clinton had burped, he would never have told anyone. By and large, the White House domestic staff was so loyal to each president that they were harder for the press to penetrate than the FBI or CIA. Nonetheless, this free-floating mistrust of the professional staff and the press affected the way they viewed Clinton. Like Carter, Clinton came into office with a chip on his shoulder, one that created even more obstacles for him.

"The paranoia comes from the isolation and the power and the perks," said Dr. Brown.

207

The silly games played by Clinton and his aides said as much about their intelligence as their judgment. The fact is that when people guess about reporters' sources, they are almost always wrong. Only dull-witted people blindly accuse others of misdeeds without any evidence. Yet Clinton acted on his unfounded suspicions, transferring John W. Magaw, the director of the Secret Service, to head the Alcohol, Tobacco, and Firearms Bureau. White House aides let on that the reason was Clinton's belief that it was the Secret Service that had leaked information about his personal life.

Just when it seemed the Clinton presidency was about to self-destruct, Clinton made a move widely hailed as brilliant—hiring David R. Gergen as counselor to the president. Gergen, who had served the Nixon, Ford, and Reagan administrations, was a spin master, an insider who knew all about the presidency and how to package it using symbolism.

Gergen and Clinton had known each other since 1984, having shared New Year's weekends together at the Renaissance Weekend gatherings of political, news media, and business leaders on South Carolina's Hilton Head Island. Over the years, Clinton had called on Gergen for advice. Besides his expertise at spin doctoring, Gergen knew how to ingratiate himself with the powerful. On the night of Clinton's disastrously long speech nominating Michael S. Dukakis for president in 1988, Gergen slipped a note to the then Arkansas governor. It said, "Chin up. A lot of your friends out there think you're terrific."

But in the months before he was hired, Gergen the journalist had given Clinton failing marks. As editor-at-large of *U.S. News & World Report*, he had written that the Clinton administration had gone from "poor to perilous," lacked a clear philosophy, and had a "wobbly domestic policy" that threatened to infect the foreign arena as well.

". . . the president himself has kidded that his cabinet looks like America but his staff looks like a Head Start program," Gergen said on ABC's "Nightline." "As much as I think he needs a few people of much greater experience . . . I think there's another problem that is probably deeper and that is, more than people, he needs a set of principles so that people can understand what he is doing."

Gergen had just concluded a speech at Louisiana State University critiquing the Clinton administration when he returned a call to McLarty from a pay phone at a gas station.

"We'd like you to come on board," he said.

On May 29, 1993, Clinton announced Gergen's appointment. Serving as Clinton's de facto chief of staff, Gergen immediately began turning things around, undoing much of what the Clinton staff had done in the previous six months. The most obvious change was Gergen's reversal of the self-defeating policy of treating reporters as pariahs.

"The only truth any president is exposed to is the press," Reedy said. "Every president dismisses the press as biased. Every president back to George Washington has gotten into a fight with the press except perhaps Ford. They look on the press as the enemy, and when they read a story, it's to figure out how to counter it. They always assume that anything critical being written about them is because the press hates them. That's because everyone else is obsequious to them."[184]

But unlike most other presidents, Clinton had picked a fight with the press early on, as he was entering the White House. Most presidents do not assume an adversarial posture with the press until later in their administrations, and none in recent memory has enunciated shunning the national press as policy.

Well before Gergen's appointment, Michael Deaver, Reagan's communications director, had told the *Wall Street Journal* that while Clinton might have thought he did not need the press, when his approval rating dipped—as it later did—the president would be "having them up to the residence for cocktails or having them out for dinner."

Sure enough, Gergen not only lifted the prohibition on letting reporters wander into the offices of the White House communications staff, he began inviting journalists and publishers to small dinners with Clinton and his wife. All of a sudden, Katherine Graham, chairman of the Washington Post Co.; Jack Nelson, Washington bureau chief of the *Los Angeles Times*; and R. W. Apple, Jr., Washington bureau chief of the *New York*

Times, were guests of the Clintons. Instead of snubbing them, Clinton invited White House regulars to a barbecue at the White House. Later, when vacationing on Martha's Vineyard, Clinton threw a party for the press. Gergen arranged the same private meetings for Clinton's political adversaries. For example, he set up a dinner for Clinton with Senator Bob Dole. He also made sure that Dole's wife, Elizabeth, who heads the Red Cross, was invited to a meeting Clinton held in St. Louis to discuss how the government would help communities ravaged by floods.

Gergen knew that Washington is an insular town where social contacts can be more important than policy issues.

"This town works to an extraordinary degree on human chemistry," Gergen would say, "who you know, who you trust. If you don't get that, you don't understand how this town works."

Gergen knew how to schmooze reporters, making them feel like valued insiders, bolstering their egos, admitting to his own mistakes or shortcomings. He would put his own spin on stories by leaking them to reporters before they were announced publicly. He would pass along tidbits, such as the fact that after ordering an attack on Iraq for having plotted to kill George Bush, Clinton watched a movie with his wife, then slept for a solid eight hours. This conveyed the image of a self-confident commander in chief. Then Gergen laid on a stop in flood-stricken Iowa en route to a meeting in Tokyo to show the president was concerned about domestic problems even while attending to foreign affairs. After Clinton gave his state of the union address in January 1994, Gergen told the *Washington Post* that Clinton had done a *USA Today* crossword puzzle on the way over to Capitol Hill. This was meant to show that Clinton was an ordinary fellow, not a policy wonk, who was not overawed by his responsibilities.

Meanwhile, Gergen advised Clinton to cut down on his well-publicized cavorting with Hollywood types, including producer Harry Thomason, who had characterized the amount of money he might get from obtaining the White House travel business as being the equivalent in his income bracket to earnings from a lemonade stand.

Within days of Gergen's hiring, the new strategy began working. Where before the Clinton administration could do nothing right, now the press was full of stories that portrayed the president as a forceful leader. Even when Clinton grotesquely violated protocol at a dinner given for him by President Kim Young Sam of South Korea, the press buried the story. Because of obviously poor staff work, Clinton referred to the wife of the president as Mrs. Kim. In Korea, a woman keeps her maiden name, which in this case was Mrs. Sohn. When Clinton stepped to the microphone to give a speech, he invited a translator to stand between him and Kim, another gross snub. In South Korea, it is an insult for anyone to stand between two heads of state. Then, when Clinton realized the translator was translating from his printed speech rather than what he was actually saying, Clinton skipped part of the speech, confusing members of the audience who had the printed version.

In earlier days, the press might have run the story on page one. But the *New York Times* referred to the repeated gaffes only in a few paragraphs in a jump, while the *Washington Post* ran an Associated Press story on the incident on page A-19.

Helen Thomas, the dean of White House reporters, cautiously ventured that relations were beginning to improve.

"I think definitely it's lightened up a lot," Thomas said a month after Gergen began spreading his charm. "There's been a lot of give and take on both sides, and a lot of the tension is gone. It doesn't mean that this is paradise . . . but I think everybody feels more accommodating."

Instead of being ostracized, she had been asked to sit next to Clinton at one of the White House dinners. When she asked Clinton to respond at a press conference to Senator Robert Dole's rebuttal to Clinton's nationwide address on his budget package, Clinton said, "My response to Senator Dole's rebuttal is to wish you a happy birthday." She had just turned seventy-three.

While the journalists would deny even to themselves that Clinton's belated coziness had had any effect, the fact is that journalists are human beings. When doors are slammed in their faces, they cannot help but let it influence how they perceive the people who have shut them out. When treated with respect, they will tend to give people the benefit of the doubt on subjective issues. When it comes to evaluating a president, nearly every issue is subjective.

Even Travelgate might never have arisen had Clinton not alienated the press. After all, every new administration replaces some White House employees with its own appointees. On the surface, the firings of seven travel office employees could have been considered part of a president's prerogatives. Faced with constant deadlines and an endless stream of possible stories to pursue, journalists have to decide where to focus their energies. If a president is stiffing them, they will be more likely to focus on the negative side. That decision may not be an act of retribution. Rather, journalists honestly believe that a president who is not open with them probably is hiding something. Therefore, journalists who are shut out by presidents become more suspicious when an action such as the firing of seven employees occurs. Conversely, in cooperating with journalists, presidents and their aides are able to fill their reports with self-serving observations that might otherwise not appear in their stories.

To probe a president's personal life would be considered an act of war, a breach of the rules of the game as developed over the years. It means a journalist or media outlet may be banned from having access to the leaks and behind-the-scenes tidbits that the media crave. Similarly, writing a tough story about the fact that the president had lied in claiming he would reduce the White House staff by 25 percent would also deviate from the range of criticism considered acceptable by the White House.

For the most part, reporters have integrity and do not consciously decide to ignore sensitive areas because they fear the consequences of being cut off. But faced with the amount of time that would be required to take an investigative approach, it is easy for them to rationalize to themselves working on less taxing stories instead. Since Watergate, the change in the perceived importance of the press has meant the White House and other centers of power try to woo editors and publishers even more than before. That coziness, along with the intimidating effect of an increase in libel suits, has led to the virtual disappearance of investigative reporting of any kind at most major newspapers.

Eugene L. Roberts, Jr., the former executive editor of the *Philadelphia Inquirer*, related what happened when he tried to help a student from Japan study how investigative reporting was done in the United States. Except at a handful of papers, the student "found it difficult to find reporters who were spending time on projects," Roberts said. "Some investigative reporters had been reassigned. Some were leaving journalism. Still others were retiring. All gave the same reason. Their newspapers had lost interest in in-depth reporting."

"I interviewed quite a number of investigative reporters in this country for this project," the student, Susumu Shimoyama, said. He found they all described themselves in the same way: as "dinosaurs."[185]

Even during the Watergate era, the national staff of the *Washington Post* looked down their noses at the kind of investigative reporting practiced by Bob Woodward and Carl Bernstein. It was considered unseemly, ungentlemanly, even rude. Then, as today, the herd instinct governed as well. No one wanted to stray from the pack into possibly risky areas that required extensive research to pin down.

"They grind you down," Howard Kurtz's *Media Circus* quoted John Yang, a *Washington Post* reporter who has covered the White House, as saying, "When you travel, the logistics are so difficult and convoluted. You have incredible delays. They have a 5 A.M. baggage call for a 10 A.M. speech. They drain all the curiosity and initiative out of you, so when they come out and tell you ridiculous things in the pressroom, you say, 'Okay, okay,' and just write them down."

Unconsciously, Jeffrey Birnbaum, who covers the White House for the *Wall Street Journal*, revealed in a January 1994 C-SPAN interview just how much control the Clinton White House exercises over the press. To show that the Clinton White House goes out of its way to cooperate with the paper, he said someone in the press office is assigned to make sure the paper's calls are returned by the end of the day.

That, after all, is the job of the press office. But having become inured to White House manipulation, Birnbaum saw this self-serving crumb—the White House returns calls only so it can push its own agenda—as evidence that the Clinton press office favors his paper.

"You're preoccupied by trivia, and I think that's by design," said Michel McQueen, who previously covered the White House for the *Wall Street Journal.* "You're running around all day covering idiotic events. They keep you moving so quickly you don't have time to talk to anybody."

So, in covering Clinton, reporters continued to focus where every president wants them to focus—on their political activities. When they occasionally stray into reporting on the human sides of presidents, journalists tend to soften characterizations of negative traits as "presidential" or, in the case of Clinton, "Clintonian." For example, in recounting one of Clinton's temper tantrums, a *Wall Street Journal* story said White House aides "who have lived with such Clintonian eruptions for months relish the memory of the first time the presidential lava began flowing . . ." Thus, instead of sounding vengeful, childish, and arrogant, Clinton came across as magisterial.[186]

Fearful of the possible consequences, those who know the human sides of presidents staunchly participate in the cover-up. Even after they have left the White House, they hope they will be called back someday and so they keep mum.

"They don't want to bring up any embarrassment," a Secret Service agent said. "They still think they are going to have a role down the line."

But only through understanding the personal side of a president can anyone make sense of his policies and the way they are carried out. Rather than being brilliant, Clinton's decision to hire Gergen was what previous presidents had done routinely—hire competent help. And while journalists were now invited to intimate White House dinners, they still were given spin, just as they had been given fluff in previous administrations. Reporters interviewed McLarty for hours without ever finding out anything new or insightful, much less critical, about the president.

"This is a difficult issue," McLarty, Clinton's kindergarten classmate, would say when asked about the latest controversy surrounding Clinton. "That decision has not been made," he would allow about another issue. "There are days when you wish you had done things differently," he would pontificate when asked about the latest horror story in the White House.[187]

If handed such self-serving prattle by the head of another agency or company, bored reporters would run away shrieking. But because of the power and access he had, journalists continued to listen to McLarty or his successors and to report what they said as if it were profound.

"The White House does not provide an atmosphere in which idealism and devotion can flourish," George Reedy wrote in *The Twilight of the Presidency*. "Below the president is a mass of intrigue, posturing, strutting, cringing, and pious 'commitment' to irrelevant windbaggery. It is designed as the perfect setting for the conspiracy of mediocrity—that all too frequently successful collection of the untalented, the unpassionate, and the insincere seeking to convince the public that it is brilliant, compassionate, and dedicated."

While Gergen could repackage the president, he was no substitute for a man or woman of ideas. He was a flack—albeit a very good one—whose services were available to any president, Republican or Democrat. He dealt in symbolism and image rather than substance.

"The most serious problem a president has is finding someone who can talk frankly but is intelligent enough to say useful things," said Dr. Brown. "Dave Gergen can do a lot, but can't tell the president he is acting like a fool."

If anyone thought David Gergen could professionalize the Clinton White House, that idea was quickly dispelled when two months after his appointment, the White House repeatedly bumbled in handling announcements about Vincent Foster's death.

"Presidents have this misconception that they are going to prevent information from getting out," Reedy said. "They can't, but the atmosphere of the White House contributes to making them think they can. If they have some bad news coming up, presidents should announce it themselves. They should announce the whole thing. That way, they don't have to live with it for a full year. They become the authority on it."

Reflecting the amateurish nature of the rest of the White House staff, the White House press office continued to perform at the level of third graders, illustrated by the way Clinton aides handled press inquiries into the Whitewater Development Co. in Arkansas and the Clintons' investment in it. On January 1, 1994, Stephanopoulos said on television that all Clinton's records relating to his investment in the project had been turned over voluntarily to the Justice Department. A day later, Dee Dee Myers said no records had yet been turned over. Two days after that, the White House issued a statement saying it would actually be turning over the documents in response to a Justice Department subpoena. Meanwhile, Nussbaum was meeting with Treasury Department officials to get updates on an investigation into Madison, conduct the *Washington Post* said even a first-year law student would know is improper. Finally, after more than a year of repeated shocking displays of poor judgment, Nussbaum resigned on March 5, 1994, saying he could best serve Clinton by returning to private life.

To be sure, every administration's press office eventually stubs its toe. "In the end, in the White House, nobody really helps you," Marlin Fitzwater, Bush's press secretary, said. "You're alone. When it comes to finding the real facts about an issue, people are self-serving. They tell you whatever is their idea, whatever helps their cabinet department. In the end, you can never trust anyone entirely. You have to do the work yourself."[188]

If that was true, Clinton's press office was so inept that it did not know how to—or did not care to—verify facts itself. Simply scheduling appointments and clearing reporters into the White House was beyond its capabilities.

David Shaw, the media critic of the *Los Angeles Times*, outlined in shocking detail his experience in trying to set up interviews through the press office for a series he was preparing on media coverage of the Clinton administration. Arriving in Washington on July 16, 1993, Shaw left messages for Stephanopoulos, Gergen, and Gearan. Meanwhile, he attended a press briefing that had been scheduled for 11:30 A.M. but actually started at 1:30 P.M.

"That's typical, I'm told," he wrote in the *Washington Monthly*. "Nothing at the White House ever starts on time. Clinton is habitually late. So is Gergen. Together, they are setting *Guinness Book of World Records* standards for tardiness."[189]

Later that same afternoon, Shaw planned to attend a background briefing given by Stephanopoulos and Gergen. The briefing was supposed to start between 3 and 4 P.M. It started at 5:07 P.M.

After the briefing, Shaw told Gergen he'd like to interview him. Gergen told him to call "Diana," who would set it up. But Diana was busy and did not return Shaw's call. Nor did Stephanopoulos or Gearan.

The next day, the press briefing was scheduled for 11:30 A.M. but was rescheduled for 12:30 P.M. It actually started at 12:45 P.M. After the briefing, Shaw again called Diana, who was on another line. He talked with Stephanopoulos's assistant, who said she didn't know her boss's schedule yet and therefore could not set up an interview.

On Tuesday, July 20, Shaw arrived at the White House, only to be told that his temporary White House press credentials, which were supposed to be available each day at the northwest entrance, weren't there. After receiving the credentials, Shaw again called Diana, who had not returned his previous calls. She was in a meeting, then on another line. Shaw got through to Diana later that day. She said she would get back to him. She didn't.

The next day, Shaw called the press office before arriving at the White House to make sure his credentials would be waiting for him. "Don't worry. We'll take care of it," he was told.

"When I get to the northwest entrance, the Secret Service agents in charge say they have no record of any request for credentials for me," he wrote. "I phone in but no one there remembers my call from fifteen minutes ago."

On Thursday, July 22, Shaw called the press office to make sure the credentials would be ready. When he arrived, there were no credentials. The previous day, press aides had blamed the Secret Service for the mix-up. This time, Shaw told the agent that the press office had blamed the Secret Service. The agent bristled.

"If they fax it to us, it's here; if they don't, it isn't," he said.

After a week in Washington, Shaw finally got his interviews, but not before the press office again screwed up in providing him with his credentials. This time, the press office only provided a pass to the old Executive Office Building, not the west wing. When Shaw complained, a press aide said, "We'll take care of it."

By now, Shaw had learned to fear the reassurance "We'll take care of it." When Shaw returned to the White House that day, he asked for his credentials. The Secret Service agent checked the computer.

"I'm sorry," he said, "you're only cleared for OEB."

In this way, Clinton's press office daily displayed its own incompetence to the press. Upon taking office, Clinton had taken a hostile attitude toward the press, deciding he did not need it. Finally, Clinton had lied to the press, claiming, for example, that he had cut the White House staff when it was obvious he had not. Then Clinton wondered why the press did not treat him with adoration.

The "knee-jerk liberal press" is ignoring or distorting the administration's record to the benefit of "the do-nothings . . . and the right-wingers," Clinton complained to William Grieder in a *Rolling Stone* magazine interview. The magazine quoted Clinton as saying that the news media are too quick to judge and too harsh when they do so, trivializing the presidency without informing the public.

His outburst came at the end of a wide-ranging discussion touching on such topics as gun control, the "change-averse" culture in Washington, and humorous moments of his months in office. The angry comments were triggered by a report that a former supporter had questioned his commitment.

"That's the press's fault, too, damnit," Clinton said. "I have fought more damn battles here for more things than any president has in twenty years, with the possible exception of

Reagan's first budget, and not gotten one damn bit of credit from the knee-jerk liberal press, and I am sick and tired of it, and you can put that in your damn article."

Clinton said he had gotten little credit or positive coverage for his accomplishments: tax changes, a family leave bill, national service legislation, among others.

"You get no credit around here for fighting and bleeding," he said. "And that's why the know-nothings and do-nothings and the negative people and the right-wingers always win."[190]

Like the former law school professor that he was, Clinton seemed to think that the press had an obligation to report on his programs as if they were the subject of the next exam. When Ann Devroy of the *Washington Post* complained in a forum at the John F. Kennedy School of Government that the press has difficulty covering the White House because Clinton's press office does not come up with new angles that will make news, Gearan professed himself perplexed. He said he did not understand how programs that Clinton had been talking about for months could be presented in a new way—something any public relations person worth his salary knew how to do. But Clinton's staff, for the most part, had had no previous experience in anything but going to college and helping Clinton win election. In contrast, every key aide in the Bush and Reagan administrations had had some White House or at least executive branch experience.

If Gergen could not alter the flakiness of the White House staff, he certainly could not change Clinton's nature. While many of his ideas such as health care reform and deficit reduction were admirable, he continued to be a bumbler—a provincial man who, as Ross Perot said, would never rise in a corporation above middle management. Nowhere was that better illustrated than by the way Clinton and his wife managed the White House residence staff. Luxurious as living in the White House is, the residence staff has never been as hard working as the staff of a good hotel.

"Individually, the domestic workers in the White House were some of the most loyal, conscientious government employees any government could have," J. B. West, the chief usher until the Nixon administration, wrote in his book *Upstairs at the White House*. "But as a workforce, they were considerably less effective than their counterparts in any private house in America." Their attitude toward the first family, West said, was, "We'll be here after you're gone."

West said, "As eight-hour-a-day, time-clock employees, the domestic staff were bureaucrats pretending to be old family retainers. And you simply can't have both at the same time."[191]

The Reagans and the Bushes managed to keep tight control of the staff. But under the Clintons, according to Sean T. Haddon, an assistant chef, the staff took over.

To be sure, Haddon had an axe to grind. He was suing Gary Walters, the chief usher, because he claimed that after Haddon married a black woman, Walters downgraded his performance evaluation and told the FBI that Haddon had threatened the president and first lady. However, after being escorted out of the White House by the Secret Service, Haddon passed a Secret Service lie detector test on the issue and was returned to work. Walters denied telling the FBI that Haddon had threatened the president and his wife, but he declined to take the test.

Haddon was engaged in litigation against Walters, but many of his observations have been corroborated independently. Haddon said that besides having married a black woman, he was out of favor with Walters because Walters and the White House are rigidly wedded to French food and chefs with European backgrounds. A former chef in Atlanta, Haddon had no European training.

When Haddon asked Walters why he had not received a promotion when another chef left, "Gary told me to my face he did not want American, nouveau, or eclectic in the White House," Haddon said. "He wanted French cooking."[192]

But that is not what the Clintons wanted. Almost as soon as she entered the White House, Hillary Clinton ordered the chef, Pierre Chambrin, to prepare menus in English instead of French. The Clintons also told the chef that they wanted light American meals. But Chambrin stubbornly continued to make cream-based, classical French meals.

In early February 1993, a *New York Times* story reported,

"In a departure from past practice, Mrs. Clinton said, the White House kitchen will emphasize American food rather than a French-style menu, and restaurant chefs will be consulted about menus."

"Hillary Clinton gave us thirty cookbooks and a broad idea [of what she wanted]," Haddon said. "Very healthy, light, a lot of pasta and vegetables. She doesn't want pesto. She likes green vegetables, no fried food. Quickly sauteed or steamed vegetables. She wants color and contrast. On desserts, we have a free hand as long as they are not cream based. She likes chocolate. But they are more into fresh fruit, light things. They say they get enough heavy things when they go out."

Chelsea Clinton—who is widely respected by the White House staff as an unspoiled teenager—likes to eat apples. "Chelsea is a wonderful kid," Haddon said. "She tries very much not to be a problem. Whatever you want to give her is okay with her. We say what we have, and she'll give you a nay or yea. She might want a grilled cheese sandwich. We give her three or four meal choices. Chelsea never touches sweets or chips or hot dogs. She is into soups, sandwiches, fresh fruit."

Her father, on the other hand, loads up on ginger ale and diet Coke.

"Mrs. Clinton is forcing American cuisine down the kitchen's throat," Haddon said. "Pierre says it is 'junk food, finger food, no sophistication.' He was at Maison Blanche [one of Washington's top French restaurants] for ten years. It is hard for him to accept any change like that."

President Bush had gone through the same exercise with Chambrin.

"When they wanted a lighter meal, he said he was going to teach them how to dine," Haddon said.

But Bush himself intervened by making sure Haddon cooked for him as often as possible. For his last dinner in the White House, Bush insisted that Haddon make him one of Haddon's specialties—a southwestern blackened shrimp with a light sauce and pasta. The dish was one of the few Bush had more than once.

"One requirement is we never have the same menu twice,"

Haddon said. "In the eight years of Reagan or the four years of Bush, we never did, unless they asked for it again."

When Hillary Clinton moved in, she said she wanted the chefs to consult with other chefs to obtain more American regional dishes. That, too, was subverted.

"They tried to consult," Haddon said. "Gary said it will never happen."

According to Haddon, Chambrin wanted only to be associated with meals that generate publicity.

"If the menu is not released [to the press], he has no interest in it," Haddon said.

Under the Reagan and Bush administrations, Gary Walters tried to get the first family to order food through him. But both Nancy Reagan and Barbara Bush circumvented him, dealing directly with Chambrin and specifying lighter dishes. When the Bushes liked a dish, they would ask that it be made for large gatherings, Haddon said. Walters or Chambrin would say ever so politely that it couldn't be done. Naive as they were, the Clintons accepted their explanations.

"They would ask for simple American things," Haddon said. "We told them we can't do that for large dinners." But Barbara Bush consulted other experts, who told her, "Of course you can," Haddon said.

When Nancy Reagan asked for a dish that was not French, Chambrin knew he could not circumvent her. "Mrs. Reagan would say, 'I want that dish.' The kitchen would have to go and modify it," Haddon said.

When the Clintons came in, Walters sensed that he could regain the control he had lost under the Bushes and Reagans. As illustrated by his response to a Freedom of Information Act request filed by Haddon, Walters considered his territory to be none of the public's business. Responding to Haddon's request, Walters claimed "the executive residence at the White House is not subject to the Freedom of Information Act."[193]

Within a few weeks of moving into the White House, Hillary Clinton was walking down the hall outside the family kitchen on the second floor when she saw two maids dart into a closet in the kitchen. According to Haddon, Hillary followed them into the closet and asked what they were doing. The maids told her they had been ordered to make themselves scarce when the first family was around.

"He [Walters] told us we are not supposed to be on the second floor when they are there. If you are there when they come, they want you to go away," Haddon said. "They [the staff] were trying to develop individual relations, and Gary was trying to destroy that."

Haddon said individual butlers play games with the Clintons. If the Clintons order a meal through one butler, another butler or the kitchen in the northwest corner of the ground floor will make sure the order is late, teaching the Clintons that they should deal next time with a more favored butler.

This sort of power game goes on in any administration. Just as leaders of industry grovel before the president, the butlers, maids, and chefs play the same game, competing with one another to curry favor with the president.

"They each think they are higher in the pecking order or have greater access to the president," a Secret Service agent said. "They really play that game of who has the greatest access. They all think they do, but in reality they don't. You would think the chefs personally fork the food into their mouths, but they don't. It's the power of the White House."

If they don't have access to the president, staffers take to trying to ingratiate themselves with his pets. The Bushes' dog Ranger, one of Millie's puppies, showed the effects.

"Ranger was getting overweight," said David C. Tiffany, who was in charge of responding to letters to Bush that required personal replies. "Staff people would feed him and give him a treat. The president sent a memo around requesting people not to feed Ranger."

Under Clinton, Haddon said, the power games got out of control. The staff would delay responding to the Clintons' orders to teach them who was boss. Walters demanded that any requests for food from overnight guests go through him or through his office. When guests called Chambrin directly, he would say they must call Walters. Even when Hillary Clinton called, Chambrin sent a butler to obtain her order rather than taking it on the phone—another way to teach her to go through Walters if she wanted her food quickly.

"Pierre would say to the house guests, 'Why are you calling here? You have to talk to Gary,' " Haddon said. "More and more, they go through the usher's office. If the first lady calls the kitchen, they will deliberately sabotage it. They are not giving them service. They didn't do that to the Bushes. Mrs. Bush would say, 'Come in here.'

"The idea is so the president understands, 'If you want something done, come directly to me,' " Haddon said.

Despite the orders of the first lady, Chambrin continued to prepare classic French dishes but began giving them American names.

"They write [the menu] in French and translate it into English for the menu," Haddon said. "But it is still French."

The Clintons told Chambrin that Clinton is allergic to dairy products and breaks out in a rash if he has cream-based sauces. Nonetheless, Haddon said Chambrin continued to make cream-based meals. When the rashes continued, "Gary said, 'Maybe it's the flowers in the second floor.' So they started taking out the flowers."

Haddon said he informed a Clinton aide what was going on. Chambrin was told again to cut out the cream. So instead of cream, Chambrin began using greasy chicken stock base as a thickener.

"They put garbage in, chicken base with grease," Haddon said. "We have all the best ingredients money can buy, and they will go out and buy salt and grease mixed together. Normally, it's when you can't afford to buy the bones [for a stock]."

The formulation is kept hush-hush. "We are not allowed to say anything," Haddon said.

Irked that Clinton was often late for meals and did not let him know he would not be on time, Chambrin took to making Clinton wait once he finally showed up.

"Pierre has kept Clinton waiting on purpose," Haddon said. "He says, 'They'll have to learn to wait.' They may be twenty minutes late or ten minutes early, much like the Bushes. But President Bush, if he was going to be late, would say, 'I'll be twenty minutes late.' That has not happened in this administration. So Pierre says they'll have to wait as retribution."

"All that stuff is bullshit," Chambrin said of Haddon's charges. "I have nothing to say."[194]

But guests confirm that the quality of the cooking has plummeted under Clinton. One guest at the White House dinner celebrating jazz said the food was "mediocre." Another guest said the food—barbecued chicken—"was not as good as a dozen of Washington's better restaurants. Tasteless. Under Bush, it was better. Even the food at the White House mess is better."

"The service has gone downhill since the Clintons came in," Haddon said. "Before the Clintons, silverware was always polished before it was used for every meal. Now it is tarnished. They [staff members] don't care. They have more free time. They sleep. Watch TV. Some are busier than they have ever been. Maids are working more. There are larger parties. More houseguests. But the butlers get away with murder. The butlers are putting in more hours but doing less work. They sleep for two hours in the afternoon in the locker room in the basement."

In contrast to the Clintons, "Mrs. Reagan was on it constantly," Haddon said. "Mrs. Bush was concerned about the family. They both dealt directly with the staff. Whatever they can get away with, they will get away with. This administration doesn't know the details, and no one is going to bring them forward."

Finally, a year after entering the White House, Chambrin resigned over the conflict.

"He is an expert in French cuisine," Dee Dee Myers said. "That's his specialty and his vocation. That's not what we serve here at the White House."

Why it took a year for such a simple decision to be made tells a lot about the Clinton White House. So does Chambrin's replacement. The Clintons chose Walter Scheib from the Greenbrier resort in White Sulphur Springs, West Virginia. Like the rest of Clinton's staff, he was relatively inexperienced compared with more distinguished and well-known chefs.

"The big question is: Who is this person?" said John Mariani, food and travel correspondent for *Esquire* magazine. "He's not a superstar chef. There are scores of fabulous American chefs who would bring enormous luster to the White House's kitchens. It doesn't appear that they did an exhaustive search."[195]

Even Hillary Clinton's professed desire to introduce more healthy food to the White House diet was a sham. The Greenbrier, said noted cooking instructor Peter Kump, is not known for its contemporary low-fat cuisine.

"The president is known for his love of food, particularly traditional fare. They've gone for somebody who can duplicate that," Kump said.

In fact, reported the respected *Washington Post* restaurant critic Phyllis Richman, food made by the new chef at the White House turned out to be akin to hotel food.

If the Clintons had trouble managing their own domestic staff, they were in no position to manage the rest of the White House or the government. While Clinton achieved some successes like getting a deficit-reduction package through Congress, he spent most of his time spinning his wheels. The result could be seen in the slow pace of making appointments. Clinton insisted on choosing even sub-Cabinet officials himself. As a result, vacancies remained in key positions more than half a year after Clinton had become president. By August 1993, the White House had yet to nominate someone to head the Office of Thrift Supervision, which regulates savings and loans, or the Federal Deposit Insurance Corporation. Because no replacements had been named, the five-person Commodity Futures Trading Commission had to make do with only two members. The National Highway Traffic Safety Administration, which regulates auto manufacturers, had no administrator.

"Bush is in charge of the agency, for all intents and purposes," Ralph Nader said.[196]

Meanwhile, the Justice Department lacked a new candidate to fill the top civil rights job at the agency, and the Environmental Protection Agency had to enforce key provisions of the Clean Air Act without a top official over air quality. Republican signatures even continued to be printed on new dollar bills because

Clinton had not named a new treasurer, according to the *Wall Street Journal*.

Seven months into his presidency, Clinton had gotten only 253 candidates for top government jobs confirmed, compared with 372 for Carter and 345 for Reagan. While Bush had gotten only 212 candidates confirmed, Bush felt less need to replace high-ranking government officials because he followed a Republican president.

With a quarter of his presidency over, Clinton had not filled 27 percent of the top positions in the executive branch. At the independent agencies, the vacancy rate was 39 percent. Along with preparing a budget, making appointments is one of the few direct obligations a president has—one that carries with it direct benefits for his own party. Yet the Clinton White House was incapable even of performing that function.

Clinton's press office remained amateurish, rarely well prepared with information and inconsistent in its policies.

"One day, they'll let you photograph anything," a *Time* photographer said. "The next day, they won't let you take anything."

Clinton's White House meetings resembled graduate school seminars. He would throw out ideas and endlessly circle the subject rather than come to a conclusion. Only Clinton's vice president, Al Gore, knew anything about managing the government.

"He's like a piece of artillery in a meeting, he's so efficient," a Gore aide said of his boss.

Gore had a fondness for tabbed binders and detailed talking points. He ticked off what needed to be accomplished and ran through the list.

Gore plunged into an ambitious effort to reduce needless bureaucracy, focusing on such minute but important details as how the government procures goods and services. As one example, he would trot out the regulations for procuring an ashtray.

"This is the specification for how you test it," Gore would tell reporters. "You put the ashtray on a maple plank. It has to be maple, 44.5 millimeters thick. And you hit it with a steel punch point, ground to a 60 percent included angle, and a hammer. The specimen should break into a small number of irregularly shaped pieces, not greater in number than 35. But wait! Now we get to the specification of the pieces. To be counted as regulation shards, they must be 6.4 millimeters or more on any three of their adjacent edges."

The federal personnel manual, which spells out the rules for hiring and firing, was 10,000 pages long. It included 900 pages alone on how to fill in Standard Form 50, the Notification of Personnel Action. The General Services Administration's process for buying computers generally took three years. By then, the items were either obsolete or had been discontinued. And the Drug Enforcement Administration and the Alcohol, Tobacco, and Firearms Bureau needlessly tracked over the same ground as the FBI on drug and firearms investigations. It was like having two police departments in the same town, both responding to the same crimes.

Gore proposed to save $108 billion over five years by slashing 252,000 government jobs that were not needed and by revamping the way the government buys supplies and services, modernizing computer and information systems, and simplifying paperwork.

Gore backed up the administration's case for boosting government efficiency with a demonstration of the government's method of safety-testing an "ash receiver, tobacco (desk type)" on CBS's "Late Show with David Letterman." He and Letterman donned safety goggles and smashed a specimen ashtray with a hammer on a United States–mandated maple plank.

"Cool," Letterman said as he surveyed the regulation-size pieces of broken glass on his desk.

If the Clinton administration made good on streamlining the government or reforming health care, it would be considered a very successful administration. In retrospect, most presidents have little to show for their four years or eight years in office. But whatever achievements Clinton managed to pull off were in spite of his maladroit administration of the White House and its staff.

"The Clinton White House is in a lot of confusion," a Secret Service agent said. "They still don't know what they have ahold of there. It's like high school. He [Clinton] pays attention one day, and the next day doesn't pay attention to anything. There is no strategy. He still doesn't know that he's the president. He knows he was elected president, but hasn't started acting like one."

The agent said Clinton's habit of throwing temper tantrums over petty inconveniences discourages his staff from bringing him negative news.

"He'll blow up in a heartbeat over minor things or his perception of the way something is supposed to be handled," the agent said. "They [Clinton and his staff] are inept."

For example, within the space of five days in August 1993, Clinton twice blew up at staffers in full view of reporters. When Clinton arrived in St. Louis, he realized somebody had left his briefcase behind. His face reddened as he yelled at trip director Wendy Smith. In Vail, Colorado, Clinton was thumbing through his papers on the hood of his limousine when he suddenly turned toward aide Andrew Friendly. Reporters saw Clinton's face contort with anger, and the president appeared to yell at Friendly at length. Aides said the president, who was about to board *Air Force One* for Tulsa, Oklahoma, was apparently angry because he was supposed to make some telephone calls but did not have the numbers or a cellular phone.[197]

Raymond Young, Clinton's chief of security in Arkansas, said the temper tantrums were not uncommon.

"He has temper fits occasionally," Young said. "When he gets stressed out and something goes wrong, he could have a temper fit. Whoever was standing closest caught the brunt of it."

While the failure to provide Clinton with his briefcase and a cellular phone illustrated the clumsiness of Clinton's staff, Clinton's overreaction underscored the fact that he felt over his head. Beset by demands that he could not adequately handle, he responded by lashing out in anger, invariably followed by abject apologies. The fawning atmosphere of the White House contributed to Clinton's impatience when anything went wrong.

"One of the real problems of the presidency is he gets no

resistance to his personality," George Reedy said. "That is very unhealthy. Most of us go through life meeting all sorts of resistance: the hotel clerk who gives us a fishy look when we try to cash a check; the old maid aunt who flushes bright red when you happen to say damn or when you light a cigar; the people who stand up and say, 'Oh, no, you don't.' There's a healthiness to that. But suppose you're a person whom everybody says yes to. You want a Coke, and all of a sudden there it is in your hand. You want a cheeseburger and all of a sudden, it's there in front of you. You want to go to Texas at 4 P.M., and you just have to say it out loud and by 4:30 P.M., there's a helicopter on the lawn ready to take you to *Air Force One* to take you to Texas. Think of what that would do to you every day for four years."

Because of that mind-set, a perfectly reasonable question from ABC-TV correspondent Britt Hume threw Clinton into a frenzy. In announcing the nomination of Ruth Bader Ginsburg to the Supreme Court, Clinton seemed transfixed as she told the story of her rise. Then the irascible Hume brought him back to reality. Addressing Clinton with deference, Hume asked if Clinton would explain "a certain zigzag quality in the decision-making process here."

Clinton was furious. "How you could ask a question like that after the statement she just made is beyond me," the president said. He turned on his heel and refused further questions.

In contrast to her husband, who tends to be unfocused, Hillary Rodham Clinton is controlled and well organized.

"She is the real power," a Secret Service agent said. "She is very systematic in her thinking and very influential. The president consults her on everything."

"The indications are that she was Bill Clinton's number one adviser throughout the time he was governor," said *Arkansas Democrat-Gazette* editor John Robert Starr, citing "the number of times Bill would say, 'Well, Hillary thinks,' when we were discussing an issue."

In contrast to Bill, "She has backbone," Starr said. "She has integrity. He doesn't. Bill Clinton will tell you what you want to hear, and Hillary will look you in the eye and tell you the truth whether you want to hear it or not, but she'll tell it to you in a way that makes you like it."

Because Hillary Clinton often wears her hair down with no makeup and sunglasses, Secret Service agents began calling her "Woodstock" because she looked like a hippie from the sixties.

"She is very intelligent, very quick," an agent said. "She does share in a lot of Bill's decisions. 'Invite them in. Don't talk to those people.' Nancy Reagan did the same thing with Ron. She is a manipulator. I don't see that with Hillary."

But the agent said the Clintons' personal relationship is cold.

"They argue a lot," the agent said. "There seems to be some kind of tension [between them]. There is an uneasiness."

On those rare occasions when Clinton was photographed kissing his wife, he looked uncomfortable, and she had a look of distaste. After Clinton was sworn in, he moved to kiss his wife, but she turned away.

The Secret Service agent said their arguments are often about policy as well as marital matters.

"It is about what they are going to do and how they are going to do it," the agent said. "It is who is going to win out. It's when they go upstairs. The ushers hear it. Late at night sound travels in that place."

"I have heard from people there that they scream at each other," said Nelson Pierce, a former assistant usher. "They can hear it down on the first floor."

According to William Bell, a former Secret Service agent, Hillary Clinton did not throw a lamp at Bill Clinton, as was widely reported and denied by the Clintons. Instead, she threw a briefing book at him—and missed. Bell said the incident occurred when two Secret Service agents were driving the Clintons in Arkansas a month before the election.

"Hillary got upset and threw a briefing book at Bill and hit the driver, the Secret Service agent," Bell said. "She was hot [angry] before she got in the limousine."[198]

Before Clinton was elected, a current agent said, he would meet alone with pretty young women in his hotel rooms late into the night. While the Secret Service agents guarding the presidential candidate never actually saw him having sex with them, they believed that was the purpose of the late night meetings.

"It's your job to notice," the agent said. "Did that person leave or not? We can figure out why they are in there. We know who the players are, who has no function."

The agent said Clinton disguised assignations as working meetings.

"Clinton is the type of individual who likes to work late," the agent said. "He will call at 2 A.M. and say, 'I need to talk to you about something, come to my room.' He is not dumb. It sets a precedent. He tries to keep it professional-looking." But, the agent said, "People of the opposite sex were going there at all hours of the night for three or four hours with no one else there."

In the agent's opinion, Clinton's insistence on continuing to jog through Washington's streets instead of using the jogging track built for him is a symptom of his frustration with being under constant observation in the White House, which Clinton has referred to as a "splendid prison." The jogging track was built because Clinton's early morning forays through Washington disrupted traffic. A dozen vehicles trailed behind him as he displayed his trademark white legs on his way to the Mall. All the while, Clinton expressed irritation that any Secret Service agents had to accompany him.

"They built the jogging track, and he is out jogging at the Tidal Basin," an agent said. "I have a feeling this is an excuse to get out—to pick up girls or whatever. He is finding it hard. There is no privacy. It was a convenient way when he was governor to do what he wanted without the wife even raising an eyebrow."

In fact, according to Gennifer Flowers, Clinton made sure her apartment was on his jogging route, so he could conceal his assignations with her by saying he was out jogging. Things were not that simple once Clinton came to Washington. Nor could he ask Janet Reno to let him use her loft, as John F. Kennedy had done with his brother Bobby.

Meanwhile, Clinton managed to conceal anything in his personal life that might reflect badly on him. Roy Neel, Clinton's deputy chief of staff, issued a memo on July 20, 1993, to the staff of the executive residence reminding them to keep their mouths shut.

"There is always considerable curiosity about the private lives of the first families," he wrote. "While this president has an open relationship with the public and the press, all first families are entitled to privacy regarding matters in their living quarters. Maintaining the privacy of the first family is the responsibility of all employees, particularly those in the executive residence. Discussions by staff members of the first family's activities of any kind, or any other matter which breaches their privacy, with anyone outside of the immediate staff is prohibited."[199]

Thus the president who claimed to be open and who used a confessional style to get his points across was the only one in recent memory to issue a directive banning talk about his private life. Even Clinton's allergies were considered too touchy to talk about publicly—an extension of the difficulty the press had in obtaining information about Clinton's health during the campaign. The fact that Clinton was allergic to dairy products was kept well hidden, as was the fact that he rarely visited Camp David because the atmosphere exacerbated his allergies. Instead, the White House put out the word that Clinton had visited Camp David only three times in his first six months in office because there was little to do there except read.

When the *Wall Street Journal* reported in December 1993 that Clinton had begun taking afternoon naps, the White House press office claimed he had just begun taking them in the fall of 1993 when he was trying to push through health insurance legislation. Moreover, the White House claimed the naps were "occasional." In fact, Clinton began taking afternoon naps within a month of entering the White House, and he took them almost daily.

There is, of course, nothing wrong with presidents taking naps. Clinton worked well beyond the hours expected of a federal employee, and if naps helped him to think more clearly, it was in the public interest that he take them as often as possible. But once again, the White House had succeeded in fooling the press and the public by distorting the facts in order to create an image of an ever-vigilant president who succumbed to drowsiness only when faced with such an arduous task as reforming the health insurance system.

Choreographed by Gergen, Clinton had learned to play the role of president. When Clinton visited South Korea in July 1993, television cameras showed him peering through binoculars at the Korean Demilitarized Zone, evoking the image of a strong commander in chief. The script had been written ten years earlier by Gergen, who had had Ronald Reagan do the same thing when he visited the same border.[200]

On his first day on the job, Gergen had found the Clinton administration floundering over the nomination of Lani Guinier to a top Justice Department post. Gergen told Clinton to decide *something*. If Clinton decided to continue to back her, he should make sure he believed in her, Gergen said. By that evening, Clinton had decided to drop her.

The fact that orchestrating displays of leadership could help Clinton's popularity so much—his approval ratings in a *Wall Street Journal*/NBC News poll shot up from 47 percent to 54 percent within two months of Gergen's takeover—demonstrates how much being perceived as a good president depends on showmanship. For while the function of the president is to make decisions, it is also to display leadership—as Reedy put it, to at least "keep people marching in the same direction." To do that, a president must command respect. For all the good Clinton tried to do, he was constantly hampered by the fact that people did not respect him. His timorous approach, green staff, temper tantrums, and show marriage undercut his image as a leader. Eventually, Clinton's parochial staff managed to cut Gergen out of key decisions, so that one of the few aides in the White House who knew what he was doing was powerless. Soon, he began making plans to leave the White House and its unruly children.

Ultimately, the shortcomings lead back both to the way presidents are elected and to the heady atmosphere of the White House. In most cases, the character flaws of recent presidents were known before they were elected. Clinton's arrogance in carrying on a lengthy affair with Gennifer Flowers while he was in public office; Carter's disingenuousness in claiming he had cut spending by the Georgia government when the budget had in fact skyrocketed; Bush's use of Willie Horton to exploit racial prejudice; and the ethics problem that was the subject of Nixon's famous "Checkers" speech were all known to the electorate. But because of the dominance of television, candidates who give good sound bites are able to mesmerize voters into overlooking politicians' track records. The staged photo opportunity is confused with reality. Although routinely broken, campaign promises are naively accepted as having significance. Politicians are held to different standards than the rest of the population.

"I'm a politician, and as a politician I have the prerogative to lie whenever I want," said Charles Peacock, a former director of the Arkansas savings and loan association at the center of the Whitewater matter, explaining why he had lied about writing a check to help cover a debt of Clinton's gubernatorial campaign.

In earlier years, the press covered up for presidents, failing to print matters that might be embarrassing. The fact that Franklin Roosevelt was crippled from a bout with polio came as a shock to most people because the press had gone along with his wishes to keep it quiet. Thomas P. (Tip) O'Neill, the former speaker of the House, recalled how amazed he was when, as a college freshman, he met Roosevelt in the White House.

"When I saw the president sitting in a wheelchair, I was so shocked that my chin just about hit my chest," he said. "Like most Americans, I had absolutely no idea that Franklin Roosevelt was disabled. It's hard to imagine in this day of television, but in those days the president's handicap was kept secret out of respect for the office."[201]

More accurately, the press kept such matters quiet out of fear of the consequences either from presidents, from their powerful allies, or from the public. Probing into what was considered people's personal lives not only contravened the prevailing standards of decency, it was also, in the case of the presidents, considered unpatriotic. For the most part, the press no longer overlooks presidential affairs, medical disabilities, or other problems when confronted with them. But the media still tend to regard probing deeply into such issues as unseemly, ungentlemanly, or tawdry. The fact that a tabloid first revealed Gennifer Flowers's affair with Bill Clinton is significant and damning. And the press's treatment of later revelations about the Clintons' personal life shows that many in the media are still starstruck when it comes to honestly reporting on presidents.

8

"God! God! God!"

Two weeks after Bill and Hillary Clinton moved into the White House, the *New York Times* ran a story at the top of page one about the Clintons' preferences in food and entertaining. Based on an interview with Hillary Rodham Clinton, the story revealed that a typical Clinton family meal consists of broiled chicken breasts, steamed fresh vegetables, rice, green salad, fruit, and iced tea. If dessert is served, it is usually fruit-based—a sorbet or apple crisp.

The Clintons do not like smoking, the story went on, and they have banned it from the White House. The ban on broccoli in the White House, imposed by George Bush, would be rescinded. As for her dual role of wife and policy adviser, Mrs. Clinton said she was no different from "every woman who gets up in the morning and gets breakfast for her family and goes off to a job of any sort where she assumes a different role for the hours she's at work, who runs out at lunch to buy material for a costume for her daughter or to buy invitations for a party that she's going to have, and after work goes and picks up her children and then maybe goes out with her husband: Our lives *are* a mixture of these different roles."[202]

Aside from the story's play—it ran from the top of page one to five inches below the fold, with a photo of Hillary—the piece was no different from thousands of other stories that had appeared since Clinton became a candidate for president. The stories portrayed a happy, all-American family—devoted to one another, health conscious, clean-living. Nor were these stories appreciably different from thousands of others run about the personal lives of every first family, whether they are making Christmas ornaments, serving Christmas cookies, playing with their pets, changing the decor of the White House residence, buying clothes, or doing their homework. The personal lives of America's presidents and their families have always been news, and legitimately so. As a symbol of America, the first family is a focal point, projecting the president's values and helping define his leadership. But when the personal lives of presidents turn out to be different from the carefully crafted image, that should also be news, or so it would seem. In fact, that is not the case. A classic example presented itself when four Arkansas state troopers decided in 1993 to relate their experiences guarding Bill Clinton when he was governor of Arkansas.

The troopers said that while on the state payroll, they spent much of their time helping Clinton meet young women for sexual encounters and covering up these affairs from Hillary Clinton. According to the troopers, when Bill Clinton got wind of the fact that the troopers were going public months before any stories had appeared, he and his aides began offering federal jobs to the troopers in an implicit attempt to buy their silence. According to the troopers, the affairs continued into January 1993, just before Clinton was inaugurated.

The charges first appeared in *American Spectator*, a conservative publication, under the byline of David Brock, who had written a book critical of Anita Hill. On December 20, 1993, the same day the *American Spectator* article was faxed to news organizations, two of the troopers appeared on CNN to repeat their charges. The following day, the *Los Angeles Times* ran its own interview with them and with two other troopers who did not want to be quoted. The article corroborated some of their charges with records of hundreds of telephone calls, some lasting an hour and a half, made by Clinton to some of the women the troopers had named as his girlfriends.

"We were more than bodyguards," said Larry G. Patterson, a twenty-six-year veteran state trooper who spent five years on Clinton's security unit. "We had to lie, cheat, and cover up for that man."[203]

Both Patterson and Roger L. Perry, a sixteen-year state police veteran who served on the security detail for four years, signed affidavits outlining their allegations. Backed by the two other troopers who did not want to be quoted, they portrayed Bill and Hillary Clinton as having a political and business partnership rather than a marriage. By their account, Bill Clinton's sexual appetites were so voracious, and his need to deceive his wife and the public so constant, that he spent virtually every day lying, sneaking around, and covering up.

Apparently aware of Bill's obsessive philandering, Hillary Clinton reportedly had little respect for him and, according to the troopers, appeared to be having her own affair going with Vincent Foster, the family friend and lawyer who later committed suicide.

Buttressing Gennifer Flowers's claim that she had had a twelve-year affair with Clinton, the troopers said they took "hundreds" of calls from her. If Hillary was in the governor's mansion when Flowers called, they alerted Bill, who came to the troopers' guard house outside the mansion and called her back from a telephone in the back of the guard post. That way, the troopers said, Hillary could not pick up on the line.

The troopers said they routinely drove Clinton to Flowers's apartment house, where he often spent half an hour and emerged smelling of perfume. Occasionally, Clinton claimed he was going to visit Maurice Smith, a state highway official who lived in the same apartment building. But Clinton liked to boast of his conquests, and one time he remarked that Flowers "could suck a tennis ball through a garden hose."

Patterson said he was in Clinton's Lincoln Town Car in the spring of 1991 when the governor used a cellular phone to call William Gaddy, a state official, to ask him to find a state job for Flowers. Both Clinton and Gaddy have denied the charge, but a state grievance panel later determined that hiring Flowers had violated the state's merit system. In a test, she had ranked ninth out of eleven candidates.

According to the troopers, Flowers was but one of a half dozen of Clinton's steady girlfriends whom he saw two or three times a week. They included the wife of a prominent judge, a Clinton aide, a local reporter, and a department store clerk. Clinton supplemented the steadies with constant one-night— or more accurately, one-hour—stands. When Clinton saw an attractive woman in an audience, he would ask one of the troopers to approach her and compliment her on her looks. The trooper would then supply Clinton's telephone number and ask her to call him. In some cases, the troopers arranged free hotel rooms so that Clinton could have sex with the women on the spot. Implausible as it sounds, he would tell the troopers to claim that he was expecting a call from then-President Ronald Reagan and needed a room so he could take the call in private.

When Hillary was out of town, Clinton entertained women at the mansion at all hours, telling the troopers he was about to give a woman "a personal tour." When Hillary Clinton was in town but out of the mansion, Clinton instructed the troopers to buzz him if he was with a woman and Hillary arrived unexpectedly.

Several times a month, Clinton sneaked out of the mansion after Hillary had fallen asleep. Clinton would claim he was "going for a drive," instructing the troopers to call him if Hillary awoke. So that he would not be spotted, he would borrow one of the troopers' personal cars for these forays. On more than a dozen occasions after Clinton had sneaked out, Patterson saw one of the troopers' cars parked outside the condominium of one of Clinton's steadies on Shadow Oaks in the Little Rock suburb of Sherwood.

While she was normally a heavy sleeper, Hillary awoke at two one morning, seething. Looking for Clinton, she called Perry in the troopers' guard post. When told that Clinton had gone for a drive, she exclaimed, "The sorry damn son of a bitch!" Following Clinton's instructions, the trooper feverishly tried to locate him. He finally found him in one of his steadies' apartments.

"God! God! God!" Clinton reportedly said when told Hillary was looking for him. Tires squealing, he raced his car back to the mansion, leaving the driver's door open as he ran into the building. As Perry dashed to close the car door, he heard screaming between Hillary and Bill. The next morning, Perry found a kitchen cabinet door hanging from its hinges. Debris was all over the kitchen floor.

So brazen was Clinton that he had the department store clerk give him oral sex in her pickup truck while they parked in a remote area of the mansion's parking lot. The pickup was parked near a security camera, which Patterson maneuvered so he could observe Clinton receiving sex in the truck on a twenty-seven-inch screen.

As Patterson watched, he noticed Mellisa Jolley, Chelsea's baby-sitter, drive up. Realizing she would be driving past the truck, Patterson waved her over and got her to go in a different direction by telling her there was a security problem on the grounds.

"When they were done, Clinton came running over to me and asked, 'Did she see us? Did she see us?' " Patterson said. "I told him what I'd done, and he said, 'Atta boy.' "

On another occasion, Clinton asked Patterson to drive him to Chelsea's school, Booker Elementary, where Clinton met the department store clerk and climbed into her car.

"I parked across the entrance and stood outside the car looking around, about 120 feet from where they were parked in a lot that was pretty well lit," Patterson recalled. "I could see Clinton get into the front seat, and then the lady's head go into his lap. They stayed in the car for thirty to forty minutes."

Clinton continued to have an affair with one of his steadies as late as January 1993, just before he was inaugurated, according to Patterson, Perry, and a third trooper. The woman, in her midforties, often met Clinton in her condominium or in the governor's mansion. The bodyguards said she sometimes picked up Clinton along his jogging route, then dropped him off along the same route.

"He'd say he ran five miles, and I'd say, 'Governor, you better see a doctor. There's something wrong with your sweat glands,' " Perry said.

After meeting the woman along his jogging route, Clinton would use the troopers' bathroom so he could splash water on his face and shirt to make it appear as if he had been sweating.

In February 1990, Little Rock reporters began examining records of Clinton's phone calls for evidence of abuse by state troopers. Patterson was one of the troopers who had made some of the unauthorized calls. According to Patterson, Raymond L. (Buddy) Young, the chief of the security detail, told Patterson that he would have to claim he had made the calls that Clinton had placed to the woman. While the records covered only a portion of the calls made by Clinton on his cellular car phone and from hotel rooms between 1989 and 1991, they showed fifty calls to the woman's home and to her office extension. On July 16, 1989, the records show eleven calls to the woman's home. Young denied Patterson's claim.

Two months later, Clinton took a state trip to Charlottesville, Virginia, where his hotel room bill shows a ninety-four-minute call placed to the woman's home at 1:23 A.M. At 7:45 A.M. the same day, another call placed from Clinton's room to the woman's home lasted eighteen minutes.

When asked about the calls to the woman, Bernard Nussbaum, then White House counsel, said, "This president calls lots of people," suggesting that Clinton had randomly chosen the woman's number and had spent an hour and a half talking with her because he was garrulous.

In the weeks after his election in November 1992, Clinton at least three times had the troopers sneak the same woman into the governor's mansion as early as 5:15 A.M. Dressed in a base-ball cap and trench coat, she would use her maiden name and tell Secret Service agents she was a staff member coming in early. One of the troopers who did not want to be named said he took her through a basement entrance of the mansion into a game room, where Clinton was waiting for her. At Clinton's instruction, the trooper then stood guard at the door to the basement in case Hillary, who was asleep upstairs, awoke.

Like others named by the troopers, the woman denied having sex with Clinton.

"There was no improper relationship," she told the *Los Angeles Times*. "I'm not going to talk to you about it."

Clearly, Hillary was aware of her husband's proclivities. When Clinton spent an inordinate amount of time with an attractive female at political functions, Hillary would say, "Come on, Bill, put your dick up. You can't fuck her here," according to Patterson.

On the Clintons' last day in Little Rock, Patterson said Clinton asked him to bring the wife of the judge to a ceremony at the airport.

"When I got there with [the judge's wife], Hillary turned to me and said, 'What the fuck do you think you're doing? I know who that whore is. I know what she's here for. Get her out of here.' Clinton was standing right there. I looked at him, and he just shrugged his shoulders, so I took her out of there and dropped her at the Holiday Inn Center City."

On another occasion in the late eighties, Patterson was sitting in the guard house when he overheard Hillary and Bill arguing on the audio monitor at the rear porch.

"I need to be fucked more than twice a year," she said.

As the troopers saw it, Hillary was the strong, decisive partner in the relationship. Power hungry and brittle, she seemed to be interested only in furthering Clinton's political career. She had no friends outside of politics, with one exception. While the troopers did not see Hillary Clinton having sex with Foster, they saw them French-kissing and saw him place a hand on her breasts and on her behind. When Clinton went out of town, Foster would immediately show up at the mansion and stay into the early morning hours. The troopers also took her to meet Foster in a cabin retreat in Heber Springs maintained by the Rose law firm, where they both worked.

"I remember one time when Bill had been quoted in the morning paper saying something she didn't like," Patterson said. "I came into the mansion, and he was standing at the top of the stairs, and she was standing at the bottom, screaming. She has a garbage mouth on her, and she was calling him 'mother fucker,' 'sucker,' and everything else. I went into the kitchen, and the cook, Miss Emma, turned to me and said, 'The devil's in that woman.' "

The troopers also got their share of abuse from Hillary. In the early morning of Labor Day 1991, Hillary drove from the mansion in her blue Cutlass. Within a minute or two, she came racing back, tires squealing.

"I thought something was terribly wrong, so I rushed out to her," Patterson said. "And she screamed, 'Where is the goddamn fucking flag?' It was early, and we hadn't raised the flag yet. And she said, 'I want the goddamn fucking flag up every fucking morning at fucking sunrise.' "

For the most part, Hillary and Bill led separate lives. When they were together, as in a long ride to a political function, they were barely civil to each other and would spend an hour or more without speaking. Hillary seemed to regard her husband as lacking in backbone and easily swayed.

"If he was dead politically, I would expect a divorce in thirty days," Perry said.

While Clinton was engaging, sometimes confiding his insecurities to them, the troopers found that he also had a childish temper and was not above playing dirty tricks. One day, Clinton asked Patterson to track down a woman who was believed to have fathered an illegitimate child by a primary opponent of Clinton's.

"On this occasion," Patterson said, "Clinton told me to go to the Holiday Inn at the [Little Rock] airport, find the woman, and offer her money or a job to sign a statement [about the illegitimate child]." Patterson said he offered the money, but she turned it down.

After he was elected president, Clinton turned aside a trooper's request for an autographed photo of himself.

"I don't have time for that shit," the trooper quoted him as saying. It was a stunning commentary on Clinton's character.

Clinton assured Patterson that he would make sure he got a lateral transfer within the state police, but then never did. Guy Tucker, the current governor, approved the request. When Secret Service agents started guarding Clinton, the troopers told them that Clinton had promised them federal jobs once he entered the White House.

"It was always that they were going to be taken care of," a Secret Service agent said. "They were waiting for these jobs, and nothing happened."

"We lied for him and helped him cheat on his wife, and he treated us like dogs," Patterson said.

On the other hand, Clinton named Buddy Young, the head of the security detail, to a $92,300-a-year job as a regional director of the Federal Emergency Management Agency in Texas. According to the troopers, whenever there was a hint that stories of his philandering might leak out, Clinton called Young, who would try to silence his former subordinates. In calling Perry, for example, Young told him he represented the president.

"This is not a threat," Perry recalled Young saying, "but I wanted you to know that your own actions could bring about dire consequences."[204]

Young denied making any such threats. But Young unwittingly documented his role in the affair to millions of television viewers when he took a call from Bruce Lindsey, Clinton's White House aide and boyhood friend, while being interviewed by ABC-TV. Since Young had put Lindsey's call on a speaker, the television audience heard both Young's and Lindsey's sides of the conversation. Sounding panicky, Lindsey told Young the White House needed to have him appear on CNN to rebut the troopers' charges. In tone and manner, he appeared to be acting as Young's boss. In fact, after Young called the troopers, two of them decided they did not want to be quoted by name.

As with anyone who talks to the press, the troopers had a mix of motives for going public. One was to show that Clinton had misled the American people by lying to them about his affairs. Another was to obtain a book contract. As their representative, they chose Cliff Jackson, a Little Rock lawyer who is a bitter political enemy of Clinton's. However, the troopers received no money for their interviews, and their financial motive was no different from the desire of a newspaper or television network to turn a profit.

It later turned out that Perry and Patterson had lied in testimony about an insurance claim filed by Perry to collect $100,000 as a result of an auto accident. But Arkansas State Police Director Tommy Goodwin vouched for the credibility of both troopers.

Perry admitted that one of his motives was revenge. In another example of the incompetence of the White House staff, Clinton never heard about a request from Perry for a federal job in law enforcement, even though he had previously promised him such a position. Perry cited Clinton's failure to keep his promise as one of his reasons for talking.

The troopers clearly were telling the truth. As eyewitnesses, they were in the best position to know what was going on. Each of the troopers' statements was supported by the accounts of the other three. Telephone records further corroborated their stories. What they said coincided with what Gennifer Flowers had previously claimed, which was in turn supported by Clinton's tape-recorded comments to her. But the troopers' statements went well beyond what Flowers knew, showing how compulsively Clinton cheated on his wife and how extensive his deceitfulness was both before and after he was elected president.

The portrait they drew conflicted sharply with the image the Clintons had created of a loving couple that believed in family values. What the troopers had to say reflected on Clinton's judgment, character, and honesty. Yet some newspapers, along with the CBS television network, chose to ignore the story, running only White House denials several days after the story broke.

Explaining his paper's decision not to run the story initially, R. W. Apple, Jr., Washington bureau chief of the *New York Times*, said, "I am not interested in Bill Clinton's sex life as governor of Arkansas. I'm certain there are a lot of readers who are interested in that, and there are lots of publications they can turn to to slake that thirst."

In contrast, the *Washington Post* reported the charges as soon as they came out, followed the next day by a page-one story focusing on Clinton's attempts to keep the troopers quiet. Leonard Downie, Jr., the *Post*'s executive editor, said, "Extramarital affairs is not the subject of our reporting. The subject of our reporting is the question of whether or not Bill Clinton, as governor and now as president, has in any way used government resources and power in any connection with his private life that would be improper."

When Hillary Clinton gave an interview to try to deflect the story and engender sympathy, the *Times* considered that story to be so newsworthy that it ran the piece on page one. Yet even the denials were nondenials. Lindsey, the president's aide, called the stories "ridiculous." While denying that he had offered a job in exchange for silence, Clinton himself never explicitly denied the specifics offered by the troopers. Instead, in a formulation he had used during the previous controversy over Flowers, he said the charges had been dealt with during the campaign. Clearly uncomfortable lying, Clinton at one point appeared not to know what to say. A radio reporter asked him, "So none of this actually happened?"

"We . . . we did, if, the, the, I, I, the stories are just as they have been said," Clinton said. Realizing he had confirmed the stories, Clinton finally sputtered, "They're outrageous, and they're not so."

During the campaign, the Clinton camp had feared that Flowers's allegations would derail his bid for the presidency. Yet now that he was president, some publications considered stories about much more substantial charges to be beneath them. Even the *Washington Post* and *Los Angeles Times*, which ran stories on the allegations as soon as they broke, acted as gatekeepers by failing to report such details as Hillary Clinton's relationship with Foster. While the troopers' information did not definitively establish that the two had been having an affair, the fact that they had engaged in fondling and French-kissing was at least as newsworthy as the fact that the Clinton White House planned to serve broccoli. Besides showing that the Clintons' pronouncements promoting family values were hypocritical, the disclosures about Hillary's relationship with Foster raised new questions about Foster's suicide and whether it had anything to do with the stress of that relationship.

What was behind some of the media's delicate handling of

the allegations was not a result of a liberal or conservative plot to suppress the news. Rather, it was a continuation of the press's long-standing reluctance to take on the president for fear of cutting off access to the White House. As in the case of the *Washington Post*'s national staff during Watergate, which shied away from tackling Watergate, organizations that depend on the White House for news look for excuses to avoid stories that might irreparably damage their well-cultivated relationships with the president and his staff. To be sure, few editors or reporters would admit even to themselves that this is the case. Yet the fact is that in covering any beat, journalists recognize that pursuing negative allegations might cut off access to sources.

While any organization tries to hide its weaknesses, the White House is perceived as all-powerful and quite capable of exacting retribution. Reporters are not about to forgo sappy, exclusive interviews with Hillary Clinton about the food tastes of the first family in return for aggressively probing irregularities that may turn out to be based on unfounded rumors.

Yet the troopers' stories required no lengthy investigation. Since the charges had first appeared in the *American Spectator*, newspapers did not have to take responsibility for breaking the story. All they had to do was recapitulate the conservative publication's story or run a wire service story on it. By any standard, it was news.

The president, said Reedy, the former Johnson press secretary, "is not just the manager of our nation. He's not just a prime minister. He is also the nation. He becomes something of a role model. People want to know every tiny nitpicking detail about him.[205]

"At one time," he said, "when you had political machines, the information was constantly going up or down. The precinct captain was in touch with everyone in the precinct, and the information went up. That doesn't happen anymore. The machines died a long time ago. In the modern age, a person can be packaged so the public does not really get a good look at him or her. Consequently, you have an urge by the voters to learn more about the candidate."

248

Paula Jones's claim that Clinton sexually harassed her on May 8, 1991, in a room of the Excelsior Hotel in Little Rock was the icing on the cake. Since Jones made her claim in a press conference announcing that she had sued Clinton, the press could not ignore it. While Jones may have been sexually provocative—her brother-in-law said she would go into restaurants and pinch men—clearly an improper encounter of some kind took place. Well before Jones filed her suit against Clinton alleging harassment, Danny Ferguson, one of Clinton's state trooper guards, said Clinton had summoned Jones to his room that afternoon. While the trooper thought the two had had sex, another witness said Jones emerged from the room looking distraught. Ferguson later said in court papers that he simply pointed out Clinton's hotel suite to Jones, and he did not know if they had sex.

Whether Clinton harassed Jones or whether she acquiesced to his advances, Jones's announcement in May 1994 that she was suing Clinton may have been the nail in his coffin, erasing whatever credibility he had left.

Aside from the public's interest in such information, hypocrisy has always been news. The politician who urges going to war, then is found to have evaded the draft, or who campaigned self-righteously against pornography, then is found to have patronized prostitutes, is rightfully subject to exposure in the press. Such duplicity should not be tolerated because it reflects on the judgment and intelligence of political candidates. When Gary Hart in effect challenged the press to catch him cheating on his wife, then was found to have been having an affair with Donna Rice, there was little question that Hart would have to withdraw from the presidential race, if only because he had made himself look like a fool. In carrying on multiple affairs while governor of Arkansas, then publicly calling one of his girlfriends a liar, Clinton was guilty of being at least as arrogant and witless as Hart.

Aside from misleading the public about the real character of the president, the biggest danger in not reporting embarrassing charges is the impression created that the president is invulnerable and can get away with even larger lapses. If the media ignore critical stories even when they are handed to them, the White House can assume it can manipulate the press on stories requiring more investigation. The corollary is that, since presidents are constantly in the public eye, people are misled into thinking they are accountable, when, in fact, they are not. The fact that Clinton could announce a 25 percent White House staff cut, then blithely increase the staff without any outcry by the press, is testimony to how unaccountable presidents really are.

In explaining its decision to run the story on Clinton's womanizing, the *Los Angeles Times* said that there has been a realization that "personal character may be as important to a leader's performance as political party or ideology." Formulating distinctions between presidents' public and private lives and drawing a line between their actions before taking office and after are meaningless exercises designed mainly to shield presidents from accountability. Such compartmentalization suggests that presidents are stick figures, not people. In reality, it is a form of self-censorship that protects the press from the consequences of taking on the president. In that respect, the disinclination to aggressively probe a president's character is not that different from the press's avoidance of the truth about the Vietnam War.

"It would have been professional suicide for us in the AP [Associated Press] to suggest that the Vietcong insurgents and Hanoi's regular forces were generally superbly trained and well motivated and seemed to believe in their revolutionary cause," war correspondent Peter Arnett noted in his book *Live from the Battlefield*. "We were dissuaded by our editors from suggesting that the Vietnam conflict contained significant elements of a civil war, even though every Vietnamese knew the truth of that description."

In suppressing the truth, the press at the time felt constrained because of President Johnson's constant suggestions that anyone who questioned the essential premise of the war—that it was a battle to save Southeast Asia from Communist aggression—was unpatriotic. Virtually the only publication that attempted to expose the myth Johnson had created was I. F.

Stone's newsletter. Similarly, the Clinton White House sounded the theme that in aggressively reporting the president's latest gaffes, the press was engaging in mean-spirited "cannibalism."

From Tonya Harding to Michael Jackson, the propagandists of celebrities have denounced the press for going too far in revealing scandals, only to fall silent as the charges initially reported in the media prove to be far tamer than the truth. In many circles, it has become fashionable to take a position of neutrality toward morality and to withhold judgment unless an individual is convicted of a crime. The corollary to that position is that only evidence admissible during a criminal trial is worthy of consideration in evaluating wrongdoing. Such a standard leaves politicians wide latitude to lie, cheat, and abuse their positions. In a democracy, voters—not judges—decide what kind of person should represent them.

That is not to say that every president who engages in extensive deceit in his private life will turn out to be a bad president. By any standard, Franklin D. Roosevelt, who had a show marriage like Clinton's, was a great president. On the other hand, his dalliances were limited to two women, compared with Clinton's reportedly numerous simultaneous affairs. Faced with such a record, any government official would be turned down for a top secret security clearance because of the possibility of blackmail and demonstration of poor judgment. Yet Clinton, who is not required as president to undergo an FBI background check, is privy to the nation's most sensitive intelligence and military secrets.

Whether they surface in an individual's personal or public life, character flaws are one way of evaluating whether a person is trustworthy enough to be president. Sleaziness may not be a crime, but it is—or should be—a disqualification for being president.

"People want to know if he is an honest man, can they trust him?" Reedy said. "The best way to determine that today is through knowing about sex. Of course, you have to report it."

Thus, given the fact that Clinton spent every day of his governorship lying about and covering up his personal life, it should not have come as a surprise that he and his wife were guilty, at the least, of engaging in gross conflicts of interest in the handling of their investment in the Whitewater Development Co., a real estate development company they jointly owned with James B. McDougal. The interconnections between McDougal and the Clintons were endless. When he was an owner of Whitewater, McDougal was also the owner of Madison Guaranty Savings and Loan, a savings and loan suspected of funneling money into Bill Clinton's 1984 campaign for governor. Clinton appointed the state regulators who oversaw Madison and allowed it to continue in business long after they should have closed it down because of improper management, costing U.S. taxpayers $47 million.

As a lawyer, Hillary Clinton represented Madison when it sought approval from state regulators for a plan to raise capital by issuing preferred stock. Her law firm later represented the Resolution Trust Co. in a lawsuit against Madison's former accounting firm. That suit was handled by Webster L. Hubbell, whose father-in-law, Seth Ward, was an executive with Madison's real estate subsidiary and had had extensive financial dealings with Madison itself. Another member of the Rose law firm, Vincent Foster, the Clintons' close friend, was the Clintons' lawyer when they sold their share of Whitewater back to McDougal in 1992. Further, Hillary Clinton borrowed $30,000 from Madison to aid Whitewater in its land dealings.

At the least, the conflicts had to compromise the Clintons' objectivity. But two facts suggested that more than conflicts of interest were involved. First, while the Clintons claimed to have lost $69,000 on their Whitewater investment, they did not deduct the loss from their federal income returns. Yet they were meticulous in deducting as charitable contributions the price of a box of Pampers and assorted cookies given to a rescue mission, and they deducted $2 and $15 apiece, respectively, for donations of Bill Clinton's used undershorts and long johns. This raised the possibility that the Clintons knew their dealings could not withstand an Internal Revenue Service audit.

Second, Bill Clinton's public statements on the matter were anything but candid. For example, during the presidential campaign, Clinton said he did not have the records of the development company. Later, he turned over more than a box full of the company's records to the Justice Department. Some of those records were in Foster's office in the White House when he committed suicide. Those records were quietly removed after his death.

"Good deeds are better than wise sayings," the Talmud says. In covering political campaigns, the press often overlooks this truism, focusing on candidates' words and on campaign strategy rather than actions. As experience has shown, the campaign promises of presidential candidates invariably are broken.

Along with a candidate's political record, examining conduct, including any kind of deceit, is the surest way to determine whether an individual will be effective as president. Even if he has good ideas, a president who is not trusted will have trouble persuading Congress and the nation to implement those ideas. In a democracy, a president cannot lead if he is not respected.

"If we would pay attention to their track records, it's all there," a Secret Service agent said. "We seem to put blinders on ourselves and overlook these frailties."

Having intimidated the press by erecting artificial barriers that define what should or should not be reported about them, presidents and their aides become even more unaccountable once the heady atmosphere of the White House envelops them. In what he called "Rumsfeld's Rules," Donald Rumsfeld, Ford's chief of staff, warned of this corrosive influence. To guard against it, he listed proscriptions violated by every administration, including Ford's. According to Rumsfeld's Rules—reproduced as an appendix to this book—aides should not accept White House jobs unless they are prepared to tell the president their opinions "with the bark off." Moreover, they should help the president allocate his time with care; they should not divide the world into "them" and "us." Under "Keeping Your Bearings in the White House," Rumsfeld advised White House aides to show their friends and family they are still the same people, despite all the publicity about them.

"Most of the fifty or so invitations you receive each week are from folks wanting the president's chief of staff, not you," he said. "If you doubt that, ask your predecessor how many he received last week." Keep in mind, he said, that if you are not being criticized, "you may not be doing much." He advised, "Don't ever conceive of yourself as indispensable or infallible. Don't let the president . . . believe that nonsense either."

It was a warning that presidents usually ignore. Simply living in the White House, always being greeted with a standing ovation, and being called by old friends "Mr. President" instead of Bill or George creates an aura of infallibility and reverence that turns the heads of all but the strongest individuals. The honorifics go back to European courts and the tension that has always existed between those who would treat American presidents as royalty and those who would prefer that they remain ordinary people. Martha Washington helped establish the royal tradition by having people curtsy before her. She dressed like a queen, wearing a high-crowned headdress, and she never corrected those who called her "the presidentess" or "Lady President." After Washington was sworn in, a crowd in front of Federal Hall in New York City cheered, "Long live George Washington, president of the United States!" The first Congress debated whether the president should be addressed as "your excellency."

Ideally, presidents would be addressed like anyone else and experience the same kinds of frustrations that other mortals encounter, living in modest homes and commuting to work. Combining residence and office only adds to the pressures, since presidents never quite feel that they are "off."

"You have no idea," President Chester Arthur told a reporter, "how depressing and fatiguing it is to live in the same house where you work." First Lady Edith Roosevelt likened it to "living above the store."

Indeed, Julia Grant vainly proposed that she and her husband continue to live in their home on Eye Street in Washington, using the White House for work and official entertaining. But even before the site of the White House was selected, George Washington set the precedent by living and working in the same rented quarters in New York, first on Cherry Street and then on Broadway. Julia Grant soon realized she could not buck that tradition, and it is unlikely it will ever change. Whether because they think the American people expect it or because they gladly seek out the luxurious atmosphere of the White House, presidents will continue to live at 1600 Pennsylvania Avenue. As Clinton remarked during his first trip on *Air Force One*, "This makes it all worth it." Having sacrificed so much to gain the presidency, it would take an individual of superhuman strength to forgo some of its gratifications.

Once they enter the White House, presidents are told that they should act "presidential," a euphemism for "regal." This exhortation leads them to think they have a divine obligation to live the lives of emperors.

Whether they live in the White House or not, the mantle is theirs.

"The essence of the president is that it is the ultimate authority," Reedy said. "Wherever he goes, the presidency is draped around him. If he lived in a rooming house, it would look like the White House in nothing flat. He has to have bodyguards and ceremonial chambers where he meets chiefs of state. The White House is not the building. The White House is the president. No matter where he goes, he is treated as the president."

The kind of homogenization that politicians go through before they become presidential contenders means that most of them will not have the strength of character to withstand the corrupting pressures. The emergence of Political Action Committees (PACs) that finance presidential campaigns has meant that only candidates who have compromised themselves to powerful interest groups become presidential contenders. Having already compromised themselves, such people may not have the inner strength of character to deal with the exhilarating atmosphere of the White House.

"There is built into the presidency a series of devices that tend to remove the occupant of the Oval Office from all the forces which require most men to rub up against the hard facts of life on a daily basis," Reedy wrote in *The Twilight of the Presidency*. Within a matter of months after taking office, Reedy said, the privileges of office "become part of an environment which he necessarily regards as his just and due entitlement—not because of the office but because of his mere existence."

"The life of the White House is the life of a court," Reedy said. "Even more important, however, he [the president] is treated with all the reverence due a monarch. No one interrupts presidential contemplation for anything less than a major catastrophe somewhere on the globe. No one speaks to him unless spoken to first. No one ever invites him to 'go soak your head' when his demands become petulant and unreasonable."

That environment inevitably leads to the kinds of misjudgments and scandals American presidents have repeatedly engaged in. Kennedy's failure to perceive the recklessness of the Bay of Pigs invasion, Johnson's stubborn refusal to bow to public demands for an end to the Vietnam War, Nixon's effort to cover up the Watergate scandal, Reagan's encouragement of the events that led up to the Iran-contra affair, and Bush's lying about his knowledge of the Iran-contra scandal are all attributable to the arrogance of power that living in the White House fosters.

To be sure, the demands on a president and first family are enormous, and the public is never satisfied with the job they do. But a president can choose to do what he wants to do. A balanced personality knows how to deal with the stress and keep it in perspective.

"The White House is a character crucible," psychiatrist Bert Brown said. "It either creates or distorts character. How does one solve the conundrum of staying real and somewhat humble when you are surrounded by the most powerful office in the land? You need to stay with your old friends and family who knew you as you were in order not to be overwhelmed by an at times pathological environment that tells you every day you are a genius."

In most cases, the White House environment takes its toll, but the cost is well concealed. Johnson's megalomania, the precariousness of Nixon's mental state, Carter's pettiness, and Reagan's slavishness to his wife did not come out until they left office. As in a movie set, the White House creates a fictional character who is a stand-in for the real president.

The twin forces of television and increased security have exacerbated the problem. Greater security has meant that presidents are isolated even further from the people and removed from everyday problems. Television has meant that presidents live in a fishbowl, giving them a heightened sense of exhilaration and power while creating an illusion that they are accountable to the people.

"The fact remains that the institution provides camouflage for all that is petty and nasty in human beings, and enables a clown or a knave to pose as Galahad and be treated with deference," Reedy wrote. "The thing that makes the system work is the fact that Congress and the Supreme Court are independent bodies," Reedy said. "That means that no matter how silly a president gets, he has to get his proposals through Congress, and he has to worry about what the Supreme Court might do to it. The division of power really works."

Even Congress occasionally falls for the reverential attitude that many have toward the president. For example, in authorizing the president to hire employees for the executive residence, Congress in 1978 passed a law that allowed the president to make such hires "without regard to any other provision of law regulating the employment or compensation of persons in government service."

In other words, the president may treat the members of the household staff as personal help rather than government employees. No other branch of government has such an exemption from the law, and the idea that the president's needs are so pressing that he cannot bear to have the salary and working conditions of a chef or dishwasher regulated like any other employee's is but another example of how the president comes to think of himself as having imperial powers. Because of that law, U.S. District Court Judge Stanley Sporkin dismissed the lawsuit brought against the White House by Sean Haddon, the White House assistant chef. On September 17, 1993, Sporkin said the law meant the court lacked jurisdiction over the matter.

Then, on November 9, 1993, U.S. District Court Judge Harold H. Greene dismissed Haddon's suit which, citing provisions of the Freedom of Information Act, sought copies of documents from the executive residence. According to Greene, the residence is not an "agency" and therefore is not covered by the act, furthering the president's lack of accountability.

Even the salaries of Clinton's assistants were considered too sensitive to disclose. When the *Washington Post*'s Ann Devroy got hold of a list and published them, the White House howled. Meanwhile, Congress routinely publishes lists of the salaries it pays aides.

For all its faults, the press more than any other institution has kept presidents accountable. Having initially accepted the government's explanation of the Vietnam War, the *New York Times* and later the *Washington Post* in 1971 published the secret Defense Department analysis known as the Pentagon Papers, which stated that the government had misrepresented its role in the war to the American people. It has been primarily the press that has uncovered the government's abuses—from the government's radiation experiments on retarded children to the CIA's and FBI's illegal surveillance of Americans. For that reason, most presidents come to hate the press and become paranoid about leaks. Nixon tried to block publication of the Pentagon Papers, and Clinton spends much of his time privately cursing members of the press and individual members of it, according to a Secret Service agent.

Yet the public is a willing partner in mythologizing the presidency. Herb Block, one of the most astute observers of the Washington scene, pointed out in his book *Herblock: A Cartoonist's Life* that Americans have come to think of the president as an institution rather than a person, shielding the president from accountability.

"It's often said that whatever we think of any current occupant at 1600 Pennsylvania Avenue, we should 'respect the office,' " he wrote. "I feel that respect for the office should begin with the person who occupies it—or who campaigns to occupy it—and his respect should extend to the other branches of government, too."

People often overlook breaches of trust by presidents on the grounds that the country cannot stand another "failed presi-

258

dency." From Richard Nixon to Ronald Reagan, presidents have presided over illegal activities and lied about it. Neither Nixon nor Reagan suffered greatly for it. When Nixon died in April 1994, Clinton proclaimed a national day of mourning and closed government offices, as if the former president had been a great leader instead of an unindicted coconspirator.

"I am boggled by the concern about 'failed presidencies'—as if the person temporarily occupying the White House is some kind of holy icon more important than the Constitution or the nation," Block said. "What I think the country cannot stand is failed justice and failure to demand that officials uphold their oaths of office."[206]

Deprived of a king or queen, Americans look to the White House for a father figure they can deify. Whether it is the rugged charm of a Ronald Reagan or the wit and sophistication of a John F. Kennedy, the public craves theater. If a president fulfills his role as actor, he may be forgiven for presiding over illegal activities such as the Iran-contra affair or engaging in flagrant illicit affairs.

As in monarchies, an attack on the integrity of the chief of state is seen almost as an attack on the nation. Many people do not want to believe the allegations about Bill Clinton's personal life because the tawdriness of it tarnishes the presidency and therefore the nation. To point out that the emperor has no clothes is to deprecate his subjects.

Over time, the tendency to overlook character flaws in presidential candidates becomes self-fulfilling. Once they enter the White House, presidents are expected to disregard their campaign promises. The need to justify publishing evidence of Clinton's blatant duplicity as governor and president-elect underscores how abysmally low standards are in evaluating presidents.

"You just shake your head when you think of all the things you've heard and seen and the faith that people have in these celebrity-type people," a Secret Service agent said. "They are probably worse than most average individuals. It just baffles me. If you could see them as they really are, they have a lot of faults and human frailties, as we all do. When you win an election, people assume that you have special qualities they do not have. You are given instant credibility and expertise that you never possessed."

For all its faults, no one has come up with a better system for selecting presidents. But Americans need to recognize that presidents are human beings, not gods, and that they must be judged and held accountable like anyone else. For only by realistically evaluating them as people can Americans select the kinds of presidents they deserve.

Notes

1. Lady Bird Johnson did not respond to a June 16, 1993, request for comment.
2. Interview on November 16, 1992, with Fields.
3. Interview on March 28, 1993, with MacMillan.
4. Interview on November 12, 1992, with Cronin.
5. Interview on January 19, 1993, with Brown.
6. DeGregorio, William A., *The Complete Book of U.S. Presidents*, Wings Books, 1991, page 571.
7. Interview on August 4, 1993, with Gulley.
8. Interview on April 5, 1993, with Cuff.
9. White House Historical Association, *The White House: An Historic Guide*, 1991, pages 70–73; letter to the *Washington Post* of February 20, 1987, from Frank J. Williams, president of the Abraham Lincoln Association, Providence, Rhode Island; *Washington Post*, January 20, 1993, page A-5.
10. Interview on November 12, 1992, with Gulley.

11. *Washington Post*, May 31, 1993, page W-14.

12. Interview on November 17, 1992, with Gulley.

13. Interview on November 17, 1992, with Gulley.

14. Interview on August 2, 1993, with Laitin.

15. Interview on April 6, 1993, with Pierce.

16. Interview on April 21, 1993, with Walzel.

17. Gulley, Bill, with Mary Ellen Reese, *Breaking Cover*, Simon & Schuster, 1980, page 21.

18. Interview on January 18, 1993, with Jones.

19. Interview on March 13, 1993, with O'Donnell.

20. Interview on March 29, 1993, with Jimmy Bull.

21. Interview on August 2, 1993, with Reedy.

22. Interview on March 28, 1993, with MacMillan.

23. Interview on February 18, 1993, with Albertazzie.

24. Interview on March 23, 1993, with O'Donnell.

25. DeGregorio, William A., *The Complete Book of U.S. Presidents*, Wings Books, 1991, page 589.

26. Haldeman, H. R., with Joseph DiMona, *The Ends of Power*, Times Books, 1978, page 66.

27. Interview on March 13, 1993, with Cox.

28. Interview on June 5, 1993, with Reid.

29. Interview on March 29, 1993, with Jimmy Bull.

30. Dean, John W., III, *Blind Ambition: The White House Years*, Simon & Schuster, 1976, page 14. In an interview, Dean said, "I never saw the stewardess again."

31. Interview on April 13, 1993, with Walters.

32. U.S. Secret Service figures, May 4, 1993. In 1992, nine Secret Service agents received reprimands, compared with fourteen uniformed officers. Another thirty-eight received suspensions, compared with twenty-nine uniformed officers. None were removed, compared with two removals of uniformed officers. The number of Secret Service agents was 2,051, compared with 1,106 uniformed officers.

33. *Washington Post*, July 24, 1990, page B-1.

34. Interview on February 15, 1993, with Khachigian.

35. Interview on September 8, 1993, with Bell.

36. Opinion of November 5, 1992, by Judge Bissell, pages 5–6.

37. *New York Times*, February 17, 1974, page A-1.

38. Interview on January 18, 1993, with Conger.

39. Interview on February 10, 1993, with Bender.

40. General Accounting Office, *Protection of the President at Key Biscayne and San Clemente*, 1974.

41. Interview on August 4, 1993, with Gulley.

42. Gulley, Bill, with Mary Ellen Reese, *Breaking Cover*, Simon & Schuster, 1980, pages 146 and 162.

43. Interview on November 12, 1992, with Cronin.

44. Interview on January 28, 1993, with Pitts.

45. Interview on November 27, 1992, with Haller.

46. Haller, Henry, *The White House Family Cookbook*, Random House, 1987, page 11.

47. Interview on March 16, 1993, with John Palmer.

48. Interview on February 12, 1993, with Chappell.

49. Interview on August 1, 1993, with Reid.

50. Interview on February 24, 1993, with Charles Palmer.

51. Interview on April 1, 1993, with Gulley. Also page 223 of Gulley's *Breaking Cover*, Simon & Schuster, 1980. The military aide could not be located to be interviewed.

52. Nixon, Richard, *RN: The Memoirs of Richard Nixon*, Grosset and Dunlap, 1978, page 902.

53. Interviews on November 30, 1992, with Gulley; December 10, 1992, with Kennerly; and December 29, 1992, with Penny. Also Bob Woodward and Carl Bernstein's *The Final Days*, Simon & Schuster, 1976, page 319. In a letter dated June 15, 1993, Ford told the author he was not aware of the incident. "In all frankness," Ford said, "I'm not familiar with a 'lessening' of Bob Hartmann's 'influ-

ence in the White House.' He was, has been, and still is a close and trustworthy personal friend." However, Terrence O'Donnell, Ford's scheduler, said on December 7, 1992, that over time, "Hartmann's duties were made more limited." Ron Nessen, Ford's press secretary, said on page 151 of his book *It Sure Looks Different from the Inside*, published in 1978 by Playboy Press, that Hartmann kept his position only because of "Ford's loyalty to longtime employees."

54. Interview on June 5, 1993, with Hartmann.

55. Interview on December 3, 1992, with Speakes.

56. DeGregorio, William A., *The Complete Book of U.S. Presidents*, Wings Books, 1991, page 612.

57. Interview on January 12, 1993, with Hopkins.

58. Interview on December 29, 1992, with Barrett.

59. Interview on October 29, 1992, with Revell.

60. Interview on November 23, 1992, with Parr.

61. Associated Press, July 7, 1993.

62. Interview on February 24, 1993, with Charles Palmer.

63. Interview on March 14, 1993, with Simmons.

64. Interview on December 1, 1992, with Rumsfeld.

65. Interview on March 16, 1993, with John Palmer.

66. Interview on December 29, 1992, with Penny.

67. Interview on December 16, 1992, with O'Donnell.

68. Interview on January 28, 1993, with Pitts.

69. *A Time To Heal: The Autobiography of Gerald R. Ford*, Harper & Row, 1979, page 187.

70. Ibid., page 279.

71. Interview on March 13, 1993, with Pisha.

72. Interview on January 28, 1993, with Conger.

73. See the author's *Moscow Station*, Pocket Books, 1989, pages 209–211.

74. *New York Times*, June 13, 1977, page 14.

75. *New York Times*, May 1, 1979, page 19.

76. Interview on February 24, 1993, with Charles Palmer.

77. Interview on April 21, 1993, with Walzel.

78. Interview on March 14, 1993, with Buzzelli.

79. Interview on November 30, 1992, with Gulley. Also Gulley's *Breaking Cover*, Simon & Schuster, 1980, page 193.

80. Interview on April 6, 1993, with Pierce.

81. *New York Times*, November 3, 1977, page C-2. Also *Washington Post*, February 9, 1977, page B-4, and February 16, 1977, page B-6.

82. Interview on June 14, 1993, with Dr. Robert Stapleton.

83. Associated Press, February 9, 1977; *New York Times*, September 3, 1976, page A-1, and January 19, 1977, page 20.

84. *New York Times*, July 21, 1978, page A-1.

85. Interview on November 12, 1992, with Gulley.

86. Associated Press, August 31, 1980.

87. Interview on February 14, 1993, with Bender.

88. Interview on March 20, 1993, with Wells.

89. Interview on March 30, 1993, with Cutler.

90. Interview on July 31, 1993, with Pisha.

91. Interview on August 3, 1993, with Gulley.

92. *Monthly Report of Federal Civilian Employment*, Office of Personnel Management, 1960–1992.

93. Interview on March 16, 1993, with Price.

94. Interview on April 6, 1993, with Pierce.

95. Interview on April 13, 1993, with Walters.

96. DeGregorio, William A., *The Complete Book of U.S. Presidents*, Wings Books, 1991, page 633.

97. Ibid., page 644.

98. Reagan, Nancy, with William Novak, *My Turn: The Memoirs of Nancy Reagan*, Random House, 1989, page 60.

99. Ibid., pages 61–63; Regan, Donald T., *For the Record: From*

Wall Street to Washington, Harcourt Brace Jovanovich, 1988, pages 66–70.

100. Interview on September 20, 1993, with Gates.

101. Kelley, Kitty, *Nancy Reagan: The Unauthorized Biography*, Simon & Schuster, 1991, pages 368–369. Also Regan, Donald T., *For the Record: From Wall Street to Washington*, Harcourt Brace Jovanovich, 1988, pages 3 and 4, which discuss the influence of Nancy Reagan's astrologer.

102. Interview on March 14, 1993, with Buzzelli.

103. Interview on May 7, 1993, with Jaworski.

104. Interview on March 22, 1993, with Lazaro.

105. Interview on February 24, 1993, with Charles Palmer.

106. Interview on March 20, 1993, with Quigg.

107. Interview on December 16, 1992, with Kelly.

108. Interview on December 30, 1992, with Kuhn.

109. Interview on February 15, 1993, with Khachigian.

110. Interview on January 8, 1993, with Weinberg.

111. Interview on November 23, 1992, with Parr.

112. Interview on February 17, 1993, with Geisler.

113. Interview on December 3, 1992, with Speakes.

114. Reagan, Michael, *Michael Reagan: On the Outside Looking In*, Zebra Books, 1988, page 219.

115. Interview on July 10, 1993, with Dr. Shumiatcher. Craigue Peters, an RCMP spokesman, said on July 12, 1993, that he was not aware of such a law.

116. Interviews with Michael Reagan on July 9 and 10, 1993.

117. *New York Times*, November 28, 1984, page A-18.

118. U.S. House of Representatives, Appropriations Committee, *Treasury, Postal Service, and General Government Appropriations for Fiscal Year 1993*, March 25, 1992, pages 10–11. Dates for White House improvements often vary in tour guides and newspaper articles.

119. West, J. B., with Mary Lynn Kotz, *Upstairs at the White*

House: My Life with the First Ladies, Coward, McCann & Geoghegan Inc., 1973, page 357.

120. Caroli, Betty Boyd, *Inside the White House: America's Most Famous Home*, Canopy Books, 1992, page 35.

121. Interview on February 10, 1993, with Bender.

122. Associated Press, *New York Times*, November 14, 1981, page A-20.

123. Interview on January 18, 1993, with Conger. Scouten declined on December 16, 1992, and April 16, 1993, to be interviewed. "I'd rather not be in books," Scouten said.

124. Interview on April 13, 1993, with Walters.

125. Interview on January 28, 1993, with Pitts.

126. Interview on December 22, 1992, with Newman.

127. DeGregorio, William A., *The Complete Book of U.S. Presidents*, Wings Books, 1991, page 681.

128. Interview on April 21, 1993, with Walzel.

129. Interview on December 29, 1992, with Penny.

130. Interview on December 22, 1992, with Newman.

131. Interview on June 23, 1993, with Trefry.

132. Interview on February 9, 1993, with Green.

133. *Washington Post*, August 12, 1992, page A-12.

134. Interview on January 21, 1993, with Untermeyer.

135. Interview on February 3, 1993, with Kanjorski.

136. Interview on November 5, 1992, with Weaver.

137. Interview on June 22, 1993, with Bateman.

138. Interview on July 13, 1993, with Trefry.

139. Interview on April 5, 1993, with Cuff.

140. *New York Times*, April 2, 1988, page A-7.

141. *Washington Post*, June 23, 1991, page A-1.

142. Interview on March 3, 1993, with Gray.

143. Interview on December 14, 1992, with Patterson.

144. Interview on March 2, 1993, with Barr.

145. *Washington Post*, June 2, 1991, page D-5. Complaining about unfairness by the media, Lee declined to be interviewed.

146. Interview on August 19, 1993, with Reedy.

147. *Washington Post*, June 4, 1991, page B-2. Bauer's book, *At Ease in the White House: The Uninhibited Memoirs of a Presidential Social Aide*, described the turkey trot.

148. *Washington Post*, July 2, 1991, page E-1.

149. *Wall Street Journal*, November 9, 1992, page C-1.

150. *Washington Post*, January 27, 1992, page A-5, excerpting the "60 Minutes" interview that aired on January 26, 1992.

151. Interview with Pellicano on September 23, 1993, and *Los Angeles Times*, January 30, 1992, page A-20.

152. Truth Verification Laboratories Inc. letter of July 27, 1992, to *Penthouse* magazine, signed by Stephen B. Laub, certified audio analyst.

153. *Congressional Record*, September 23, 1992, page H-9263, reprinting transcripts of portions of telephone calls between Bill Clinton and Gennifer Flowers from September to December 1991, as released by the *Star* at a New York press conference in January 1992. Quotes do not necessarily appear in chronological order.

154. Interview on June 30, 1993, with Flowers.

155. Interview on July 12, 1993, with Saddler.

156. *People*, July 26, 1993, page 124.

157. Interview on April 9, 1993, with Podesta.

158. Associated Press, July 4, 1993, quoting the July 1993 issue of *Computer Shopper*, and *PC Magazine*, July 1993, pages 293–294, and *Consumer Reports*, September 1993, page 570.

159. Interview on April 9, 1993, with Watkins.

160. *White House Travel Office Management Review*, July 2, 1993, pages 4–5, and *Arkansas Business*, November 16, 1992, pages 1–28.

161. *New York Times*, December 2, 1992, page B-10.

162. Kurtz, Howard, *Media Circus: The Trouble with America's Newspapers*, Random House, 1993, page 238.

163. Interview on July 12, 1993, with Saddler.

164. *Budget of the U.S.*, fiscal 1993, Appendix One, pages 201–212.

165. *Washington Post*, February 10, 1993, page A-1.

166. *Washington Post*, April 14, 1993, page A-19.

167. *Washington Post*, September 30, 1993, page A-1.

168. Interview on April 9, 1993, with Watkins.

169. Watkins did not return telephone calls made to obtain comment on the status of his plan.

170. General Accounting Office, *White House Acquisition of Automated Résumé Processing System*, June 1993, page 2.

171. *Washington Post*, September 5, 1993, page A-8.

172. Interview on June 29, 1993, with Price.

173. Anthony, Carl Sferrazza, *First Ladies: The Saga of the Presidents' Wives and Their Power, 1789–1961,* volume I, William Morrow and Co., 1990, pages 87 and 153.

174. Anthony, Carl Sferrazza, *First Ladies: The Saga of the Presidents' Wives and Their Power*, volume II, William Morrow and Co., 1991, pages 250–251.

175. *New York Times*, August 22, 1993, page A-1.

176. *New Yorker*, August 9, 1993, page 45.

177. *Washington Post*, August 11, 1993, page A-1.

178. *Newsweek*, August 9, 1993, page 29.

179. *Washington Post*, August 15, 1993, page A-21.

180. Interview on September 7, 1993, with Young.

181. Interview on September 4, 1993, with Brown.

182. *Newsweek*, August 23, 1993, page 22.

183. Interview on September 14, 1993, with Young.

184. Interview on August 2, 1993, with Reedy.

185. *American Journalism Review*, December 1993, page 4.

186. *Wall Street Journal*, December 1, 1993.

187. McLarty appearance on "Meet the Press," June 20, 1993.

188. *Washington Monthly*, March 1994, page 4.

189. *Washington Monthly*, November 1993, page 9.

190. Associated Press, November 18, 1993.

191. West, J. B., with Mary Lynn Kotz, *Upstairs at the White House: My Life with the First Ladies*, Coward, McCann & Geoghegan Inc., 1973, page 82.

192. Interview on June 28, 1993, with Haddon. Also *Sean T. Haddon v. Gary J. Walters*, Civil Action 93-1254, filed June 21, 1993, in U.S. District Court in Washington, and *Washington Post*, June 22, 1993, page A-17, and July 8, 1993.

193. Gary J. Walters letter of April 1, 1993, to Rodney R. Sweetland III.

194. Interview on July 5, 1993, with Chambrin.

195. *USA Today*, March 30, 1994, page 2-D.

196. *Wall Street Journal*, August 20, 1993, page A-12.

197. Associated Press, August 16, 1993.

198. Interview on September 8, 1993, with Bell.

199. Memo of July 20, 1993, from Neel to executive residence staff.

200. *Wall Street Journal*, August 16, 1993, page A-16.

201. O'Neill, Tip, with William Novak, *Man of the House: The Life and Political Memoirs of Speaker Tip O'Neill*, Random House, 1987, page 4.

202. *New York Times*, February 2, 1993, page A-1.

203. *Los Angeles Times*, December 21, 1993, page A-1.

204. *American Spectator*, January 1994, page 22.

205. Interview on January 3, 1994, with Reedy.

206. Herbert Block, *Herblock: A Cartoonist's Life: Self-portrait and Views of Washington from Roosevelt to Clinton*, Macmillan Publishing Co., 1993, pages 104 and 296.

White House Dates

1790   After being sworn in the previous year, President Washington signed legislation to designate Philadelphia as the temporary U.S. capital until the "first Monday in December, 1800," when the government would be located in a district "not exceeding 10 miles square . . . on the river Potomac."

1791   George Washington selected Pierre L'Enfant to plan the capital in Washington. L'Enfant envisioned a "president's palace" five times the size of the house eventually built. Congress failed to appropriate funds.

1792   The cornerstone was laid and construction began on the White House on a wooded knoll overlooking the Potomac River. James Hoban's design, borrowing heavily from architecture in his native Dublin, was selected from nine entries in a competition suggested by Thomas Jefferson. Made of gray sandstone, the Georgian-style building was called the President's House, the name preferred by George Washington. The cornerstone has never been found. The exterior was 165 feet from east to west and 85 feet from north to south.

1798 After it was painted with whitewash, people began referring to the building unofficially as the White House.

1800 John Adams, the second president, and his wife, Abigail Adams, moved in with eight servants.

1801 Thomas Jefferson had the Marine Band play at the White House. It continues to play "Hail to the Chief" and the "President's Own" as the president's official entrance march.

An iron cookstove replaced an open fireplace.

1814 The British burned the White House, leaving only the charred stone walls. Two wells were installed just outside the White House. Previously, servants hauled water from half a mile away. A bathtub was installed, but water was supplied by hand.

1817 James Monroe moved back into a reconstructed White House.

1824 A semicircular south portico was added.

1829 The north portico with covered carriage passage was added.

1834 Indoor plumbing was installed.

1837 Central heating was installed.

1848 Gaslights were installed.

1853 Hot water was installed.

1857 Congress approved the first salary for an employee to handle secretarial duties. The amount was $2,500 a year. Prior to that, presidents paid secretaries—usually family members—from their own pockets.

1865 The Secret Service was established within the Treasury Department to suppress counterfeiting.

1866 A telegraph was installed.

1879 A telephone was installed. The phone number was 1. It remained the only telephone in the White House for three decades.

Rutherford Hayes started the annual Easter egg roll on the south lawn.

1880 The typewriter was introduced.

1881 Air-conditioning and a hydraulic elevator were installed.

1889 The first female staff member, a stenographer, began work.

1891 Electricity was installed.

1901 Edith Roosevelt obtained the first staff member for a first lady, detailed from the War Department.

After the assassination of William McKinley in Buffalo, New York, in 1901, Congress directed the Secret Service to protect the president. McKinley was the third president killed in thirty-six years.

1902 The west wing was added as an office. Connected to the White House by a low-lying colonnade, it was sixty by ninety feet.

Theodore Roosevelt officially named the building the White House, the name most Americans had been using anyway. He allotted space for reporters next to his secretary's office.

The first tennis court was built. In 1909, it was moved to the south grounds.

1906 Congress passed legislation to require the Secret Service to protect the president.

1909 The Oval Office was added to the west wing. It was thirty-six feet long and thirty feet wide.

1915 The first transcontinental telephone call was placed from the Oval Office.

1921 The first radio was acquired.

1922 The White House Police was started under the White House military aide. The first formal attempt to provide security for the White House had begun during the Civil War, using four officers of the Metropolitan police and members of the 150th regiment of the Pennsylvania Volunteers.

The first vacuum cleaner was acquired.

1926 The first electric refrigerator was installed.

1927 The third floor was remodeled to add living space, including a "sky parlor" or solarium on the roof of the south portico.

1929 The first electric washing machine was installed.

Herbert Hoover began his term with three secretaries and a staff of forty.

1930 Congress placed the White House Police under the supervision of the Secret Service.

1933 An indoor swimming pool was built and later converted to a press room.

1935 Franklin Roosevelt established a library.

1942 The east wing was built. It included a movie theater.

1947 The first television set was acquired.

1949 Margaret Truman's piano began to fall through the second floor, and the commissioner of public buildings said the floor was "staying up there purely from habit." A renovation, finished in 1952, included gutting the inside and installing a steel frame to support the floors. Two additional basement levels were added beneath the ground floor as service areas. To give presidents a private place to sit outside, a balcony on the second-floor level of the south portico was also built.

1961 A kitchen was added to the second floor for family dining.

The White House Historical Association was formed.

1970 The White House Police was renamed the Executive Protective Service and given responsibility for protecting foreign missions.

A billiard room was built on the third floor.

1975 An outdoor swimming pool was built.

1977   The Executive Protective Service was renamed the Secret Service uniformed division.

1980   Restoration of the exterior began.

1988   The American Association of Museums accredited the White House as a museum.

Compiled from standard reference books such as *Within These Walls: A Viewer's Guide to Understanding the White House*, published by the White House Historical Association. These works sometimes differ in their accounts of when events took place.

Presidents
and Their Wives

George Washington   April 30, 1789–March 3, 1797
  Martha Dandridge Custis Washington
John Adams   March 4, 1797–March 3, 1801
  Abigail Smith Adams
Thomas Jefferson   March 4, 1801–March 3, 1809
  Martha Wayles Skelton Jefferson
James Madison   March 4, 1809–March 3, 1817
  Dolley Payne Todd Madison
James Monroe   March 4, 1817–March 3, 1825
  Elizabeth Kortright Monroe
John Quincy Adams   March 4, 1825–March 3, 1829
  Louisa Johnson Adams
Andrew Jackson   March 4, 1829–March 3, 1837
  Rachel Donelson Robards Jackson
Martin Van Buren   March 4, 1837–March 3, 1841
  Hannah Hoes Van Buren

William Henry Harrison   March 4, 1841–April 4, 1841
   Anna Symmes Harrison
John Tyler   April 6, 1841–March 3, 1845
   Letitia Christian Tyler
   Julia Gardiner Tyler
James Polk   March 4, 1845–March 3, 1849
   Sarah Childress Polk
Zachary Taylor   March 5, 1849–July 9, 1850
   Margaret Smith Taylor
Millard Fillmore   July 10, 1850–March 3, 1853
   Abigail Powers Fillmore
Franklin Pierce   March 4, 1853–March 3, 1857
   Jane Appleton Pierce
James Buchanan   March 4, 1857–March 3, 1861
Abraham Lincoln   March 4, 1861–April 15, 1865
   Mary Todd Lincoln
Andrew Johnson   April 15, 1865–March 3, 1869
   Eliza McCardle Johnson
Ulysses S. Grant   March 4, 1869–March 3, 1877
   Julia Dent Grant
Rutherford B. Hayes   March 4, 1877–March 3, 1881
   Lucy Webb Hayes
James A. Garfield   March 4, 1881–September 19, 1881
   Lucretia Rudolph Garfield
Chester A. Arthur   September 20, 1881–March 3, 1885
   Ellen Herndon Arthur
Grover Cleveland*   March 4, 1885–March 3, 1889
   Frances Folsom Cleveland
Benjamin Harrison   March 4, 1889–March 3, 1893
   Caroline Scott Harrison
   Mary Lord Dimmock Harrison
Grover Cleveland*   March 4, 1893–March 3, 1897
   Frances Folsom Cleveland
William McKinley   March 4, 1897–September 14, 1901
   Ida Saxton McKinley

---

*Cleveland served twice.

PRESIDENTS AND THEIR WIVES

Theodore Roosevelt   September 14, 1901–March 3, 1909
   Alice Lee Roosevelt
William H. Taft   March 4, 1909–March 3, 1913
   Helen Harrison Taft
Woodrow Wilson   March 4, 1913–March 3, 1921
   Ellen Axson Wilson
   Edith Bolling Galt Wilson
Warren G. Harding   March 4, 1921–August 2, 1923
   Florence Kling De Wolfe Harding
Calvin Coolidge   August 3, 1923–March 3, 1929
   Grace Goodhue Coolidge
Herbert Hoover   March 4, 1929–March 3, 1933
   Lou Henry Hoover
Franklin D. Roosevelt   March 4, 1933–April 12, 1945
   Eleanor Roosevelt Roosevelt
Harry S Truman   April 12, 1945–January 20, 1953
   Bess Wallace Truman
Dwight D. Eisenhower   January 20, 1953–January 20, 1961
   Mamie Doud Eisenhower
John F. Kennedy   January 20, 1961–November 22, 1963
   Jacqueline Bouvier Kennedy
Lyndon B. Johnson   November 22, 1963–January 20, 1969
   Claudia (Lady Bird) Taylor Johnson
Richard M. Nixon   January 20, 1969–August 9, 1974
   Patricia Ryan Nixon
Gerald Ford   August 9, 1974–January 20, 1977
   Elizabeth (Betty) Bloomer Warren Ford
Jimmy Carter   January 20, 1977–January 20, 1981
   Rosalynn Smith Carter
Ronald Reagan   January 20, 1981–January 20, 1989
   Jane Wyman Reagan
   Nancy Davis Reagan
George Bush   January 20, 1989–January 20, 1993
   Barbara Pierce Bush
Bill Clinton   January 20, 1993–
   Hillary Rodham Clinton

Rumsfeld's Rules*

By Donald Rumsfeld, Chief of Staff to President Ford

Serving the President

• Don't accept the post or keep it unless you have an understanding with the president that you're free to tell him what you think with the "bark off" and unless you have the courage and ability to carry that out.

• Visit with your predecessors from previous administrations. They know the road ahead and can help you spot potholes. You have an obligation to make original mistakes rather than needlessly repeating theirs.

• Don't think you're president. You're not. The Constitution provides for only one.

• In executing presidential decisions, work hard to be true to the president's view, both in substance and tone. Handle your responsibilities as he would were he in your position.

• The immediate staff and others in the administration will assume that your manner, tone, and tempo reflect the president's. Conduct yourself as if they did.

• Learn to say "I don't know." If used when appropriate, you will say it often.

• If you foul up, tell the president quickly and correct the error quickly. Don't dally, compounding mistakes.

• Walk around the government. If you are invisible, the mystique of the president's office may perpetuate wrong impressions about you or the office, to the president's detriment. After all, you may not be as bad as they say you are.

• The president's key assets are his words and time. Help him allocate each with care.

• In America, leadership is created by consent, not command. A president must persuade to lead. Personal contact must mold his thinking. This is critical to his ability to persuade and thus to maintain his leadership.

• Be precise. Lack of precision is most dangerous when the margin of error is smallest.

• Preserve the president's options. He'll need them.

• It is always easier to get into something than to get out of it.

• Don't divide the world into "them" and "us." Particularly avoid infatuation with or resentment towards the press, Congress, internal rivals, or political opponents. Accept them as inherent components of your world. Leaks are inevitable, too. Amidst all the clutter are the goals you set. So put your head down, do the best job possible, let the flak pass, and work towards those goals.

• Avoid speaking ill of another member of the team. In private, tell the president your fair and balanced assessments.

• Never say, "The White House wants." Buildings cannot "want."

• Leave the president's family business to the family members. Don't try to manage the first family. You will have plenty to do without that and they are likely to do fine without your help.

• Make decisions about the president's personal security yourself. He can overrule you, but don't make him be the one to counsel caution.

• Realize that being vice president is tough. Don't make his already tricky set of relationships more difficult. Work to make them easier.

• Don't automatically obey presidential directives if you disagree or if you suspect the president hasn't considered all aspects of the issue.

• The price of being close to the president is delivering bad news. You fail him and yourself if you don't tell him the truth. No matter how eager you are to do your job, others won't want to do this part of it for you.

• You and other key staff aides must be—and be seen to be— above suspicion. Set a good example, watch for trouble, face problems, and correct errors fast.

• Don't speak ill of your predecessor or successor. You didn't walk in their shoes.

• Guard the public trust. Strive to preserve and enhance the integrity of the office of the presidency. Pledge to leave it stronger than when you came in.

• Beware when any idea is pushed primarily because it is "bold, exciting, innovative, and new." Loads of such ideas are also foolish.

• Above all, don't blame the boss!

Keeping Your Bearings in the White House

• Enjoy your stint in public service. It will be one of the most interesting and challenging times of your life.

• Don't ever conceive of yourself as indispensable or infallible. Don't let the president or others believe that nonsense either.

• Show your family, staff, and friends that you're still the same person, despite all the publicity and notoriety accompanying your position.

• Choose a first-rate deputy. Don't be consumed by the job or you'll lose your balance. Keep your mooring lines to the outside world—family, friends, neighbors as well as people out of government and people who may not agree with you. Balance is the key to life in government and outside it.

• When asked for your view by the press or others, remember that reporters are seeking the president's view. Yours is far less important.

• Most of the fifty or so invitations you receive each week come from folks wanting the president's chief of staff, not you. If you doubt that, ask your predecessor how many he received last week.

• Remember, you are not all that important. It's your responsibilities which are.

• Keep a sense of humor. Remember the saying: "The higher a monkey climbs, the more you see of his behind."

• Be yourself. Follow your instincts. Success in any effort depends, at least in part, on your ability to carry out the mission. This is easiest when you are convinced that what you are doing is right.

• Realize that the amount of criticism you receive correlates somewhat with the amount of publicity you receive.

• If you are not criticized, you may not be doing much.

- Know and remember where you came from.

- If in doubt, don't. If still in doubt, do what's right.

- From the inside, the White House may look as ugly as the inside of a stomach. Sausage making and policy making shouldn't be seen close up. But don't let that panic you. Things may be better than they seem from the inside.

- Identify and develop a successor.

- Be able to resign. It will improve your value to the president and do wonders for your performance.

Doing the Job in the White House

- Performance depends on the quality of people. Be careful to select the best, train them, and back them. When errors occur, give sharper guidance. If errors persist or if you find a person doesn't fit, cut the loss and help the person to move on. The country cannot afford "amateur hour" in the White House.

- You'll have time to launch many projects but be able to finish few. So think, plan, develop. Along the way, place good people in responsible positions, give them authority, and hold them accountable. Trying to do everything yourself means that little will be done.

- Think ahead. Day-to-day operations drive out planning.

- Plan backwards. Set objectives and trace them back to see how to achieve them. You may find that no path can lead you there, which requires changing objectives.

- Plan forward to see where your steps will take you.

- Don't overcontrol. Stay loose enough so that you can observe the flow of paperwork and decisions and modify and improve upon the process.

• A president needs many sources of information. Avoid restricting the flow of paper, people, or ideas to him.

• If in doubt, move decisions up to the president.

• When you raise an issue with the president, try to come away with a decision, ideally one that sets a precedent. Pose the issue so it will produce broad policy guidance. This will help guide you when a range of similar issues arise later, saving everyone time.

• Serve the president, Cabinet, and staff by seeing that they are informed. If they are cut out of the information flow, their decisions will be poorly made, not made, or not confidently and persuasively implemented.

• Don't allow people to be excluded from meetings or other opportunities to express their views simply because their views differ from the president's or from the views of the person who calls the meeting or from your own views. The staff system must have discipline and integrity in order to serve the president well.

• When the president is faced with a decision, either be sure he has the recommendations of all appropriate people or make sure he is aware that he lacks their views and is willing to do without them. Bear in mind that those who are excluded will be unhappy and become less effective if they feel cut out.

• Don't act as a bottleneck in the flow of paper. If a decision is not important enough for you or the president to make, delegate the responsibility for handling the matter to someone else. Force decision making down and outside the White House. Find problem areas, add structure where necessary, and delegate. The pressure is to do the opposite. Resist it.

• Be sure the staff is given policy guidance against which to test decisions. Otherwise, decisions will be random.

• Test ideas in the marketplace. You should learn from a wide range of sources. The mere act of consulting helps create support for ideas.

• If a prospective presidential approach cannot be explained clearly enough to be understood well, it probably has not been thought out enough. If not widely understood by the American people, it will not be accepted anyway.

• The American people elect a president to make choices. Staff must help to identify those choices and make sure the president is aware of the real differences among those choices.

• Most people around the president had hefty egos before they entered government, many with some justification. Their initial press notices do little to deflate those egos. This may include you.

• Resist referring to "we" in the White House and "they" outside the White House.

• Control your time. Don't let it be done for you. If you're working off your In box, you're working off the priorities of others. Be sure the staff works off what you move to them from the president. Otherwise, the president will be reacting, not leading.

• Look for what's missing. Most advisers can tell a president how to improve proposals or how to rectify matters that have gone amiss. Few are able to see what is not there.

• Think of dealing with Congress as a revolving door. You'll be back to today's opponents for support tomorrow.

• Work constantly to trim the White House staff, from your first day to your last. All the pressures run in the other direction.

• Assume that everything you say or do will be on the front page of the *Washington Post* tomorrow. It may.

Index

Accountability, 198, 250, 253
    press and, 258
Adams, Abigail, 4, 67, 272
Adams, John, 4, 67, 272
Adamson, Terrence B., 89, 90,
    94, 103
Adolfo (designer), 113
Agnew, Spiro, 61–62
Aides, 9, 10, 14
    background clearances, 69–70
    to Clinton, 171
    favors for, 14, 15, 16
    power and responsibility of,
        150–52
Air Force One, xiv, xv, 3, 10, 15,
    16, 21, 22–24, 45, 72, 148,
    156
    Bush and, 137–38
    and Clinton haircut, 176
    costs, 23
    crew, 23, 35–37, 60–62, 100
    food, drinks on, 77–79, 90

Johnson and, 21, 24–25, 32
Nixon and, 57–58
Air force Two, 37
Air Mobility Command
    Eighty-ninth Airlift Wing,
        23
Albertazzie, Ralph, 12, 36, 37
Alcohol use, alcoholism, 66
    Carters, 90–91
    Fords, 67–68, 77–78
    Johnson, 31
    Nixons, 40–41
    Reagan White House, 111
All the President's Men (Wood-
    ward and Bernstein), 174
American cuisine, 220–21, 222,
    224
American Fur Co., 113
American Spectator, 238, 248
Ames, Aldrich H., 186
Amyx, Raleigh D., 48–49
Andrews Air Force Base, 23

INDEX

Antiques
  stolen from Bethesda Naval
    Hospital, 84–86, 89
Apple, R. W., Jr., 209–10, 246
Appointments process (Clinton),
  186–87, 191, 202, 226–27
Architectural Digest, 125–26
Arkansas Democrat-Gazette, 193
Arkansas state troopers, 238–46,
  248, 249
Arnett, Peter
  Live from the Battlefield, 250
Arrogance, 45–46, 145
  of Clinton, 160, 166, 234–35
  of Clinton staff, 160, 175, 183,
    184, 186
Arthur, Chester, 254
Atmosphere of White House, xiv, 26,
  93, 131, 146–55, 160, 255–56
  effects of, 234–35, 253–54

Baird, Zoë E., 186
Baker, James A., III, 128–29, 145
Baldridge, Letitia, 155
Barlow, Joel, 187
Barr, William P., 148
Barrett, Robert E., 72
Bartley, Robert, 192
Barucci, Piero, 185
Bateman, Herbert H., 47
Bateman, Paul W., 142, 147
Bauer, Stephen M., 154
Bay of Pigs invasion, 204, 256
Beautification Program, 187
Begin, Menachem, 90
Bell, William J., 49–50, 75, 83,
  109, 112, 231
Bender, Shirley, 55, 68, 91, 93,
  99–100, 125
Bernstein, Carl, 213
  and Bob Woodward; *All the
  President's Men,* 174
Bethesda Naval Hospital, 84–86,
  89
Birnbaum, Jeffrey H., 174–75,
  213–14
Bissell, John W., 50
Blass, Bill, 113
Blind Ambition (Dean), 45
Block, Herb
  Herblock, 258, 259

Bloomingdale, Betsy, 113
Bluem, Norbert, 185
Boeing 707's, 22, 37, 57, 100, 137
Boeing 747's, 22, 93–94, 137–38,
  156
Bourne, Peter G., 92
Brandt, Willy, 91, 94
Branscum, Larry, 135–36
Britt, Donna, 149
Brock, David, 238
Brooks, Jack, 201
Brown, Bertram S., 9, 149–50,
  207, 215
  on Clinton, 202, 205
  on Ford, 68
  on Foster, 195
  on Johnson, 31–32
  on Nixon, 40
  on White House, 256
Brown, Jim, 62
Brzezinski, Zbigniew, 97
Buchanan, James, 148
Buchanan, Pat, 107
Bull, Jimmy R., 23, 24, 44–45,
  81, 101
Bull, Steve, 45–46, 62–63
Burka, Jane, 168
Bush, Barbara, 75, 128, 130, 131,
  132–33, 134, 153–54, 155,
  168
  adult literacy programs, 187
  and domestic staff, 224, 225
  as first lady, 187, 188
  and White House food, 222
Bush, George, 10, 22, 97, 113, 167,
  168, 174, 210, 235
  and domestic staff, 220
  favorite restaurants, 76–77
  food preferences, 138, 237
  and information about White
    House finances, 146–47
  Iran-contra affair, 156, 256
  post-presidential income, 157
  presidency, 130–42, 143,
    147–50, 152, 153–57, 175,
    177, 178, 204, 227
  removed from everyday life,
    83, 130–31
  vice-president, 118–19, 128,
    139–40

and White House food,
221–22, 224–25
Bush, George Prescott, 130, 131
Bush, John E. "Jeb," 130
Bush administration, 53, 176–77,
219
Butlers, xiv, 11, 223–24, 225
Butterfield, Alexander, 58, 59
Buzzelli, James A., 89, 110

Calligraphers, 7, 123
Camp David, xv, 7, 10, 90, 100,
233
Code name: Cactus, 12
Camp David Accords, 90
Campaign promises, 259
Bush, 155–56
Carter, 90
Clinton, 176, 177, 180–81
Carter, Amy, 93–94, 96
Carter, Billy, 91, 122
Carter, Hugh, 99
Carter, James Earl (Chip), III,
91–93
Carter, Jimmy, 16, 60, 107, 110,
111, 122, 128, 138, 235
code name, 87
cuts promised by, 84, 86–87,
90, 99–101
election, 82
food preferences, 62
mail received, 137
planned attack on, 119–20
post-presidency protection of,
75
presidency, 84, 86–92, 94–103,
135, 203, 207, 227, 256
relationship with wife, 96
Carter, John William (Jack), 92
Carter, Lillian, 91
Carter, Rosalynn, 11, 90, 92,
93–94, 95–96, 98, 99–100,
126, 131
role taken by, 187
Carter administration, 159
Casey, William, 107
Catoctin Mountain Park, 12
Central Intelligence Agency (CIA),
5, 28, 30, 258
Chambrin, Pierre, 220, 221–22,
223–25

Chappell, William J. (Joe), 61–62
Character flaws in presidents,
234–36, 244, 246, 249–51,
256–57, 260–61
Chefs, 59–60, 76, 123, 220–22,
223, 226–27
Cheney, Dick, 204
Chief(s) of staff, 11, 195, 204
Chief usher(s), 105, 135
Children of presidents, 43, 68,
91–94, 120–22
Children's Defense Fund, 166
China, 39
Citizens for a Sound Economy,
179
Clarke, Kenneth, 185
Clean Air Act, 226
Cleveland, Frances, 187
Clinton, Bill, 76, 119, 138, 142,
194
code name, 71
and domestic staff, 223–24
favorite restaurants, 77
governor of Arkansas, 167
hair cut (Los Angeles), 24, 58,
175, 176
interest in people, 203
lack of discipline, 203–04
presidency, 8, 147, 159–60,
167–87, 189, 202–12,
218–19, 226–36, 237–38,
255, 259
and press, 173–75, 196,
209–19, 258
relationship with wife, xiii–xiv,
166
temper, 165, 214, 229–30, 234
threats to, 52
and Whitewater, 251–52
Clinton, Chelsea, 73, 94, 105, 189,
221, 241
code name, 71
Clinton, Hillary Rodham, 139,
169, 171, 187–90, 197,
237–38, 248
and B. Clinton alleged sexual
affairs, 238, 239, 240–41,
242, 243–44, 247
code name, 71
health care task force, 192

Clinton, Hillary Rodham (*cont.*)
    marriage, xiii–xiv, 160, 165,
        166, 207, 231
    relationship with husband,
        230–31
    and White House food, 220–26
    and Whitewater, 252
Clinton, Roger, 71–72
Clinton administration, 184–87,
        228–29
    Gergen critique of, 209
    ineffectiveness of, 159–60
Clinton White House, 201–02,
        207, 225
    inadequacy of, 183, 195, 197,
        199, 228–29
    paranoia, 206, 207–08
    and press, 251
Clough, Susan, 101–02
Code names, 71–72
    Air Force One: Angel, 22
    Bush: Timber Wolf, 130
    Camp David: Cactus, 12
    Carter: Deacon, 87
    Clintons, 71
    Ford: Passkey, 68
    Green Ball (fund code), 19
    Johnson: Volunteer, 10
    Nixon: Searchlight, 40
    presidential limousine: Stage-
        coach, 70
    Reagan: Rawhide, 109
    White House: Crown, xiv
    White House garage: Headlight,
        47
Collingwood, John E., 172
Collor de Mello, Fernando, 154
Commodity Futures Trading Com-
        mission, 226
Condon, George, 175
Conger, Clement E., 22, 54–55,
        84–85, 125–27
Congress, 6, 8, 144, 257, 258
    House Judiciary Committee, 39
Corder, Frank Eugene, 54
Cornelius, Catherine A., 170–71,
        172
Council of Economic Advisers,
        115
Country Club of Little Rock,
        194–95

Cox, Edward F., 15
Cox, Kenneth L., 43, 44
Cronin, John, Jr., 7, 58
Cuba, 187
Cuff, William F., 14, 18, 19, 22,
        145–46, 151
    on Carter, 88, 100
Cuomo, Mario, 162
Curator(s), 54–55, 86, 125, 126
Cutler, Lloyd N., 96–97, 114–15,
        122, 190

Davison, Steve, 172
Dean, John W., III
    Blind Ambition, 45
Deaver, Michael, 128, 146, 153,
        209
Defense Department, 7, 8, 19, 30,
        57, 71, 143, 145, 179, 258
Defense Intelligence Agency, 5
Democratic National Committee,
        39
Detailees, 20, 86, 176–77
Devroy, Ann, 179–80, 219, 258
Dole, Elizabeth, 210
Dole, Robert, 210, 211
Donaldson, Sam, 154
Donovan, Raymond J., 107
"Doomsday" planes, 15
Downey, Thomas J., 152–53
Downie, Leonard, Jr., 246–47
Dreyer, David, 186
Drug forfeiture fund, 178–79
Dukakis, Michael, 131–32, 208

Ehrlichman, John, 57
Eisenhower, David, 41–42, 44
Eisenhower, Dwight, 12, 22, 34
Eisenhower, Mamie, 43, 188
Eller, Jeff, 171
Employees (White House)
    background checks on, 76
    detailed, 8
    Executive Office of the Presi-
        dent, 8, 101, 176, 178,
        183–84
    non-detailees, 142
    see also Detailees; Staff
Environmental Protection
        Agency, 226
Executive Clerk(s), 119

Executive Office Building (EOB), new, 6
Executive Office Building (EOB), old, 6, 7, 14, 20, 102, 114, 119, 136
  security, 46, 47
Executive Office of the President, 6
  employees, 8, 101, 176, 178, 183–84
Executive Protective Service, 46, 274, 275
Executive Residence, 6, 7
Exner, Judith Campbell, 2

"Faddle" (secretary), 2, 35
Federal Aviation Administration, 23
Federal Bureau of Investigation (FBI), 30, 53, 69, 75, 118, 186, 202, 220, 258
  National Crime Information Center (NCIC), 71
  and White House travel office affair, 171, 172, 173, 191, 196–97, 200, 201, 207
Federal Deposit Insurance Corporation, 226
Ferguson, Danny, 249
Ficklin, John, 42
"Fiddle" (Secretary), 2, 35
Fielding, Fred F., 122, 145
Fields, Alonzo, 2
Fields, Louis, 139
Fillmore, Millard, 187
First family(ies), 123–24
  Clintons, 238
  Secret Service protection, 122–23
First lady(ies), 11, 133–34
  designer dresses, 113
  list, 277–79
  office, 4
  role of, 187–88
Fischer, David C., 113–14
Fiske, Robert B., Jr., 200
Fitzgerald, Jennifer, 139–40
Fitzwater, Marlin, 216
Flowers, Gennifer, 160–66, 173, 176, 232, 234–35, 236, 239–40, 246, 247

Food in White House
  Clintons and, 220–26
  Secret Service and preparation of, 76
Food preferences of presidents, 77
  Carters, 98–99
  Clintons, 237
  Johnsons, 25, 32–33, 59–60
  Nixons, 59, 60–61, 62, 124
  Reagans, 111–12
  snacks, 62, 138
For the Record (Regan), 114
Ford, Betty, 77, 81, 83, 96, 188
  alcoholism, 67–68
  project of, 187
Ford, Gerald R., 58, 60, 63, 65, 66, 67, 72, 79–82, 83, 97, 102, 204, 209
  assassination attempts on, 69, 74
  code name, 68
  drinking, 77–78
  food preferences, 77
  loss to Carter, 82
  mail received, 137
  and nuclear football, 120
  pardoned Nixon, 68–69
  post-presidential protection of, 75
  relationship with wife, 96
  Time to Heal, A, 81, 124
Ford, Susan, 68, 188
Ford administration, 51, 208
Former presidents, 92
  protection of, 74–75
  townhouse for, 92, 102–03
Foster, Brugh, 194
Foster, Lisa, 194
Foster, Vincent, Jr., 206, 207, 238–40, 243, 247, 252
  suicide, 190–201, 215, 253
Founding Fathers, 144
Freedom of Information Act
  requests for information under, 63, 145–46, 222, 258
Freeh, Louis J., 190
Friendly, Andrew, 229
Fromme, Lynette "Squeaky," 69
Furniture
  EOB, 102
  stolen, 10, 54, 55, 84–86

INDEX

Gaddy, William, 239–40
Galanos (designer), 113
Gamarekian, Barbara, 126
Gannett News Service, 139
Garfield, James, 5
Gates, Robert M., 97–98, 107–08, 147, 148
Gearan, Mark, 186, 217, 219
Geisler, Ron, 119, 178
General Accounting Office (GAO), 6, 7, 56, 58, 142, 183
General Services Administration (GSA), 7, 56, 92–93, 101, 102–03, 158, 159, 179, 183, 228
Gergen, David R., 208–11, 214, 215, 217, 219, 234
Giancana, Sam, 2
Ginsburg, Ruth Bader, 190, 230
Goldwater, Barry, 9, 28
Goodwin, Stanley J., 24
Goodwin, Tommy, 246
Gore, Al, Jr., 167, 186, 204, 227–28
Graham, Katherine, 209–10
Grant, Julia, 254–55
Graux, Nancy, 128–29
Graux, Yves, 128–29
Gray, C. Boyden, 139, 147–48, 149, 150, 156
Gray, Robert, 139
Green, Shirley M., 136–37
Greene, Harold H., 257–58
Greenstein, Fred, 204
Gregg, Judd, 133
Gridiron Club, 80
Grieder, William, 218
Gronouski, 25, 30
Guinier, Lani, 186, 234
Gulley, Bill, 10–22, 42, 55, 62, 100, 101, 126
    on budget, 145
    on Carters, 89, 90, 92, 96
    on Nixon, 56–58

Haddon, Sean T., 220, 221–25, 257–58
Hagin, Joseph W., 130
Haig, Alexander M., Jr., 118
Haiti, 187
Haldeman, Bob, 12, 40, 57, 62, 63

Haller, Henry, 59–60, 76, 77, 91, 111, 112, 125
Hamilton, George, 33–34
Hart, Gary, 160, 249
Hartmann, Robert T., 65–67
Hayes, David, 113
Hayes, Rutherford B., 113, 273
Health care reform issue, 187, 189, 206, 209, 228
Herblock (Block), 258
Hickey, Edward, 145
Hickey, James V., Jr., 118
Hickok, Lorena, 2
Higby, Larry, 55, 61, 62
Hinckley, John W., Jr., 117–18, 119–20
HMS Resolute, 113
Hoban, James, 3, 271
Hockersmith, Kaki, 197
Homosexuals, homosexuality, 48, 49, 131, 187
Hoover, Herbert, 8
Hopkins, William, 8, 69
Horton, Willie, 131, 156, 235
Hotel security, 72–73, 98
Hubbard, Lewis, 133
Hubbell, Webster L., 194, 252
Hume, Brit, 230
Humphrey, Hubert, 26
Hunt, Al, 175
Hussein, Saddam, 188

Imperial presidency, xiv, 131, 141, 147
Investigative reporting, 212–13
Iran-contra affair, 9, 106, 107, 191, 259
    Bush and, 156, 256
Isolation of president, xiv, 3, 207
    Nixon, 44–45
    security and, 257

Jackson, Andrew, 178
Jackson, Cliff, 245
Jackson, Michael, 161
Javits, Jacob, 40
Jaworski, Joseph A., 110, 138
Jefferson, Thomas, 4, 55, 106, 144, 271, 272
Jenkins, Walter, 69
Johnson, Andrew, 67

Johnson, Eliza, 67
Johnson, Lady Bird, 1–2, 21, 36,
    37, 38, 75, 106
  Beautification Program, 187
  food preferences, 60
Johnson, Luci, 33
Johnson, Lynda, 33–34
Johnson, Lyndon Baines, 3, 38,
    62, 85, 123, 206
  and *Air Force One,* 21, 24–25,
    36–37
  corrupted by power, 9–10,
    26–28, 30–34
  food preferences, 59–60
  illegal expenditures by, 18–22
  mail received, 137
  megalomaniac, 32
  sexual indiscretions, 1–2, 13–14
  and White House security, 69
  Vietnam War, 250–51, 256
Johnson, Sam Houston, 16
Jolley, Mellisa, 241
Jones, James R., 19, 22
Jones, Paula, 249
"Just Say No" campaign, 108
Justice Department, 200, 202, 216,
    226–27, 234, 253

Kanjorski, Paul E., 7, 141–43,
    146–47, 156
Kelly, Frank J., 114
Kennedy, Anthony, 154
Kennedy, Caroline, 5, 124
Kennedy, Jacqueline, 2, 34, 36,
    54, 188–89
  and privacy issue, 124
Kennedy, John F., 2–3, 9, 22, 27,
    32, 34, 35–36, 61, 62, 113,
    149, 202, 232, 259
  assassination of, 69
  Bay of Pigs, 204, 256
  memorabilia, 49
  sexual activities, 35
Kennedy, Robert F., 2, 32, 34, 232
Kennedy, William H., III, 171,
    186, 187, 191, 207
Kennedy administration, 55, 155
Kennerly, David Hume, 81–82
Khachigian, Kenneth L., 49,
    115–16
Kim Young Sam, 211

King, Martin Luther, 74
Kissinger, Henry, 60–61, 62, 82,
    99
KPMG Peat Marwick, 171
Kroft, Steve, 160
Kuhn, James F., 110, 113, 114
Kump, Peter, 226
Kurtz, Howard, 174
  Media Circus, 213

Laimbeer, Bill, 154–55
Laitin, Joseph, 20, 25, 30, 32
Lake, Anthony, 187, 204
Laurie, Madame, 108
Lawrence, Louis J., 60–61, 80–81
Lazaro, Robert A., 110
LBJ Ranch, 18–19, 21
Leaks, 25, 150
  Clinton and, 205–07
LeBlond, Dorothy, 156–67
Lee, Burton J., III, 148–49
Lee, Jessica, 154–55
L'Enfant, Pierre, 144, 271
Letterman, David, 228
Lightfoot, Jim, 183–84
Lincoln, Abraham, 14, 15
Lincoln, Mary Todd, 14, 108, 187
Lindsey, Bruce, 173, 186–87,
    245, 247
Live from the Battlefield (Arnett),
    250
Los Angeles International Airport,
    24, 175
Los Angeles Police Department, 188
Los Angeles Times, 139, 238–39,
    247, 250

McCain, Carol, 152–53
McCarthy, Dennis, 118
McDougal, James B., 252
McGovern, George, 39
Machiavelli, Niccolò
  Prince, The, 26
McKinley, Ida, 67
McKinley, William, 67, 148, 273
McLarty, Thomas F. (Mack), 171,
    176, 178, 181, 194, 195,
    204–05, 209, 214–15
MacMillan, Robert M., 3, 24–25,
    30–31, 32, 33, 34–37, 44,
    60, 61

McQueen, Michel, 214
McQueen, Steve, 113
Madison, Dolley, 67, 113, 187
Madison, James, 67
Madison Guaranty Savings and
    Loan, 252
Magaw, John W., 208
Magaziner, Ira, 204, 206
Maids, xiv, 11, 223, 225
Mail, 135–37, 177
Manson, Charles, 69
Mariani, John, 225–256
Marine Corps, 7
Media Circus (Kurtz), 213
Military aides, xiv, 17
    and nuclear football, 72, 89
Military social aides, 154
Minor, Catalino, 21
Monroe, James, 272
Monroe, Marilyn, 2
Moore, Sara Jane, 69, 74
Morris, Anthony, 187
Mosbacher, Georgette, 155
Mosbacher, Robert, 155
Moseley-Braun, Carol, 194
Mount Weather, 15
Moyers, Bill, 25
Muskie, Edmund, 75
My Turn (N. Reagan), 5, 107
Myers, Dee Dee, 177, 179, 186,
    199, 216, 225

Nader, Ralph, 117, 226
National Airborne Command
    Posts, 15
National Association of Broad-
    casters, 75
National Enquirer, 125
National Highway Traffic Safety
    Administration, 226
National Park Service, 7, 102, 105,
    170, 199
National Security Agency (NSA),
    72
National Security Council, 6, 82
Naval Investigative Service (NIS),
    85, 86
Neel, Roy, 204–05, 232–33
Nelson, Jack, 209–10
New York Post, 139

New York Times, 20, 54, 91, 126,
    184, 201, 211, 220–21, 237,
    246, 247, 258
Newman, J. Bonnie, 130, 133–35,
    137–38, 140–41, 146, 152,
    169
Newsweek, xiii, 175, 190, 199,
    200, 206
Nixon, Julie, 38, 44
Nixon, Pat, 11, 38–39, 57, 124
    alcohol problem, 41
    "volunteerism," 187
    and White House remodeling,
    55–56
Nixon, Richard, 12, 22, 38–41, 42,
    43, 44–45, 46, 49, 56–57,
    61, 63–64, 97, 98, 102, 125,
    149, 161, 202, 205, 235
    and *Air Force One,* 78, 80–81
    favorite restaurants, 77
    food preferences, 62, 77, 124
    haircuts, 58–59
    illegal activities, 259
    mail received, 137
    pardoned by Ford, 68–69
    and the press, 258, 259
    relationship with wife, 96
    resignation, 39–40
    threats to, 52
    Watergate affair, 174, 256
    Watergate tapes, 58, 62–63
    and White House remodeling,
    54–55
Nixon, Tricia, 15, 38, 43–44,
    78–79
Nixon administration, 127, 208
Nixon White House, 171, 200
Nofziger, Lyn, 108
Non-detailees, 142
North, Oliver, 192
Nuclear football, xiv, 10, 17–18, 89
    in presidential motorcades, 72
    presidents separated from, 120
Nuclear threat(s), 66, 89, 118
    relocation centers, 15
Nuclear war codes, xiv, 17
Nussbaum, Bernard W., 115, 186,
    187, 242
    and Foster suicide, 190–91,
    193, 198, 199
    resigned, 216

O'Brien Larry, 25, 30
O'Donnell, D. Patrick, 22, 36–37
O'Donnell, Terrence, 80
Office of Administration, 6, 87
Office of Management and Budget
    (OMB), 6, 23, 115, 176,
    204, 273
Office of National Drug Policy, 178
Office of Personnel Management
    (OPM), 7–8
Office of Thrift Supervision, 226
Ogle, Charles, 144
Oldenburg, Herb, 72
O'Neill, Thomas P. (Tip), 235
Oval Office, 4, 17, 18, 29, 62, 113,
    152, 158, 197

Palmer, Charles, 39, 56, 59, 61,
    62, 79
  on Bush, 138
  on the Carters, 87–88, 90,
    93–95, 96, 98, 99
  on Ford, 77–78
  on Kissinger, 60
  on the Reagans, 110, 111
Palmer, John E., Jr., 60–61, 79
Panetta, Leon E., 205
Parr, Jerry S., 74, 117–18, 119, 155
Patterson, Bradley H., Jr., 159, 204
  Ring of Power, The, 148
Patterson, Larry G., 239–46
Peacock, Charles, 235
Peden, Carl A., 44
Pellicano, Anthony J., 161
Pennsylvania Volunteers, 46
Penny, Don, 79–80, 133
Pentagon, 12–13
Pentagon Papers, 258
Perot, Ross, 167, 219
Perquisites (perks), 8–9, 22, 148,
    151–55, 207
  Carter reduction, 100
  living in White House, 123–24
  mess, 16
  upgrading, 182
Perry, Roger L., 239–42, 244,
    245, 246
Persian Gulf War, 152, 167
Personal life of presidents, xiv
  Clinton, 232–33, 235–36, 238
  press and, 246–48

Pets, 105, 223
Pierce, Nelson C., Jr., 20, 81, 88,
    90, 104–05, 106, 231
Pincus, Walter, 193
Pisha, Gerald F., 31, 43–44, 82,
    93, 98–99
Pitts, Milton, 58–59, 81, 128–29,
    138–39, 175–76
Podesta, John, 168
POTUS, 133–34
Power, 10, 22, 26, 198
  corrupting influence of, 8–9
  derived, 9
  Johnson corrupted by, 26–28,
    30–34
  obtained and used by Gulley,
    10–17
  of presidency, 207
  secrecy and, 30
  of White House, 149–50, 155,
    256
Power plays, 29, 207
  domestic staff, 223–25
Presidency (the), xiv, xv, 255–56
  attitudes toward, 143, 144
  Bush and, 131
  cost of, 6–9
  as institution, 143
  mythologizing, 258–60
  Reedy's critique of, 26–32
  See also Imperial presidency
Presidential motorcades, xv
  security, 70–71
Presidents, xiv
  assassination attempts on, 69,
    74, 117–20
  character flaws in, 234–36, 244,
    246, 249–51, 256–57,
    260–61
  illegalities by, 3, 259
  image of, 175
  list, 277–79
  paying for nonofficial expenses,
    58, 123–24, 134
  role of, 234
  salary and expenses, 6, 141
  threats to, 51–53
  transfer of power, 118–19
  travel budget, 141
  See also Personal life of
    presidents

INDEX

President's House, 4
Press, 16–17, 25
  Clinton and, 173–75, 196,
    209–19, 258
  Johnson and, 14, 30
  and personal lives of presi-
    dents, 35, 212–13, 214, 235,
    246–48, 249–51
  and presidential accountabil-
    ity, 258
  presidents and, 28
  and travel office, 197
  used by staff, 12–13
  and White House, 212–14, 248,
    253
Press corps
  and Clinton, 173–74, 175
Press office, 173–74
  Clinton, 216–18, 219, 227
Preston, Robert K., 53–54
Price, Lucille P., 93, 102, 103,
  159, 185
Prince, The (Machiavelli), 26
Privacy, xiv, 128
  Air Force One, 24
  Carter and, 89
  complaints about lack of,
    124–25
  issue with Clintons, 169,
    189–90, 233
Procrastination (Burka and
  Yuen), 168
Procurement process, 182–83,
  227–28

Quayle, Dan, 82, 83, 132, 154, 205
Quayle, Marilyn, 132, 154
Quigg, Glenn A., 112–13
Quigley, Joan, 108
Quinn, Sally, 175

Reagan, Maureen, 122
Reagan, Michael, 120–22
Reagan, Nancy, 104–06, 112–13,
  127, 128, 152–53, 182
  astrologer, 108, 114
  character, 106–07, 108–09
  controlling R. Reagan, 107–10,
    111, 231
  designer dresses, 113
  and domestic staff, 225

drug abuse program, 187
food preferences, 111–12
and Michael Reagan, 121–22
My Turn, 5, 107
and White House food, 222
and White House renovation,
  125–26, 134
Reagan, Ronald, 10, 41, 49, 54, 80,
  97, 102, 168, 234, 240
  assassination attempt on, 74,
    117–20
  code name, 109
  and domestic staff, 220
  food preferences, 62, 138
  and food preparation, 76
  illegal activities, 259
  Iran-contra affair, 192, 256
  personal relations, 89
  post-presidency protection of,
    75
  presidency, 106–07, 108,
    109–12, 113–17, 120, 122,
    125–29, 137, 148, 152–53,
    173, 174, 219, 227
  relationship with wife, 96, 112
  and White House food, 222
Reagan administration, 155, 159,
  169, 208, 219
  presidential motorcade, 72
  White House finances, 146
  White House security, 51
Reedy, George, 35, 111, 117, 144,
  153, 206, 230, 234, 248, 251
  on Clinton, 189, 202
  on leaks, 207
  on Nixon, 63
  on the press, 209
  Twilight of the Presidency, The,
    xiv, 25–32, 215–16,
    255–56, 258
Regan, Donald, 107, 115, 116,
  127, 128
  For the Record, 114
Rehnquist, William H., 167–68
Reid, Russ, 25, 39, 44, 61–62, 82
Renaissance Weekend(s), 208
Reno, Janet, 196, 232
Resolution Trust Co., 252
Respass, Charles B. (Buddy),
  102–03
Restaurants, 76–77

Revell, Oliver B. (Buck), 73
Rice, Donna, 160, 249
Richman, Phyllis, 226
Ring of Power, The (Patterson), 148
RN: The Memoirs of Richard Nixon (Nixon), 63
Roberts, Eugene L., Jr., 213
Roberts, Juanita, 12
Rogers, John F. W., 102, 108, 117, 127, 133, 169, 173, 197
Romano, Lois, 175
Roosevelt, Edith, 124, 254, 273
Roosevelt, Eleanor, 2, 67
Roosevelt, Franklin Delano, 12, 22, 62, 235, 251, 274
memorabilia, 49
sexual dalliances, 2
Roosevelt, Theodore, 4, 14–15, 124, 273
Roosevelt administration, 69
Rose law firm, 191, 192, 243, 252
Royal Canadian Mounted Police (RCMP), 120, 121, 122
Rumsfeld, Donald, 74, 78, 253–54
"Rumsfeld's Rules," 253, 281–87
Russell, Richard, 26
Rutherford, Lucy Mercer, 2
Rutherford, Skip, 194

Sadat, Anwar, 60, 90
Saddler, James R., 111, 168, 176
Safe house(s), 72
Saunders, George E., 69–70
Schatteman, Cristophe, 58, 175, 176
Scheib, Walter, 225–26
Scouten, Rex W., 102, 125–28
Scrowcroft, Brent, 10, 137, 147
Secrecy, 125–28, 206
presidents' obsession with, 29–30
Secret Service, 1, 7, 179
budget, 145
establishment of, 272
intelligence division, 51
"one-voice policy," xiii–xiv
and presidential motorcades, 70–71
protection of former presidents, 63, 74–75

protection of presidents, 7–8, 119–20, 140, 141–42, 273
as source of leaks, 206, 207, 208
and theft of antiques, 84–85
uniformed division, 46–47, 48, 54, 127–28, 275
and White House security, 50–54, 117
Secret Service agents, xiv, 66
and *Air Force One,* 23
color-coded pins, 71
and Ford White House, 66–67
improper behavior by, 49–50
presidential security, 46–47, 72–74
on presidents and first families, xv, 2, 16, 38–39, 40–43, 44, 56, 64
on presidents and first families: Bush, 131
on presidents and first families: Carters, 88–89, 92–94
on presidents and first families: Clintons, 230–32, 253, 259–60
on presidents and first families: Reagans, 108–09, 112, 113, 120–21
protection of children, 68
Secretaries, 8, 11–12
to Johnson, 13–14, 36, 37
Security, 5, 46–48, 75–76, 117, 273–74
Bethesda Naval Hospital, 85–86
children of presidents, 94
presidential, 3, 69–74, 75–77, 257
problems with, 50–54
and travel, 72–73
Security clearances, 70, 186
Sequoia (presidential yacht), 100, 143
Sessions, William S., 202, 205
Sexual activities of presidents, allegations of, 259
Bush, 139
Clinton, 160–66, 231–32, 234–35, 236, 238–51, 246–47, 249, 250, 251
Johnson, 1–2, 13–14
Kennedy, 2
press and, 35

Sexual activity of aides, 14–15, 16
Shattuck, Ray, 117
Shaw, David, 216–18
Shimoyama, Susumu, 213
Shumiatcher, Morris C., 121
Sidwell Friends School, 73
Simmons, Lee F., 56, 62
"60 Minutes," 160
Smith, J. Dorrance, 156
Smith, Maurice, 239
Smith, Wendy, 229
Smith, William French, 128
Snyder, Richard A., 153–54
Somalia, 187
Speakes, Larry, 10, 67–68, 102,
    120, 128
Spence, Craig J., 48, 138
Sporkin, Stanley, 257
Springer, Rick, 75
SR-71 (spy plane), 12–13
SS *Mayaguez,* 82
Staff
  Bush, 141, 147–49, 155
  Clinton, 159–60, 168–71, 173,
    175–87, 190, 191, 195–96,
    199, 201–02, 203–05, 207–09,
    216–18, 219, 229, 234, 246
  Reagan, 116
Staff (White House), 9, 105,
    127–28, 151, 221, 257
  and Carter, 87
  and Clintons, 223
  domestic, 219–26
  jockeying for favors, 11
  permanent, xiv, 8
  and press, 174
  and privacy, 124–25
  size of, 8, 10
Staff reduction
  claimed by Clinton, 176–81,
    212, 250
Stapleton, Robert T., 91
Stapleton, Ruth Carter, 91
Star (tabloid), 160–61, 164
Starr, John Robert, 230–31
State Department, 5, 7, 22
State Department building, 54–55
State dinners, 153–55
Stephanopoulos, George, 172,
    173, 174–75, 201–02,
    216–17

Stockman, David, 128
Stone, I. F., 250–51
Sununu, John H., 147–48, 155
Sununu Syndrome, 147
Supreme Court, 257

Taft, William, 178
Talbott, Strobe, 204
Tate, Sheila, 125
Taylor, Margaret, 124
Taylor, Zachary, 124
TelePrompTer, 115, 185–86
Television, 235, 257
Thomas, Helen, 12, 20, 126, 211
Thomason, Harry, 170, 210
Tiffany, David C., 223
Tillotson, Mary, 139
Time (magazine), 177
Time to Heal, A (Ford), 81, 124
Travel (presidents)
  security measures, 72–73
Travelgate, 159, 196, 212
  see also White House travel
    office
Treasury Department, 15
Trefey, Richard G., 134, 143–44
Trento, Joe, 139
Trento, Susan B., 139
Trinkets, presidential, 48–49
  as gifts, 11–12, 21
Truman, Bess, 67
Truman, Harry S, 8, 22, 34–35, 56,
    68, 202
Truman, Margaret, 4
Truth Verification Laboratories,
    Inc., 161
Tucker, Guy, 244–45
Turkey trot, 154
Twilight of the Presidency, The
    (Reedy), xiv, 25–32, 215,
    255–56
Tyler, Julia, 108

U.S. Information Agency, 151
U.S. Park Police, 198–99, 200
U.S. Trade Representative, 176
University of Arkansas, 167, 169
University of Arkansas Law
    School, 193
Untermeyer, Charles G. (Chase),
    139, 151, 156

INDEX

Upstairs at the White House
(West), 220
USA Today, 149
Ushers, xv, 105–06, 231
chief usher, 105, 135

Valenti, Jack, 20, 31
Van Buren, Martin, 145
Vanity Fair, 139
Vice-president(s), 133–34
Secret Service protection,
141–42
Victoria, Queen of England, 113
Vietnam War, 9, 26, 27–28, 30, 34,
52, 250, 256, 258
Nixon and, 39
prisoners of war, 64
Vise, Buddie L., 44
Visitors to White House, 47, 53
Voles, Lorraine, 177

Wall Street Journal, 174–75,
191–92, 193, 198, 206, 209,
213–14, 227, 233, 234
Wallace, George, 28
Walsh, Lawrence, 106, 156
Walters, Gary, 46, 105–06, 128,
135, 145, 207, 220, 222,
223–24
Walzel, Frederick H., 20, 88–89,
127–28, 132
Walzel, Rena, 132
Ward, Seth, 252
Washington, George, 4, 144, 198,
209, 254, 271
Washington, Martha, 254
Washington Post, 17, 139, 145,
148–49, 174, 179–80, 181,
210, 211, 213, 216, 226,
246–47, 248, 258
Washington Star, 14
Watergate scandal, 9, 39–40, 41,
59, 68–69, 174, 212, 213,
248, 256
Nixon tapes, 58, 62–63
Watkins, W. David, 169–73, 176,
181–84
Weaver, Mary E., 7, 142
Webster, William, 140
Weinberg, Mark D., 116, 150, 181
Wells, Brad, 93

West, J. B., 49, 106, 124, 219–20
White House, xiv–xv, 3–9
career employees, 206
computers, 168–69, 177,
182–83
concept(s) of, 144–45
cornerstone, 3, 271–72
dinner invitations, 153–55
domestic staff, 207
east wing, 4, 6
effects on presidents, 35
"garden pavilion," 117
Green Room, 55
Jacqueline Kennedy Garden, 123
jogging track, 123, 182, 232
letter-writing unit, 136–37
Lincoln Bedroom, 14, 15, 16
living quarters, 6
organization chart, 135
porticoes, 4
rats at, 101–02, 134
remodeling/renovation, 4,
54–55, 125–26, 127, 134,
197, 274
Rose Garden, 123
sport/recreation facilities, 123
as stage, xiv
state floor, 6
subterranean tunnel, 15–16
technological additions improvements, 4–5
telephone system, 168, 169, 177
tennis court, 87, 89, 123, 135
transition between presidents,
158–59
west wing, 4, 6, 106, 114–15,
158
see also Atmosphere of White
House; Oval Office
White House Communications
Agency, 8, 72, 179
White House counsel, 122, 186,
187, 193, 199
White House dates, 271–75
White House finances, 6–9, 20,
58, 134
under Clinton, 126–27, 177, 179
cost of flowers, 124
cost of paint removal, 105, 146
secrecy about, 141–47
staff, 105

INDEX

White House Historical Association, 55, 126–27
White House mess, 7, 16, 76, 143, 151
White House military office, 16, 17
White House Office, 6, 7
White House Police, 45–46, 273, 274
White House Situation Room, 5
White House tours, 47
  as perk, 151–53
White House travel office, 169–73, 191, 206, 207
  investigation of, 196–97, 200–01
White House-itis, 146–50, 169–70
Whitewater affair, 189–90
Whitewater Development Co., 216, 252
Wilson, Woodrow, 14–15
Winder Building, 6

Wise, Phil, 99
Wolf, Frank R., 181
Women's Christian Temperance Union, 188
Wong, Mr., 20–21
Wood, Kimba, 186
Woods, Rose Mary, 12, 57, 62–63
Woodward, Bob, 213
  and Carl Bernstein: *All the President's Men,* 174
World Wide Travel (co.), 172, 173, 200
Wright, Betsey, 163
Wright, Zephyr, 59–60
Wyman, Jane, 120

Yang, John, 213
Young, Raymond L. (Buddy), 189, 203, 205, 207, 229, 242, 245

Zamaria, Rose M., 135
Ziegler, Ron, 57